ALL THE Aires

BELGIUM, LUXEMBOURG & THE NETHERLANDS

3rd Edition

Vicarious Shop

One Stop Motorhome and Caravan Bookshop

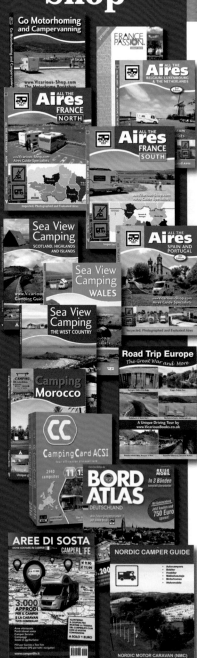

Go Motorhoming and Campervanning

- MMM, 'Essential, pleasurable reading for novice or old hand.' *Barry Crawshaw.*
- Practical Motorhome, '... it's jam-packed with information on touring...' *Sarah Wakely.*
- Motor caravanner, 'It really is a powerhouse of information plus hints and tips based on real active motorcaravanners' experiences both at home and abroad.' *Gentleman Jack.*

All the Aires

- Inspected and photographed Aires.
- GPS coordinates taken on site.
- Aires for large motorhomes identified.
- Best Aires guides for France; Spain & Portugal; Belgium, Luxembourg and the Netherlands.

ACSI Camping Card

There are other low season discount schemes, but none rival the quantity and freedom of this no commitment guide. Buy the book, it's as simple as that, and camp across Europe for a maximum of €19 a night. The card presses out of the cover.

Sea View Camping: West Country, Scotland and Wales

These unique campsite guides show you all the sea view campsites around England's West Country, Scotland and Wales. All you have to do is choose where you want to go and be ready for a fantastic time as you explore some of the most diverse coastlines in the world.

France Passion

Like a glass of wine? Then why not spend a night at the vineyard where you can see, smell and taste the process. Similar guides for Italy and Germany.

Road Trip Europe

The Great War and More tour encompasses five cities, four countries and two world wars. It details walking tours; where to stay: Aires, campsites and hotels and where to eat and drink.

Stopover Guides for all of Europe

We specialise in importing stopover guides from Europe: Reise Mobil Bord Atlas for Germany, Camper Life for Italy, and Camperstop Europe for a general guide across Europe.

Campsite Guides for all of Europe

We also stock the superb ACSI DVD, Caravan Club's guides to France and Rest of Europe, Alan Rogers and a range of other guides including Camping Morocco.

Map and Tour Guides

Wherever you are going in Europe, we have all the road atlases, sheet maps and tourist information guides you will need. Walking maps for France and the UK are also stocked.

0131 208 3333   www.Vicarious-Shop.com

Freedom of Benelux

Motorhoming in Benelux (Belgium, the Netherlands and Luxembourg) is easy if you know where you are going to stop for the night, but don't expect to stumble across municipal Aires. You will have to plan your night stop and to assist you we have inspected and provided comprehensive details about all the municipal and low cost commercial Aires. All of the Aires featured in this edition were inspected during the latter half of 2015 by Meli and Chris, the editors of this guide and directors of Vicarious Media.

Aires can be full, occupied by the funfair, or simply closed for maintenance. Vicarious Media is not responsible for any Aires. This book is a guide only and was correct at the time of going to press. Should you have any complaints about an Aire or wish to know why an Aire has closed, please speak to the local town hall and remember to let us know about any changes.

Front cover main image: Neede page 156.

Motorhome used for research: Pilote Aventura G600 purchased from Hayes Leisure, Birmingham, www.hayesleisure.co.uk

First published in Great Britain by Vicarious Books LLP, 2009. This edition published April 2016.

© Vicarious Media Ltd 2016.

Copyright © text Vicarious Media. All rights reserved.

Copyright © photographs Vicarious Media unless otherwise stated.

ISBN: 978-1-910664-06-3

Editorial Team, Vicarious Media, Unit 1, North Close Business Centre, Shorncliffe Industrial Estate, Folkestone, CT20 3UH. Tel: 0131 2083333

Chief editor: Meli George

Editor: Chris Doree

Assistant editor: Pami Hoggatt

Editorial assistant: Ben Taylor

Design and Artwork: Chris Gladman Design Tel: 07745 856652

GLOSSARY

Abbreviations and Glossary of Terms

5 mins	Estimated walking times.
Adj	Adjacent.
CC	Credit card.
CL style	Small grass parking area.
Commerce	
Local commerce	One or more: bar, baker, restaurant, convenience store, hair dresser.
Small town commerce	As above plus a mini market and bank.
Tourist commerce	Kiss me quick or seasonal restaurants and boutiques.
Town commerce	Big enough to have a wedding dress shop.
Commercial Aire	Set up for profit, often pay at barrier or Service Point.
Dead quiet	Peaceful location adj to cemetery.
Grass parking	Will not be marked as open all year, but can be used whenever conditions allow.
Inc	Included in price.
Inside barrier	Service Point behind barrier at pay Aire. Access may be free or reduced cost for short duration.
May feel isolated if alone	Normally locations without habitation nearby, but don't lose sleep over it.
Open access	No fence or barrier.
Opp	Opposite.
Oversubscribed	Often too many motorhomes for official space.
Popular	Aire likely to be busy.
Poss	Possible.
Private Aire	Run by an individual, often at home or business.
pp	Per person.
Sp	Signposted 'Town name'.
Signed	Aire signed with symbol or text.
'text'	Extracts from signs.
TO	Tourist Office.
Tolerated	Unofficial motorhome parking.
Trucking hell	Noisy trucks hurtling past day and night.
Inspected	Inspected by Vicarious Media staff.
Reinspected	Previously inspected and reinspected for this edition.
Visited	Customer submission.
Submitted	Owner supplied information.

Editors enthralled at Hansweert

What's new?

The way that people go motorhoming in Benelux has not changed significantly since the last edition, but the number of Aires has. The previous edition of this guide was published in 2013, since then the Aires increased in Belgium from 78 to 127, in the Netherlands from 121 to 190 and in Luxembourg from 10 to 12. Disappointingly, Belgium has banned overnight parking along the length of the coast except at private Aires and campsites, however there is a significant increase of waterside Aires inland.

Inspections

100% of the Aires featured in this guide were inspected during the late summer and autumn of 2015. Meli and Chris, the editors of this guide, drove their Pilote camper to every known municipal Aire and every inexpensive commercial Aire. They inspect up to 1500 Aires each year and stop overnight at a different one every night, so they know what you want and need to know.

Who goes where?

Benelux cannot be considered a seaside destination unless you stop at campsites. During 2015 Belgium banned night parking at all of its coastal municipal Aires. Furthermore, there is just one Aire in the Netherlands with a sea view. But don't 'Cry Me a River' because there are enough waterside Aires in Flanders and the Netherlands to float everybody's boats no matter how big. We find it enthralling watching the barges and ships navigating the canals and rivers. Unsurprisingly, any Aire with a good view of a navigation has the potential to be full or oversubscribed; so arrive early and wait for a space. Traditional Aires that are located at tourist destinations or on the main migratory routes are also likely to be full or oversubscribed in the evenings, but Aires in seemingly uninspiring locations are likely to be empty. We have provided as much information as possible to help you understand what the place is like and what there is to do nearby.

Do you need to Aire on the side of caution?

The one thing you need to understand is the youth culture that is often observed in the Netherlands and Flanders. If you park in a remote section of a public car park, it is likely that young people in cars will drive in calmly and park nearby. They will probably faff about a bit, turn their music off or down, then unwind their windows from which clouds of smoke will billow out. They will probably drive off in a relaxed manner after 15 to 30 minutes. Quite a lot of the municipal Aires are located at the sports centre and the allocated motorhome parking is often in the area least used by visitors, but most used by smokers. During our inspection tour we mostly parked overnight at such car parks without incident or animosity. We found the youths to be respectful, and they rarely got out of their cars.

Surely there are no motorhomers that have not heard about break-ins at motorway rest areas, but does it happen in Benelux? Simple answer: rarely. Over the past 15 years we have heard of very few incidents involving motorhomes in Benelux. But why take the risk? As always, in big cities you should be vigilant against pick-pocketing and bag snatching.

Further information

See page 10 where we have provided further information about motorhoming in Belgium, Luxembourg and the Netherlands and their Aires. If you bought your guide direct from Vicarious Books you have also been given a double-sided fold out map in a bigger scale. For ease, use the map in conjunction with this book when choosing your next Aire or LPG station.

HOW TO USE THIS GUIDE

Inside covers. Maps colour coded by country. All Aires numbered 1-2-3... in each country.

Cartes codées par couleur selon la pays. Toutes les aire de service numérotées 1-2-3... dans chaque pays.

Karten farblich nach land codiert. Alle Stellplätze nummeriert 1-2-3... in jeder Land.

Mappe a colori di un codice paese. Tutti le aree di sosta numerati 1-2-3... in ciascuna paese.

Mapas codificados por color según la país. Todos área de servicio numerados 1-2-3... en cada país.

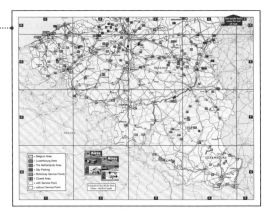

• **Page 10-17. Further information.**

Before you depart read the further information.

Avant votre départ lire les informations utiles.

Bevor Sie abreisen lesen Sie die nützliche Informationen.

Prima di partire leggere le informazioni utili. Antes de partir leído la información útil.

Page 19-189. Colour coded chapters by country.
All countries use map numbers 1-2-3...

Code couleur chapitres par pays.
Toutes les pays utilisent des numéros de carte 1-2-3...

Kapiteln farblich nach Land cudiert.
Alle länder verwenden map Zahlen 1-2-3...

Codice colore capitoli per paese. Tutte le paese usare i numeri 1-2-3...

Código de colores capítulos según la país. Todas las país utilizar los números del mapa 1-2-3...

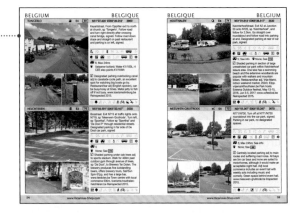

HOW TO USE THIS GUIDE

Page 191-193. Day Parking, Motorway Service Points and Closed Aires.

Parking de Jour, Aires de service autoroute aménagée pour les camping-car, Aires de services fermé.

Tag Parkplatz, Raststätte mit Einrichtungen für Wohnmobile, Wohnmobil Stellplätze geschlossen.

Parcheggio giorno, Area di servizio autostradale con servizi per camper, Aree di sosta chiuso.

Aparcamiento día, Área de servicio de autopista con servicios para autocaravanas, Área para autocaravanas cerrada.

Page 195-213. Fuel stations with LPG by country.

Stations d'essence au GPL par pays.

Tankstellen mit Flüssiggas nach Land.

Stazioni di servizio con GPL per paese.

Estaciones de combustible con GLP por país.

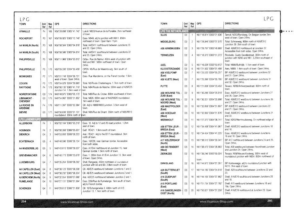

Page 215-220. Alphabetical index by town name.

Index alphabétique par nom de ville.

Alphabetischer Index nach Ort Name.

Indice alfabetico per nome paese.

Indice alfabético por nombre de ciudad.

HOW TO USE THIS GUIDE

1 Town Name.
* The inspectors rate the Aire or location to be better than most. Often the view or surrounding area is of interest.
2 Surroundings, see cover flaps for key.
3 Map grid reference.
4 Map number or letter.
5 GPS coordinates.
6 Postcode.
7 Photographs of Aire.

8 Directions.
9 Service Point details, see cover flaps for key.
10 Parking details, see cover flaps for key.
11 🚐 Number of parking spaces; Cost per night; Time limit.
12 🚰 Service Point type; Payment type if not cash; Cost.
13 Description.
14 Local amenities, see cover flaps for key.
15 Fuel station brand.
16 Large motorhome access.

Note: *Symbols in grey = unavailable*

Français
1 Nom de ville.
2 Ambiance.
3 Localisation cartographique.
4 Numéro de carte.
5 Pointage GPS.
6 Code Postal.
7 Photographies de l'aire.

8 Indications.
9 Services proposées; eau, électricité, WC etc.
10 Détails de stationnement.
11 🚐 Le nombre de places de stationnement disponibles, avec tarif et durée maximale d'occupation.

12 🚰 Type de borne camping-car et prix.
13 Description.
14 Commodités locales.
15 Marque de station service.
16 Accès pour les grandes autocaravanes.
* Aire bonne.

Deutsch
1 Stadtname.
2 Masseinheiten.
3 Gitterkoordinaten.
4 Karten-Zahl.
5 GPS-Koordinaten.

6 Postleitzahl.
7 Stellplätz-Photos.
8 Richtungen.
9 Einrichtungen.
10 Eigenschaften.
11 🚐 Zahl der Parzellen.

12 🚰 Näheres und Gebühren für Service.
13 Beschreibung.
14 Lokale Annehmlichkeiten.
15 Kraftstoffstationmarke.
16 Großer wohnmobile Zugang.
* Gute Stellplätz.

Italiano
1 Nome della città.
2 Le unità hanno accettato.
3 Riferimento di griglia.
4 Numero del programma.
5 Il GPS coordina.

6 Codice postale.
7 Fotografie del luogo.
8 Sensi.
9 Facilità.
10 Caratteristiche.
11 🚐 Numero dei passi.

12 🚰 Particolari e spese per servizio.
13 Descrizione.
14 Amenità locali.
15 Marca della stazione del combustibile.
16 Grande accesso del camper.
* Buono Aire.

Español
1 Nombre de la ciudad.
2 Las unidades aceptaron.
3 Referencia de rejilla.
4 Número del mapa.
5 El GPS coordina.
6 Código Postal.

7 Fotografías del sitio.
8 Direcciones.
9 Instalaciones.
10 Características.
11 🚐 Número de echadas.
12 🚰 Detalles y cargas para el servicio.

13 Descripción.
14 Amenidades locales.
15 Marca de fábrica de la estación del combustible.
16 Acceso grande del autocaravanas.
* Buena Aire.

Explanation of an entry

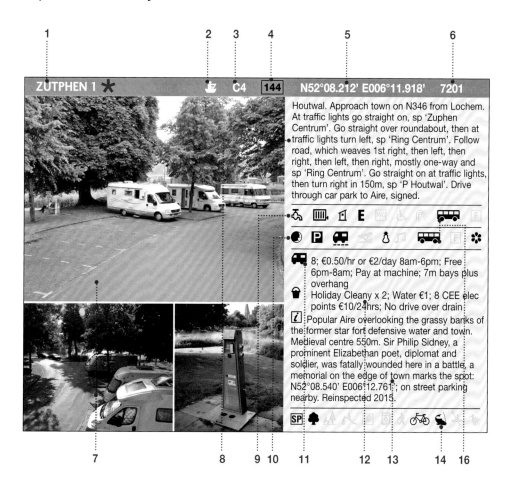

1 2 3 4 5 6

ZUTPHEN 1 ★ C4 144 N52°08.212' E006°11.918' 7201

Houtwal. Approach town on N346 from Lochem. At traffic lights go straight on, sp 'Zuphen Centrum'. Go straight over roundabout, then at traffic lights turn left, sp 'Ring Centrum'. Follow road, which weaves 1st right, then left, then right, then left, then right, mostly one-way and sp 'Ring Centrum'. Go straight on at traffic lights, then turn right in 150m, sp 'P Houtwal'. Drive through car park to Aire, signed.

8; €0.50/hr or €2/day 8am-6pm; Free 6pm-8am; Pay at machine; 7m bays plus overhang

Holiday Cleany x 2; Water €1; 8 CEE elec points €10/24hrs; No drive over drain

Popular Aire overlooking the grassy banks of the former star fort defensive water and town. Medieval centre 550m. Sir Philip Sidney, a prominent Elizabethan poet, diplomat and soldier, was fatally wounded here in a battle, a memorial on the edge of town marks the spot: N52°08.540' E006°12.761'; on street parking nearby. Reinspected 2015.

SP

7 8 9 10 11 12 13 14 16

Explanation of LPG entry

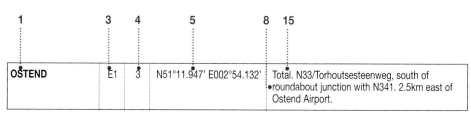

1 3 4 5 8 15

| OSTEND | E1 | 3 | N51°11.947' E002°54.132' | Total. N33/Torhoutsesteenweg, south of roundabout junction with N341. 2.5km east of Ostend Airport. |

FURTHER INFORMATION

What are Aires and what does Aire mean?

All the Aires is a series of books which started with France, but this particular book would be better named *All the Camperplaats*. Camperplaats is the name most used for official motorhome areas in Benelux, except in the French-speaking half of Belgium where the phrase 'aire de service camping car' is used.

Municipal Aires provide motorhome travellers with the freedom to come and go as they please. Generally municipal Aires are allocated sections in unsupervised public car parks, thus it is not possible to reserve a space. They are designed to be convenient stopovers rather than holiday destinations. In contrast, commercial Aires are privately run and normally have a reception, toilets, and electric hook-up.

Facilities range from a single allocated parking bay in a public car park to marinas and private enterprises offering fully serviced motorhome areas that look like campsites. The duration of stay is normally indicated on signs and is typically 24-72 hours.

Who can use Aires?

Law forbids caravans and tents from using the municipal Aires in this guide, but motorhome users are permitted to park, cook, eat and sleep within the confines of their vehicle. This law actually enabled Aires to develop in the first place. The law does not permit camping activities at municipal Aires, such as winding out awnings or putting out tables and chairs. Some commercial Aires may tolerate limited camping equipment, but please check the rules when you arrive.

Vicarious Media champions responsible tourism

Motorhoming is booming and offsite parking is illegal across Benelux, so as a result the Aires network is under pressure, except at unserviced Aires located off the beaten trail. When reading our comments keep an eye out for words like 'popular' and 'oversubscribed'. Some otherwise uninspiring Aires are popular due to geographical location, and some Aires are oversubscribed because everyone knows about them. We encourage you to be adventurous and to help you we have provided useful information about what to see and do in the lesser known locations.

We would all like to see the Aires network continue to grow; so before you bend the rules a little remember that the locals see lots of individuals over a long time, but the ones they remember either offended or befriended them. Most people in Benelux speak English, so it is especially rewarding to spend your money in the local commerce. Take the time to have a chat and thank them for maintaining their camperplaats.

We can all be valued visitors if we are RESPONSIBLE and:

R espect the environment
E lect to use un-crowded Aires
S pend locally
P ark sensibly
O rganise your recycling
N o camping
S ave water
I mpeccable behaviour
B e quiet
L eave before you outstay your welcome
E valuate your impact

Finding Aires

Satellite navigation: The GPS coordinates provided in this guide were taken on site and it should be possible to drive to the spot where they were taken. However, this does not mean to say that your navigator will get you there. Check the directions against your printed map and look at the suggested route on your navigator.

Directions: The directions are written to assist you with map navigation. We have attempted to select the simplest route that is free of height and weight restrictions. Where possible you should follow road signs, abbreviated 'sp' in the directions, and look for Aires signs, abbreviated to 'signed'. In Benelux the standard motorhome symbol is frequently used to indicate the parking spaces, but the area and direction signs are often written as camperplaats.

Overnight parking and time limits

Known time restrictions are provided in the listings. Many Aires restrict use to 48hrs, which is logical because it should be enough time to visit the local attractions. Aires not displaying time limits should be assumed to be 48hrs.

Designated parking

Municipal Aires normally share space in pre-existing car parks. To assist you we have provided the number of marked bays. Where bays are restricted in size we have given definitive bay lengths, amount of overhang and width if relevant. In unmarked parking areas it is normal to park close to your neighbour when necessary, so try to leave enough space for another motorhome to slot in if the need arises. Everybody enjoys a view, so share them as much as possible. Never park overnight on the Service Point or obstruct roadways. It is not uncommon for municipal Aires to be commandeered during events. Where possible we have provided the municipality website URL so that you can see what events are planned.

Service Points are few and far between at municipal Aires in Benelux. Many are simply signed parking areas, described as 'designated parking' in this guide. Aires with services are identified with a red outline box on this guide's supporting mapping. Always check the Aire details to ensure that the facilities are adequate.

Who turned out the lights? The illumination symbol ☖ is highlighted when the inspectors have seen light fittings. There is no guarantee that lights work and it has become common practice to turn the lights off during the middle of the night to save electricity.

FURTHER INFORMATION

Large motorhomes (RVs) >7.5m:

The highlighted coach symbols 🚌 identify Aires where the inspectors believe it should be possible for motorhomes over 7.5m to access the parking and Service Point. There is normally more space at marina Aires and someone will probably make decisions for you. Many of the municipal Aires have been designed to accommodate motorhomes up to 7m long. In general it is unacceptable to park across bays. We sometimes write that there are more bays than allocated, or extra space if it appears that the space is not normally used by cars. Remember to put your responsible tourist hat on when you are making parking decisions. During busy periods Service Point access may not be possible.

Using Aires all year: Aires make suitable night stops all year round and, unlike campsites, few close for the winter. Most Aires have a hard surface. Grass covered parking areas often have reinforcing. The open all year symbol is not highlighted for grass parking, but it can usually be accessed as long as weather conditions allow. Water may turned off during the winter to prevent frost damage.

Marina Aires

The Aires network is growing across Benelux, but it would be insufficient for demand if the marinas stopped accommodating motorhomes. These marinas fill the gap between Aires and campsites. They differ significantly, but many have excellent facilities and toilet blocks for boaters and campers. We set a budget of €15 per night because there are 470 Benelux campsites in the ACSI CampingCard scheme. To find details of all the marina Aires in the Netherlands, acquire copies of De Havengids from a marina. It is published in two volumes, north and south.

Oosterwijk marina

Custom Service Point

Service Point at Gouda

Service Points

Service Points provide three main functions: to replenish fresh water, and to dispose of waste (grey) water and toilet (black) waste. Service Points may facilitate one or all of these functions and some provide electricity. Park on the Service Point for no longer than it takes to exchange fluids.

Most Service Points are branded, simple and durable. Electricity is frequently provided and is mostly euro coin-operated and metered by kWh used. Sometimes the layout of a Service Point is confusing or a facility is a little way from the parking, especially at marinas.

Damme day parking

SERVICE POINTS

Drinking water: Benelux tap water is very palatable and consistent throughout the region. Thoughtless users are known to contaminate taps when rinsing toilet cassettes. Using disinfectant wipes or spray before drawing water will improve hygiene. Taps are normally threaded to assist the connection of hoses. Flot Bleu, Euro and Pacific Service Points have all the facilities located in one enclosed space increasing the risk of cross contamination. In addition, we have found the drinking water hose down the toilet emptying point on several occasions, so consider disinfection essential.

Waste water: Drive over drains differ widely in construction. Typically a shallow metal sink is set in concrete near the Service Point. Some drains are so badly designed or located that it is necessary to use a length of flexible pipe to direct waste water accurately. Some Service Points do not have a drain, but it is often possible to direct a pipe to the toilet emptying point. Flot Bleu, Euro and Pacific Service Points often have a short flexible pipe instead of a drive over drain.

Toilet cassette emptying: Cassette emptying points differ so widely that you may have to think about it before you work out the correct place. It may be necessary to remove a grid. Some drains are too small, so do not rush this operation as spillage will occur. In Benelux the drive-over emptying point is often the only facility. Local motorhomers usually travel with some bottled water for rinsing and flushing. Many commercial Aires have waste height toilet emptying points referred to in this guide as Seijsenser WC sinks. Make sure that your toilet is not too heavy to lift.

Maintain a hygiene gap.

Seijsener WC sink

HOLIDAY CLEANY water selection

Electricity: The electricity symbol **E** is highlighted for every Aire that has an electricity supply, regardless of cost or duration. No further information is provided if the electricity supply is less than one hour. Aires that offer unlimited or practical electricity supplies have the details written in the further information of either the Service Point or the Parking. Branded Service Points that charge for use, such as Aire Services or Euro Relais, normally have one or two electricity points. 55-60 minutes of electricity and 100 litres or 10 minutes of water is distributed upon payment, typically charging €2-€3. Flot Bleu Service Points normally provide 20 minutes of 'environ', access to water and electricity. Seijsener electricity bollards are common in Holland and often charge per kWh. Normally these bollards take euro coins. Flot Bleu electricity bollards normally provide four hours of electricity per token and up to 12 hours of electricity can be paid for in one go. Token costs differ from Aire to Aire.

Commercial and marina Aires often include electricity in their nightly charge. Be aware that in busy periods there may not be enough electricity points for the number of motorhomes staying.

Should you be lucky enough to stay at an Aire with free electricity, you will be expected to share it with several motorhomes.

Toilets and showers: Public toilets are inconvenient in Benelux due to their almost total absence. In the Netherlands you will literally need to spend a penny (50 cents) because it is normal to use café/restaurant facilities. The facilities at commercial and marina Aires are normally impeccably clean. Where necessary, prices and further information is detailed within the text of the entry.

Seijsener bollard

BRANDS OF SERVICE POINTS

HOLIDAY CLEANY: These are practical machines that have an accessible WC emptying point at the bottom. When two taps are fitted one is fresh water and one is for cassette rinsing. The cassette rinsing tap may work without payment. Ensure the switch, located on one side, is correctly positioned and press button 6. They usually have CEE electric points requiring payment with euro coins.

HOLIDAY CLEAN: These are practical machines that have an accessible WC emptying point at the bottom and are fitted with both a WC rinse tap and a drinking water tap. They do not have electricity.

MARYCAMP XL: These are practical machines that have an accessible WC cassette emptying point at the bottom with a WC rinse tap above. The drinking water tap is on the other side. When payment for water is required it is normally euro coins. Electricity is not provided.

SEIJSENER BOLLARD: These simple Service Points do not have a WC point. Both water and CEE electric are usually metered and payment is by euro coins.

SEIJSENER WC SINK: The stainless steel sink is designed for WC cassette emptying and can be encased in a variety of surrounds. Often they are at waist height, so cassette lifting is required. There is usually a tap for rinsing.

SANI STATION: These Service Points should require payment by euro coins before WC cassette emptying possible, however the roller shutters are often broken and left open. A rinsing tap is located inside the shutter. On the payment side there is a threaded tap. Ensure you connect your hose before payment is made. A hose is essential because of the tap's location.

Holiday Cleany

Typical drive over drain

FLOT BLEU: The Flot Bleu Euro and Pacific have all the services located behind a locked, narrow door on the left side of the cabinet. Be aware, the drinking water hose is prone to fall into the toilet disposal point, so clean the dispensing pistol before use. Flot Bleu Service Points normally provide 20 minutes of 'environ', access to water and electricity. These units are very robust and designed to be used all year around. Flot Bleu electricity bollards normally provide four hours of electricity per token and up to 12 hours of electricity can be paid for in one go.

Side view Flot Bleu Euro or Pacific

DEPAGNE: These oversized units are easy to use and normally provide an accessible WC emptying point. A WC rinse tap is located on one side and a fresh water tap on the other.

EURO RELAIS/RACLET and AIRE SERVICES: Euro Relais and Raclet are the same and Aire Services are very similar. These are practical machines that have an accessible WC emptying point at the bottom. Often there are two water taps. The one for toilet rinsing normally works without payment. When tokens or payment is required, 100 litres of water and one hour of electricity is dispensed.

CUSTOM: These Service Points are built by local craftsmen to individual designs. Take your time to find all the services as a facility may be a little way from where you expect.

Sani Station

Sani Station rear

Vicarious Shop

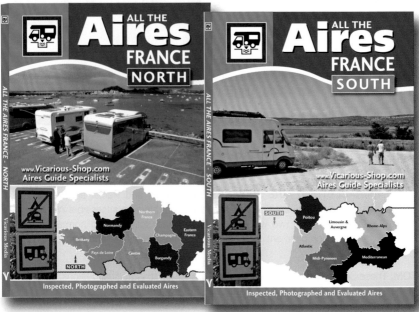

St Vith

Bouillon Day Parking

BELGIUM

Strépy-Thieu Ascenseur

Commonwealth War Memorial Plugstreet

VEURNE 🏛 E1 [1] N51°04.226' E002°39.889' 8630

Kaaiplaats. Exit A18 at Junction 1a and follow sp 'Veurne'. At roundabout by small windmill turn right, sp 'Nieuwpoort N39'. Turn left at next roundabout, with mixing bowl in centre, sp 'Veurne - Centrum'. Go straight over next roundabout, then turn right at following roundabout, sp 'Politie' and 'P'. Aire 200m on left, signed. Service Point just past parking on right.

🚐 5; Max 7m; See info
☂ Seijsener WC sink; By boat marina; Toilets €0.50; Showers €1.50

ℹ️ Popular parking area for motorhomes and locals alike. Barriers are installed on the official bays to prevent overhanging the pavement. For many years motorhomers have been parking adj to the Service Point on 25 unlevel 7m marina-side bays. www.toerisme-veurne.be Reinspected 2015.

NIEUWPOORT ⛺ E1 [2] N51°07.815' E002°45.909' 8620

De Zwerver, N367. Turn off N34 near the Albert memorial onto N318, sp 'Lombardsijde'. Then turn 1st right onto N380, sp 'Diksmuide'. Then turn left onto N367, sp 'Diksmuide'. In 650m turn left opp cemetery, sp 'De Zwerver'. Enter through barrier.

🚐 28; €16.50/1st 24hrs, then €12/24hrs; Inc 10amp CEE elec and WiFi (code on ticket)
☂ Custom; Inside barrier; Water €0.50/50L; €5/30 mins service only; Pay at machine

ℹ️ Landscaped, automated Aire adj to nursery greenhouses. The reinforced grass parking area is enclosed by a hedge preventing any views. SEP key card for shower (open 8am-8pm) and washing machine. Albert I monument, N51°08.214' E002°45.330', 1km along cycle path. Beach 4.5km. www.nieuwpoort.be Reinspected 2015.

LOMBARDSIJDE

E1 | 3 | N51°09.350' E002°45.583' | 8434

Strandjuttersdreef. Turn off N318 at KM-13.7, sp 'KACB camping'. Turn 2nd right into Bassevillestraat. Turn 1st left in 200m and Aire on left. Enter through barrier.

🦽 ▥ 🏚 E wc ♿ 🅿️ 🚌 F

● 🅿️ 🚐 ⚓ 🎵 🚌 F ❄️

🚐 35; €12/20hrs or €20/44hrs (low season); €17/20hrs or €30/44hrs (high season); Inc service and 10amp CEE elec; 9m x 4.5m bays; Reinforced grass parking

🪣 Seijsener bollard; Inside barrier

ℹ️ Landscaped Aire in between the suburbs and several large campsites, mostly occupied with static caravans. Local commerce adj to N318. Beach 800m: from entrance turn left and follow road for 400m, follow footpath straight through dunes, crossing N34 at zebra crossing, to beach. Reinspected 2015.

SP 🌳 🏕️ 🏃 📷 🔭 🚴 🚣 🦆

WESTENDE

E1 | 4 | N51°09.340' E002°45.994' | 8434

Heidestraat. Travelling towards Nieuwpoort on N318 drive past Camping Westende and take next turning on left, not signed. Aire 200m on right, signed. Enter through barrier.

🦽 ▥ 🏚 E wc ♿ 🅿️ 🚌 F

● 🅿️ 🚐 ⚓ 🎵 🚌 F ❄️

🚐 30; €15.50-€20/2pm-11am inc facilities; Advance booking poss

🪣 Seijsener WC sink 2pm-11am inc service, 10amp CEE elec and facilities; Advance booking poss

ℹ️ Nicely landscaped commercial Aire opp static holiday park. Pleasant hardstanding pitches, each with own grassy area. Use of seasonal swimming pool and café at campsite opp. WiFi available. www.camperparkwestende.be Local commerce and bus stop 300m on N318. Large sandy beach 1km. www.nieuwpoort.be Inspected 2015.

SP 🌳 🏕️ 🏃 📷 🔭 🚴 🚣 🦆

KEIEM ('t Nesthof) E1 | 5 | N51°04.300' E002°51.910' 8600

Zijdelingstraat 2A. From Diksmuide head north on N369 towards Middelkerke. Drive past Beerst, then after the right turn to Keiem turn left into Leimolenstraat. Follow road, then turn left into Zijdelingstraat. Aire on left at farm 't Nesthof, signed. Drive up drive to parking.

🚐 14; €9/night; Mar-Oct; Grass parking

🚰 Custom; WC emptying by entrance; Water tap by house; CEE elec €2/night

ℹ️ Pleasant commercial Aire at rural family farm house with goats and chickens. WiFi included, English spoken and daily bread orders taken. Conveniently located for following the WWI memorial cycle path visiting Diksmuide peace tower: N51°01.925' E002°51.187' and the Trench of Death: N51°02.746' E002°50.582', both also have day parking. Inspected 2015.

OUDENBURG E1 | 6 | N51°11.620' E003°00.330' 8460

Stationstraat. Exit A10 at Junction 5b following sp 'Oudenburg'. Service Point on left on northern outskirts adj to N358 main route. Clearly signed.

🚐 2; Max 30 mins; See info

🚰 Sani Station; €1 (2 x €0.50); No drive over drain

ℹ️ 2 Service Points located in roadside lay-by. Signs indicate 30 mins parking, however additional parking is unrestricted; 5m bays plus overhang. WC emptying opens for 5 mins only. Hose needed for fresh water. Reinspected 2015.

OSTEND E1 7 N51°12.277' E002°54.153' 8400

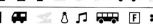

N33. Turn off N33 at roundabout junction with N341 into URBANO motorhome dealers. If travelling away from Ostend, entrance on right before roundabout. If travelling towards Ostend, turn left at roundabout and entrance off side road, not N33. Day parking available in town: N51°14.181' E002°56.158'.

Poss

Marycamp XL; Water €1/90L; 6 CEE elec points €1; No drive over drain

ℹ️ Service Point outside motorhome dealer adj to noisy main route in retail/light industrial area. Poss to park overnight, ask at dealership; open Mon-Sat 9am-6pm, Sun 10am-5pm. Dealership will work on most motorhomes. www.urbano.be Possible to catch a bus into Ostend at bus stop on opp side of roundabout. www.visitoostende.be Inspected 2015.

KORTEMARK E1 8 N51°01.913' E003°02.515' 8610

Ichtegemstraat. Turn off N35, sp 'Kortemark'. At roundabout adj to church follow sp 'Ichtegem' and 'Sportcentrum'. In 250m turn left, sp 'Sportcentrum' and 'Ichtegem'. In 180m turn right, sp 'Sportcentrum' and signed. Aire immediately on right, signed.

🚐 2

Sani Station x 2; €1; WC emptying opens for 5 mins only

ℹ️ There is no time limit, but the designated bays are adj to the Service Points and intended for their use. Other parking is unrestricted, but small 5m bays. www.kortemark.be Reinspected 2015.

AARTRIJKE   🏛 E1   9   N51°06.797' E003°05.396'   8211

Sint-Aarnoutstraat. Turn off N368 opposite church, sp 'Torhout'. In 400m turn right into the parking area before the Proxy minimarket, sp 'Zonnehart'. Follow road through parking area and around to left. Designated parking on left opp back entrance to Proxy minimarket, signed.

🚐 3; Max 48hrs
🚰 None; See 8

ℹ️ Conveniently located in a peaceful residential parking area behind a mini supermarket. Small town commerce 750m. Coastal parking restrictions make this one of the few practical night stops in the area. Reinspected 2015.

BRUGES   ⚓ E1   10   N51°11.783' E003°13.510'   8000

Vaartdijkstraat, at southern point of Bruges R30 ring road, signed. Designated night parking to left (22 spaces) and right (33 spaces), both via barrier. Take a ticket and pay at booth before departing.

🚐 55; €25/night Apr-Sept; €19/night Oct-Mar; Inc service and 6amp CEE elec; Pay at machine
🚰 Custom x 2; Water €0.50 (free at time of inspection); Inside barriers both sides

ℹ️ Pleasant landscaped commercial Aire just 500m from historic Bruges centre. Parking to right is more popular as further from ring road and closer to canal. The Brugge City Card, www.bruggecitycard.be, offers discounts and freebies across the city. www.discoverbruges.com Reinspected 2015.

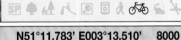
Parking to right

Parking to left

BEERNEM ⚓ E1 | 11 | N51°08.060' E003°20.083' 8730

Oude Vaartstraat. Exit A10/E40 at Junction 10 and follow sp 'Beernem'. Turn right before canal bridge, sp 'Kanaaloever' and signed. Follow road to right along canal. Aire on left in 600m, signed.

🔧 ▥ 🏠 E wc ♿ 📶 🚌 F

● P 🚐 ⚓ 🜖 🎵 🚌 F ❋

🚐 6; €10/night; Pay at machine; Max 72hrs
💧 Seijsener bollard; 4 unmetered 16amp CEE elec points

ℹ️ 6 shaded landscaped bays adj to a canal and marina, no view or access but pedestrian bridge 300m. Open access Service Point before parking. Town commerce 600m. Adj cycle path runs all the way to Bruges. www.beernem.be Reinspected 2015.

SP 🌳 🏕 🚶 📷 🗑 🚶 🚲 🛶 🎣 🐾

EEKLO ⚓ E2 | 12 | N51°10.733' E003°32.979' 9900

Eeklose Jachthaven. Exit Eeklo to south on N499 towards Ursel. At Eeklose boundary sign turn right, sp 'Niewendorp'. Follow road to left then go straight on, sp 'Jachthaven', into marina.

🔧 ▥ 🏠 E wc ♿ 📶 🚌 F

● P 🚐 ⚓ 🜖 🎵 🚌 F ❋

🚐 12; €10/24hrs; Collected, Reinforced grass parking
💧 Custom; Behind blue building; Water €0.50/100L; 6amp CEE elec €5/24hrs; Showers €1/10 mins (Closed Thurs)
ℹ️ Commercial marina Aire with large hedged bays overlooking canalside marina and main road. Some road noise. Toilet block open during day. Service Point is basic. The marina is dotted with sculptures, especially along the edge of the canal. Catch a steam train 10km to Maldegem where you can visit the Steam Centre, www.stoomcentrum.be www.eeklo.be Reinspected 2015.

SP 🌳 🏕 🚶 📷 🗑 🚶 🚲 🛶 🎣 🐾

MARIA AALTER   E2   13   N51°05.955' E003°22.291'   9880

Schuurlo. Turn off N370, sp 'Ruiselede'. Follow road for 2km, then turn left, sp 'St Maria Aalter'. Drive 2.6km, through village, and Aire is in the 3.5t weight restricted car park on left opp chapel, signed.

🚐 2; 9m bays plus 2m overhang
🚰 Seijsener bollard; Water €1/100L

ℹ️ Pleasant, peaceful designated parking on edge of village with local commerce. Cycle path adj; woodland walks from village. Café opp Aire serves cakes, pancakes and waffles. Catch a train from the station, 1.4km, and visit Bruges, 15-35 mins, or Ghent, 26 mins; see www.belgianrail.be Inspected 2015.

WINGENE   E1   14   N51°04.447' E003°15.920'   8750

Noordakkerstraat. Turn off N370 in Wingene, sp 'St Elooi'. Follow road for 2km, then in St Elooi turn 1st right. Aire 500m on left, signed.

🚐 6; €8/24hrs inc elec; €4/24hrs if eat in café; Max 72hrs; 10m bays
🚰 Custom; 6 unmetered CEE elec points

ℹ️ Rural, landscaped, commercial Aire with open feel at family dairy farm and ice cream makers. Café open Fri-Sat 2-10pm, Sun 11.30am-10pm all year, and Tues-Thurs in high season. Fresh milk and ice cream available to take away. Rural views across grazing fields owned by dairy farm. www.smart-ijs.blogspot.be www.wingene.be Inspected 2015.

LICHTERVELDE

E1 | 15 | N51°01.445' E003°08.170' | 8810

Nieuwstraat. Turn off N32 onto N370, sp 'Lichtervelde' and 'P OC De Schouw'. Follow road for 1.8km, then turn right onto Nieuwstraat, sp 'P OC De Schouw'. Designated parking 200m on left, signed. This route avoids 2.3m height restriction.

2; Max 48hrs   None; See 8

ℹ Small designated parking to rear of municipal building backing onto fields with an additional large car park adj. Sheltered from road noise, but only 300m from small town commerce. The town has a small cinema dating to 1924, www.cinemadekeizer.be, and the info panel outside the church details the kapelroute, a 26km cycle ride passing 22 chapels. www.lichtervelde.be
Inspected 2015.

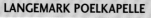

LANGEMARK POELKAPELLE

E1 | 16 | N50°54.618' E002°55.072' | 8920

Boezingestraat. Turn off N313 opp Canadian memorial, Monument St Julien: N50°53.964' E002°56.398' (parking adj), sp 'Langemark'. At traffic lights turn left, sp 'Poperinge'. In 400m turn right, sp 'Sportscentrum'. Drive through car park to right, signed, and Aire on left, signed.

8; €12/night; Reinforced grass parking
Custom; 8 unmetered CEE elec points

ℹ Adj to sports facilities with bar; sports centre open 9am-10pm. Small town commerce and Voie Verte cycle path from Kortemark to Pilkem, 800m. Photo panels around town show WWI destruction. German War Cemetery of Langemark remembers 44,000 dead, 1.3km north, signed: N50°55.303' E002°55.075'. www.langemarkpoelkapelle.be
Reinspected 2015.

German Cemetery

ROESELARE   E1   17   N50°56.645' E003°08.015'   8800

Trakelweg, adj to Onze-Lieve-Vrouwemarkt. Exit A17 at Junction 7 and follow sp 'Roeselare'. In 800m turn left at roundabout, sp 'Haven Noord'. Follow road along canal, past canal loading bays. At traffic lights turn left, cross canal, then turn immediately right, sp 'Haven Zone 1'. Follow road in same direction but on other side of canal. Aire at end of road/canal on right, signed.

🚐 2; Other additional parking locally
🚻 None; See 19

ℹ️ Designated parking overlooking canal at the end of a working wharf. Noise from road, train line and industry, however this is pleasant waterside parking near the town centre. Town centre and train station 500m, via cycling/walking; cross under railway, turn right and follow path to large square before train station. www.roeselare.be Inspected 2015.

MESEN   E1   18   N50°45.830' E002°53.883'   8957

Zwijnemarkt. From Ypres follow sp 'Mesen' onto N365. Follow road through Mesen, then when road bends sharply to right turn left. Designated parking 10m on right outside the church, signed.

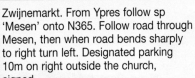

🚐 2; Max 24hrs; Max 10m
🚻 None; See 19

ℹ️ Designated parking in town known as Messines during WWI. The crypt of the adj church was a German military hospital and Adolf Hitler was treated here during WWI. The church bells play well known war songs every 15 mins during the day. Small town commerce 200m. www.mesen.be Reinspected 2015.

WEVELGEM   E1   19   N50°48.878' E003°12.125'   8560

N8/Kortrijkstraat. Travelling south on A17 exit at Junction 5, sp 'N8 Wevelgem'. At roundabout turn right, sp 'Kortrijk'. Drive past the VanoMobil motorhome dealer on left. At next roundabout, by LIDL, go right round and return to VanoMobil motorhome dealer on right. Service Point immediately on right, signed.

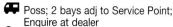
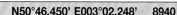

🚐 Poss; 2 bays adj to Service Point; Enquire at dealer

🚰 Euro Relais Mini; Token (ER); Large motorhomes would impede entrance when servicing

ℹ️ Service Point located on motorhome dealer forecourt adj to noisy road. Opening hours: Mon-Fri 9am-6.30pm (closed noon-1.30pm), Sat 10am-6pm, closed Sun. 12 parking bays on forecourt are accessible outside of opening times. Adj roadside parking is 3.5t weight restricted. www.wevelgem.be Inspected 2015.

WERVIK   E1   20   N50°46.450' E003°02.248'   8940

De Balokken. Exit N58 at Junction 5 and follow sp 'Komen' onto N531. Drive through industrial estate, then at the roundabout by LIDL turn left, sp 'Wervik'. In 800m as enter Wervik turn right opp cemetery, sp 'Centrum'. Turn immediately right, sp 'De Balokken'. Follow road and cross river bridge, then turn left. Follow road to end and turn right, signed. Aire on left through barrier, signed.

🚐 8; €10/72hrs inc 16amp CEE elec; Pay at barrier with 10 x €1 coins!; Max 72hrs; Reinforced grass parking

🚰 Marycamp XL; Inside barrier; Water €1/100L

ℹ️ Popular landscaped Aire in hedged section of car park within a pleasant 36 hectare recreation park. Café adj, open daily Jul-Aug, weekends rest of year. Small town commerce and tobacco museum across river via pedestrian bridge. Cycle path along river Leie or follow Tabaksroute around the former tobacco plantations. www.wervik.be Inspected 2015.

KORTRIJK   🏛 T   E1   [21]   N50°49.961' E003°16.037'   8500

Parking Broeltorens, IJzerkaai. From north on N50 turn left at traffic lights at end of road, sp 'Harelbeke' and 'R36'. Go straight across roundabout, sp 'P Broeltorens'. Cross river bridge and turn right at roundabout, sp 'Buda' and 'P Broeltorens'. Follow road and Aire in barriered car park on left. Press buzzer for assistance and access. Aire on far side of car park, signed.

🚰 ▥ 🔲 E 🚾 ♿ 🐾 🚌 F

⊕ P 🚐 ⛵ 🗑 🎵 🚌 F ✳

🚐 8; €10/24hrs up to 72hrs, then €15/24hrs; CC; Max 9m

👕 Marycamp XL; Inside barrier; Inc

ℹ Aire in designated corner of pleasant, barriered car park on island in town centre; some shaded parking. River adj, but no views. Riverside park to one side, town centre with large town commerce to other including Broelt towers and museum, 150m. www.toerismekortrijk.be Inspected 2015.

SP 🌳 ⛺ 🎿 📷 🖥 🚶 🚴 🛶 🦅

HEULE (KORTRIJK)   🏛   E1   [22]   N50°50.697' E003°14.126'   8501

Lagaeplein, at rear of church off Zeger Van Heulestraat. Exit R8 ring road at Junction 8, sp 'Heule', and follow sp 'Heule'. In centre turn left, sp 'Lagaeplein'. In 100m turn left, sp 'Lagaeplein'. Follow road and parking signed on far side of car park.

🚰 ▥ 🔲 E 🚾 ♿ 🐾 🚌 F

⊕ P 🚐 ⛵ 🗑 🎵 🚌 F ✳

🚐 1; See info

👕 None; See [19]

ℹ Designated bay in busiest part of car park closest to adj swimming pool. The car park has more suitable and level places along the bottom edge. Local commerce adj to church, 100m. Poss to cycle to Kortrijk centre (2.5km) on roadside cycle path. www.toerismekortrijk.be Reinspected 2015.

SP 🌳 ⛺ 🎿 📷 🖥 🚶 🚴 🛶 🦅

HARELBEKE   🏃 E1 ☐23   N50°50.756' E003°18.660'   8530

Sporthal de Dageraad. Turn off N43 at roundabout, sp 'Stasegem'. Follow road straight on, passing under a railway bridge, sp 'Sporthal de Dageraad', and go straight over roundabout, sp 'Sporthal de Dageraad' and signed. Turn left in 100m, sp 'Sporthal de Dageraad' and signed. Aire 100m on right, enter through barrier.

🚐 8; €5/24hrs inc service and 6amp CEE elec; Pay at barrier
💧 Marycamp XL; Inside barrier

ℹ️ Small, landscaped, commercial Aire adj to sports facilities and crazy golf. Facilities include a bar/café, open access sports fields and a large recreational lake, 400m. Town centre 1.5km. www.harelbeke.be Reinspected 2015.

SINT ELOOIS VIJVE   ⚓ E2 ☐24   N50°54.537' E003°24.260'   8793

Leiesas. From Deinze follow N43 for 12km towards Kortrijk. Turn right at traffic lights onto 5.5t restricted road, sp 'St-Eloois-Vijve', 'Waregem Zone 6b' and signed. Drive through St Eloois Vijve, turning right before river bridge, sp 'Waregem Zone 6b' and signed. Before Leievoeders building turn left, signed. Turn left before river and Aire on left, signed. Enter via barrier.

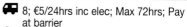

🚐 8; €5/24hrs inc elec; Max 72hrs; Pay at barrier
💧 Marycamp XL; Inside barrier; Water €1/90L

ℹ️ Landscaped, commercial Aire on reinforced grass adj to river Leie, limited views. Evening shade from a willow tree, and there is road noise from the river bridge. Small town commerce 450m, via steps up to river bridge. Towpath on opp side of river runs from Armentieres all the way to Zeebrugge. Inspected 2015.

MACHELEN

E2 25 N50°57.657' E003°28.987' 9870

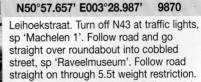

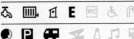

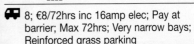

Leihoekstraat. Turn off N43 at traffic lights, sp 'Machelen 1'. Follow road and go straight over roundabout into cobbled street, sp 'Raveelmuseum'. Follow road straight on through 5.5t weight restriction. At T-junction turn left, sp 'P'. Follow road to right. Turn left into car park, signed. Aire is to rear of car park. Enter through barrier.

🚐 8; €8/72hrs inc 16amp elec; Pay at barrier; Max 72hrs; Very narrow bays; Reinforced grass parking

🚽 Sani Station; Inside barrier; €1

ⓘ Landscaped commercial Aire on edge of village backing onto green space. Self-serve chain boat adj, just jump on and drag yourself across the lake. Village 200m with local commerce. Cycle/walking path adj extends along river Leie from Armentieres all the way to Zeebrugge. www.machelen.be Inspected 2015.

TOURNAI

E1 26 N50°36.232' E003°22.859' 7500

Boulevard Bara. Exit A8 at Junction 34, sp 'Tournai', and follow sp 'Tournai' onto N50. Follow road, then turn right at roundabout onto R52 ring road, sp 'Toutes Directions'. At traffic lights veer to the right into service road, signed, and then in 100m turn right into car park, signed. Service Point at far side of car park, signed.

🚐 20   🚽 Custom

ⓘ Parking adj to ring road and open access sports fields. 800m to UNESCO World Heritage cathedral and belfry (the oldest in Belgium); climb the stairs for a fantastic view of Tournai. Annual beer festival, www.tournai-beer-festival.com Calendar of events on TO's website, www.visittournai.be Reinspected 2015.

RONSE ☆ E2 | 27 | N50°44.636' E003°35.310' 9600

N48/Engelsenlaan. From Tournai follow N48 to Ronse, sp 'Renaix'. At Ronse turn left at roundabout, sp 'Kortrijk'. At next roundabout turn right, sp 'Centrum'. Then turn right opp ALDI into swimming pool car park, signed. Aire straight on through barrier, signed.

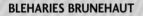

🚐 5; Access via barrier during opening hours

🐷 None; See | 26 |

ℹ️ Aire in car park behind swimming pool, accessible through barrier. Pleasant park behind. Aire on edge of town with ALDI opp. Ronse centre includes a railway station that was moved brick by brick from Bruges. Ronse is on the edge of Parc Naturel du Pays des Collines, www.paysdescollines.be www.ontdekronse.be Inspected 2015.

BLEHARIES BRUNEHAUT ⚓ F2 | 28 | N50°31.018' E003°25.308' 7620

Quai de l'Escaut, off N507/Rue des Combattants. Approach from south on N507 following sp 'Tournai'. After crossing roundabout turn right, signed, and then 1st left to designated quayside parking, signed.

🚐 10   🐷 None; See | 26 |

ℹ️ Designated parking overlooking the river Lys and the barges going by. Good cycle path on both sides of the navigation. Local commerce 200m. Saint Aybert is an interesting Art Deco-style church designed by architect Henry Lacoste and built between 1924-26. From roundabout, church is 400m on left as walk to town: N50°30.777' E003°24.893'. Inspected 2015.

Info/photos: Janet & John Watts

GERAARDSBERGEN ⚓ E2 29 N50°47.537' E003°54.169' 9500

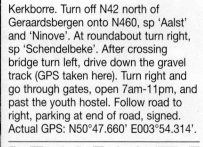

Kerkborre. Turn off N42 north of Geraardsbergen onto N460, sp 'Aalst' and 'Ninove'. At roundabout turn right, sp 'Schendelbeke'. After crossing bridge turn left, drive down the gravel track (GPS taken here). Turn right and go through gates, open 7am-11pm, and past the youth hostel. Follow road to right, parking at end of road, signed. Actual GPS: N50°47.660' E003°54.314'.

🚐 6; Max 24hrs

🚿 None; Water tap by boats; See 30

ℹ️ Popular summer parking between canal and leisure lakes, but no real view of either. Peaceful location with park and walks adj. Youth hostel with evening bar 150m. www.geraardsbergen.be Reinspected 2015.

AALST 🚶 E2 30 N50°56.309' E004°03.474' 9300

Zwembadlaan. From east on N9 turn right at traffic lights before Dats 24 fuel station onto R41, sp 'Andere-richtingen'. Turn 2nd right in 450m by ALDI, signed. In 300m turn left, signed. Drive through car park to Aire, signed. Rush hour is terrible so if poss approach from this direction during work hours.

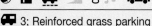
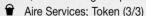

🚐 3; Reinforced grass parking

🚿 Aire Services; Token (3/3)

ℹ️ Pleasant Aire in separate area from car park adj to sports facilities and indoor swimming pool. Pleasant open access green space adj; dogs must be kept on a lead. Supermarket 350m. Town centre 2km, market in centre Sat 8am-1pm. www.aalst.be Reinspected 2015.

DONKMEER   🏃   E2   31   N51°02.506' E003°59.004'   9290

N467/Donklaan. At Donkmeer turn off N467, sp 'Festivalhal' and signed. Turn right, signed, and Aire on left, signed. 3.5t weight restriction on Aire. Actual GPS: N51°02.561' E003°58.978'.

🚐 5; Max 48hrs

🚽 None; See 30

ℹ️ Reinforced grass parking near events area and recreation space around a lake, no views. Boat hire avail. Bars/restaurants 200m. The town has a pleasant, resort feel. www.donkmeer.be Reinspected 2015.

GENTBRUGGE   🏢   E2   32   N51°02.229' E003°46.024'   9050

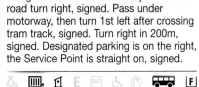

Driebeekstraat. From east exit E17/A14 at Junction 10, sp 'Gentbrugge' and 'P&R'. At traffic lights follow sp 'Gentbrugge' alongside/under the motorway. At end of road turn right, signed. Pass under motorway, then turn 1st left after crossing tram track, signed. Turn right in 200m, signed. Designated parking is on the right, the Service Point is straight on, signed.

 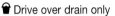

🚐 20   🚽 Drive over drain only

ℹ️ The motorhome parking is closest to the motorway, but despite suffering road noise this is one of the best used Aires in Belgium due to its convenient location. Sports facilities and private, pay kids' play area adj. Large play area and green space 200m at end of road. Tram (No. 22) adj direct to Ghent every 6 mins. http://stad.gent/gentbrugge Reinspected 2015.

BELLEM   E2   33   N51°05.851' E003°29.717'   9881

Vaart-Zuid. Exit Bellem to north towards Ursel. Before bridge turn right onto 3.5t weight restricted road. Follow road to end and turn left. Parking along canal, signed. Parking also on other side of canal, not weight restricted: N51°05.961' E003°29.620'. Cross bridge, turn right and follow road to canal. Turn right along canalside and parking is adj to canal, signed.

20+; Depending on parking

None; See 11

Pleasant and popular designated motorhome parking alongside canal with barges passing occasionally. Good bakery and chocolatier 300m: N51°05.789' E003°29.882'; local commerce 750m. Reinspected 2015.

LOTENHULLE   E2   34   N51°02.813' E003°27.841'   9880

Guldensporenplein. Exit A10 at Junction 11, sp 'Aalter'. At roundabout turn right onto N409, sp 'Deinze'. Follow N409 for 3.5km towards Deinze. 100m after turning to Nevele (on left) turn right, sp 'Feestzaal'. Parking at far side of large cycle shop.

1

None; See 11

1 designated space impeded by tree. Chip shop and large retail cycle shop adj. Reinspected 2015.

ASSENEDE 🏨 E2 35 N51°13.840' E003°44.988' 9960

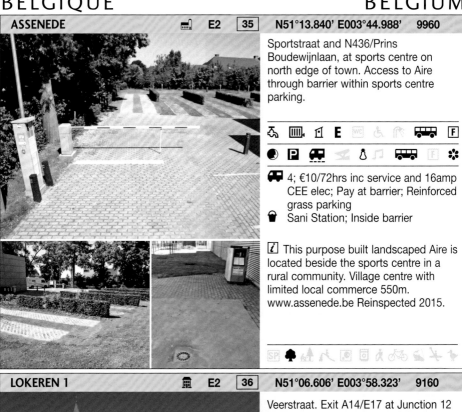

Sportstraat and N436/Prins Boudewijnlaan, at sports centre on north edge of town. Access to Aire through barrier within sports centre parking.

🚐 4; €10/72hrs inc service and 16amp CEE elec; Pay at barrier; Reinforced grass parking

🪣 Sani Station; Inside barrier

ℹ️ This purpose built landscaped Aire is located beside the sports centre in a rural community. Village centre with limited local commerce 550m. www.assenede.be Reinspected 2015.

LOKEREN 1 🏛 E2 36 N51°06.606' E003°58.323' 9160

Veerstraat. Exit A14/E17 at Junction 12 onto N47 (2nd Junction 12 if coming from Ghent), sp 'N47 Lokeren'. Follow N47 to end and turn right at traffic lights onto N70, sp 'Daknam'. Turn left at next traffic lights and the parking is in the car park on right opp church, signed.

🚐 5; Max 48hrs

🪣 None; See 40

ℹ️ An uninspiring but perfectly adequate place to stopover. Alongside the main route so expect some traffic noise, and loud church bells! Local commerce adj. Town centre 1.8km. From car park cross road and turn left walking along tree line. At river turn right and follow river through countryside 1.5km to central square with TO. www.lokeren.be Reinspected 2015.

LOKEREN 2   E2   37   N51°06.593' E003°59.694'   9160

Aardeken. From Ghent follow N70 to Lokeren and drive past 36. In 800m, after passing ALDI, turn right at traffic lights, sp 'Station'. Follow road for 500m, pass under bridge, then at roundabout turn left, sp 'Hoogland'. Follow road for 550m, then as road bends left turn right, sp 'P Aardeken - gratis'. Turn right in 70m and designated parking in corner on right, signed. Approach from Hoogland has a 2.75m height restriction.

2; See info   None; See 40

ℹ️ Slightly isolated designated parking in large car park surrounded by woods and adj to popular country park. River bridge, 240m, leads to more sports facilities and town centre. Info board adj details the scale of the park and location of a café. Paardenworst, horse meat sausages, are a regional speciality. www.verlorenbos.be Inspected 2015.

Photo: Donna Garner

Photo: Donna Garner

HAMME   E2   38   N51°06.261' E004°08.506'   9220

Hamveer. Turn off N41 at traffic lights, sp 'Hamme'. Turn right in 300m before Avia fuel station into 3.5t weight restricted road, sp 'P'. Turn right at end of road, sp 'Hamveer'. Turn right at end of road into 3.5t weight restricted parking, signed.

2; Max 48hrs   None; See 40

ℹ️ Popular designated parking in large car park adj to river Durme, no views. Mira bridge, adj, originally built in 1898, destroyed in the war and restored in 2003. It is now the beginning of popular cycle/walking paths to Temse, St Amand and beyond. Locals are known as Wuitens, the Jay bird, which is the town mascot. See the mascot at the town's festival, a 3-day event starting on Carnival Sunday. Start dates: 6.3.16, 26.3.17 and 11.3.18, www.wuitensfeesten.be www.hamme.be Inspected 2015.

TEMSE 1   E2   39   N51°07.507' E004°12.535'   9140

P De Zaat, Oeverstraat. From Puurs on N16 cross bridge and take 1st exit off N16, not signed, and turn left. Turn right at Stop junction. Follow road straight on past LIDL, then turn left, sp 'Parkeerroute'. At end of road turn right, sp 'P De Zaat'. In 200m turn left into P De Zaat. Follow road downhill and designated parking is on right, signed.

🚐 10; 6m bays plus unlimited grass overhang

🛒 None; See 40

ℹ️ Designated parking in town centre with town commerce adj. Town hall with TO 200m. www.temse.be The town is dominated by the river Schelde, no views from Aire. Cycle 4km along river to Fort van Steendorp: N51°07.385' E004°15.553', for a self-guided tour or a guided walk on the 1st Sat of the month, €2pp. Inspected 2015.

TEMSE 2 (Alpha Motorhomes)   E2   40   N51°08.211' E004°10.811'   9140

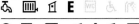

Kapelanielaan, off N16 in industrial estate at Alpha Motorhomes. Exit A14 at Junction 15 and follow sp 'Temse'. Drive past motorhome dealer on left, then turn left off N16 at 1st set of traffic lights. Turn 1st left onto service road, sp 'Zone A'. Service Point and parking on right outside motorhome dealer's gate.

🚐 5; Do not park in front of Service Point

🛒 Custom; 1 Cont + 2 CEE elec points

ℹ️ Adj to busy main road in industrial estate. Daytime access to Service Point is difficult due to parked cars, but Service Point is free and accessible 24hrs. Dealer has small accessory shop, open Tues-Fri 9am-12pm, 1-6pm, Sat 10am-12pm, 1-5pm. www.temse.be Reinspected 2015.

SINT AMANDS 🏛 E2 41 N51°03.567' E004°12.121' 2890

Emile Verhaerenstraat. From Bornem, northeast of town, travel south, sp 'St Amand'. Follow road for 5.3km going straight across all junctions. Aire is on right as enter St Amands, signed.

🛁 🚾 🔁 E 🚾 ♿ 📡 🚌 F

⚫ P 🚐 ⤳ 🗑 🎵 🚌 F ✳

🚐 2; 10m bays
🛈 Custom

ℹ️ 2 designated bays on edge of car park adj to creek off River Schelde. Walking/cycling path along river to Temse or Dendermonde or inland to Puurs. Local commerce 400m. A steam train runs from Dendermonde to Puurs on Sundays Jul-Sept, €10pp return, and a bike carriage is avail, see www.stoomtrein.be www.sintamands.be Reinspected 2015.

SP 🌳 🧗 🔫 📷 🗑 🚶 🚲 🐿 🎣 🦆

BEVEREN 🚶 E2 42 N51°12.723' E004°14.649' 9120

Klapperstraat. From town centre head towards Ghent on N70 and turn right just after AZ Nikolaas Hospital, sp 'Waasland Beveren'. Follow road to right, then in 300m turn left, sp 'P' and 'De Meerminnen'. Turn 1st right and parking on the left, signed.

🛁 🚾 🔁 E 🚾 ♿ 📡 🚌 F

⚫ P 🚐 ⤳ 🗑 🎵 🚌 F ✳

🚐 2; 8m bays; See info 🛈 None; 40
ℹ️ 2 narrow, designated bays in a very large car park that will only be busy during sporting events. The location feels secluded as it is screened from habitation by a hedge. Small town commerce 950m. Cortewalle Castle, 1.8km, offers free entry May-Sept on the 1st and 3rd Sunday of month at 3pm at castle entrance: N51°12.869' E004°15.829'. www.beveren.be Inspected 2015.

SP 🌳 🧗 🔫 📷 🗑 🚶 🚲 🐿 🎣 🦆

WILLEBROEK   🏰   E2   43   N51°03.619' E004°20.689'   2830

Dijleaan. Exit A12 at Junction 7 and follow sp 'Willebroek' onto N183. At traffic lights by Brico turn left. At end of road turn left again and the Aire is in the car park on the right in 280m. GPS taken at Service Point.

🚽 💧 🔲 E WC ♿ 🚏 🚌 F

⚫ P 🚐 ⛵ 🍾 🎵 🚌 F ❇️

🚐 20

🚰 Sani Station; €1; No drive over drain

ℹ️ Popular transitory Aire in pleasant tree-lined parking. Town centre with town commerce 600m. Star fort formerly used as a Nazi detention centre, now a remembrance museum, 400m: N51°03.485' E004°20.468'. Museum open daily 9.30am-5.30pm, €11pp; see www.breendonk.be www.willebroek.be Reinspected 2015.

SP 🌳 🚶 🏃 📷 🎣 🚴 🛶 🦢 🦅

ANTWERP (Camper Park Vogelzang) 🅰 E3   44   N51°11.399' E004°24.051'   2020

Vogelzanglaan. From west exit Ring 1, sp 'Wilrijk'. Follow sp 'Wilrijk' and 'Antwerp Expo', turning right at 2 sets of traffic lights. The Aire is on right up drop kerb. Antwerp now has a low emissions zone requiring vehicle registration. These directions avoid the low emissions zone.

🚽 💧 🔲 E WC ♿ 🚏 🚌 F

⚫ P 🚐 ⛵ 🍾 🎵 🚌 F ❇️

🚐 115; €8/night Sept-May; €10/night Jun-Aug; Closed Nov for Antwerp book fair

🚰 Custom; 16amp CEE elec €1/kW

ℹ️ This is a laidback commercial Aire at a former municipal campsite just 1km from Antwerp centre, www.camperparkvogelzang.be Tram stop by the Expo building, 150m; see www.antwerpexpo.be www.antwerpen.be Reinspected 2015.

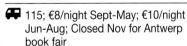

SP 🌳 🚶 🏃 📷 🎣 🚴 🛶 🦢 🦅

PUURS — E2 — 45 — N51°04.487' E004°17.056' — 2870

Kerkhofstraat. Turn off N16 at traffic lights east of Puurs, sp 'Kalfort'. Follow road 900m. At roundabout turn right to go straight on, sp 'Centrum' and 'P Route'. Turn left before no entry sign, sp 'Kerkhofstraat P'. In 150m turn left into car park, signed. Aire halfway through car park, signed.

2; Max 48hrs; 11m bays

Custom; Water avail Apr-mid Oct; 2 CEE elec points (Turned off since 2010)

Aire in car park adj to cemetery and sports facility; open access playing fields past tennis courts. 3 large bays opp are undesignated. Local bar adj, high street commerce 150m. Cycle path to St Amands. www.puurs.be Fort Liezele, a defensive bunker built in 1908, is 1km and has a path around with info panels; museum open Mar-Nov Sat/Sun/holidays 1.30-5.30pm, www.fortliezele.be Reinspected 2015.

KALMTHOUT — D3 — 46 — N51°22.619' E004°26.967' — 2920

Heibloemlaan. Exit Kalmthout on N111 towards Stabroek. Turn off, sp 'De Vroente', and the designated parking is in the car park on the left, signed.

2; Max 48hrs

None; See 48

Parking at cross-border nature park and leisure area. Adj woods have marked walking/cycling trails with info panels. Disabled access includes off-road wheelchairs, free hire from Interpretation Centre. Bee/nature exhibition with lots of taxidermy. US army gun, WWII V1 bomb defence. Restaurants adj. Small town commerce 2km in Heide. www.kalmthout.be Reinspected 2015.

BELGIQUE   BELGIUM

ESSEN 🏛 D3 47   N51°28.241' E004°27.857' 2910

N133/Essenseweg. From village centre
follow sp 'Nispen'. Turn left into car park
just before exit village into Holland. Aire
in far corner, signed.

🚐 1; Max 24hrs; Max 7m if staying
overnight
💧 Water only (Slow); See 48

ℹ️ Aire on the Dutch/Belgian border.
Really just a water point as Aire is within
car park used by residential apartments,
but poss to stay overnight if necessary.
High street commerce 300m.
www.essen.be Reinspected 2015.

BRASSCHAAT 🚶 D3 48   N51°17.144' E004°30.184' 2900

N121/Elshoutbaan. Turn off N115 at
traffic lights onto N121, sp 'Brasschaat'.
In 1.7km, before Brasschaat, turn left
into woodland parking area, sp 'Parking
5'. Turn right, signed, and then either
turn right to parking, signed, or straight
on to Service Point on left, signed.

🚐 10; Max 72hrs
💧 Seijsener bollard; Water €0.50/100L;
4 CEE elec points €0.50/0.5kW

ℹ️ Very pleasant parking under oak
trees adj to main road, some noise.
Large open access country park adj with
landscaped gardens, walks, cycle paths,
children's play area, water slides and
swimming pool. There are also
restaurants, bars and a mansion open
for private events. Reinspected 2015.

BRECHT   🏭 D3   49   N51°20.877' E004°38.485'   2960

Gemeentepark. Turn off N115 in Brecht at traffic lights onto N133, sp 'Westmalle'. In 200m turn left off N133, sp 'Cultureel Centrum'. Turn left into car park, signed. Undesignated parking in car park.

♿ 🏛 🔌 E WC ♿ 🏔 🚌 F

⚫ P 🚐 ⬗ 🛢 🎵 🚌 F ✳

🚐 2; Max 48hrs; 8m bays plus overhang; See info

🚽 None; See 48

ℹ️ The car park has long spaces with overhang opportunities, but the access road is twisty and the car park is popular. Open and shaded parking, adj to park just off town centre with cobbled high street, TO and library. www.brecht.be Reinspected 2015.

SP 🌳 🏕 🧗 📷 📺 🚶 🚴 🛶 🏊

ST JOB IN T GOOR   🏛 D3   50   N51°18.106' E004°34.141'   2960

Vaartlaan. Turn off N115 at traffic lights, sp 'St-Job-in-'t-Goor'. Cross lift bridge and turn immediately right. Designated parking in 2nd parking area on right, signed.

♿ 🏛 🔌 E WC ♿ 🏔 🚌 F

⚫ P 🚐 ⬗ 🛢 🎵 🚌 F ✳

🚐 2; Max 48hrs; Max 6m

🚽 None; See 48

ℹ️ Adj to canal, lift bridge and pleasure boat marina, but no views. Parking in standard parking bays with little overhang. High street commerce inc ALDI 250m. Reinspected 2015.

SP 🌳 🏕 🧗 📷 📺 🚶 🚴 🛶 🏊

GROBBENDONK   E3   51   N51°11.354' E004°44.171'   2280

Vaartkom. From N13 turn off at traffic lights, sp 'Grobbendonk'. Follow road over bridge and at the 1st roundabout turn left, sp 'De Volle Vaart'. Aire is 200m on left, signed.

🚐 5; 11m bays plus overhang

🚰 Sani Station; €1; 6 16amp CEE elec points €1/kW

i Aire in car park adj to fire station opp sports facilities. Centre with small town commerce 200m. Cycle/walking path along river SAS nearby. Reinspected 2015.

LIER   E3   52   N51°07.516' E004°34.455'   2500

N10/Aarschotsesteenweg. Enter town from south on N10. Go straight on at traffic lights and Aire is in car park on right, sp 'De Mol'.

🚐 2; See info

🚰 Sani Station; €1; No drive over drain

i Oversubscribed Aire with designated bays adj to main road in large car park. The undesignated parking behind the Service Point is often used as overflow motorhome parking. Fritterie adj. Green space beside river, 150m. Pretty, historic central square and town commerce 900m. Reinspected 2015.

BELGIUM

BELGIQUE

PUTTE 🏃 E3 | 53 | **N51°02.806' E004°37.538'** 2580

Heuvel. From town centre follow sp 'Mechelen' on N15. In 750m turn left, sp 'Sportscentrum'. Turn right in 500m, sp 'P'. Designated parking in car park, signed.

🚐 2; Max 48hrs; 10m bays
🚽 Custom; No drive over drain

ℹ️ Designated parking at sports centre. On the old farm building by the tennis courts there is a memorial to Frank Klepper, an American WWII soldier who was killed here in 1944 by a V1 rocket. Small town commerce 1.5km in centre. www.putte.be Inspected 2015.

ROTSELAAR 🏃 E3 | 54 | **N50°57.715' E004°43.349'** 3110

Vakenstraat. Turn off N21, sp 'Rotselaar'. Follow road for 2.5km, then turn left, sp 'VV Rotselaar'. In 1.8km turn right, sp 'Sporthal' and signed. Turn right at sports centre building, signed, and WC emptying on left. Follow road to left, signed, and designated parking on left before barrier, signed.

🚐 4; Max 7m
🚽 Seijsener bollard; Water €1/100L; 4 16amp CEE elec points €1/kW

ℹ️ Peaceful designated parking behind sports hall. Green space, café and play area adj. Swimming lake and beach with toilets and outdoor showers 100m, open Jul-Aug 10am-6pm. Leuven is 38 mins by bus. Info boards display cycle and walking routes in the region. www.rotselaar.be/toerisme Inspected 2015.

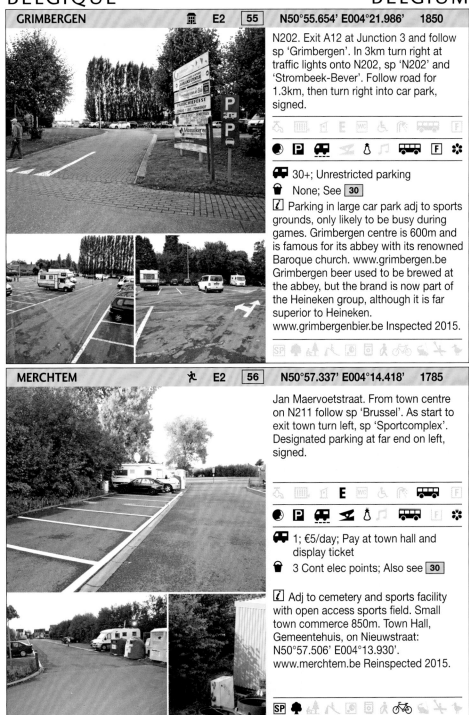

GRIMBERGEN
E2 55 N50°55.654' E004°21.986' 1850

N202. Exit A12 at Junction 3 and follow sp 'Grimbergen'. In 3km turn right at traffic lights onto N202, sp 'N202' and 'Strombeek-Bever'. Follow road for 1.3km, then turn right into car park, signed.

🚐 30+; Unrestricted parking

👜 None; See 30

ℹ️ Parking in large car park adj to sports grounds, only likely to be busy during games. Grimbergen centre is 600m and is famous for its abbey with its renowned Baroque church. www.grimbergen.be Grimbergen beer used to be brewed at the abbey, but the brand is now part of the Heineken group, although it is far superior to Heineken. www.grimbergenbier.be Inspected 2015.

MERCHTEM
E2 56 N50°57.337' E004°14.418' 1785

Jan Maervoetstraat. From town centre on N211 follow sp 'Brussel'. As start to exit town turn left, sp 'Sportcomplex'. Designated parking at far end on left, signed.

🚐 1; €5/day; Pay at town hall and display ticket

👜 3 Cont elec points; Also see 30

ℹ️ Adj to cemetery and sports facility with open access sports field. Small town commerce 850m. Town Hall, Gemeentehuis, on Nieuwstraat: N50°57.506' E004°13.930'. www.merchtem.be Reinspected 2015.

BRUSSELS E2 57 N50°51.199' E004°20.067' 1080

Rue de l'Eléphant. Approach on N8, crossing R0 ring road. Follow N8, driving around Brussels West tram/bus/train station staying on N8, then in 550m, after square, turn left by Polyclinique de la Duchesse into one-way street. Turn immediately right before Petite Restauration into one-way Vanderstraeten. Go straight on 500m, Aire at Les Auberges de Jeunesse. Aire past entrance to Auberge through gate on right, signed. Park on street/in gateway and proceed to reception. Not recommended for long/wide vehicles or nervous drivers.

🚐 7; €30/1st night; €25/2nd night; Inc elec, hostel's facilities and breakfast
Depagne; 6 Cont + 1 CEE elec points

ℹ️ Aire located in Brussels centre in compounded car park for youth hostel. Includes use of all facilities, inc WiFi; washing machine €3.50. Free walking tour Mon 2pm; daily walking tour calls at 10am and 2pm. www.lesaubergesdejeunesse.be http://visitbrussels.be Inspected 2015.

BERTEM E3 58 N50°51.806' E004°37.813' 3060

Gemeenteplein, Frans Dottermanstraat. Exit A3 at Junction 22 and follow sp 'Bertem'. Go straight over roundabout, sp 'Bertem - Centrum'. In 750m turn right at traffic lights, sp 'Centrum'. Follow one-way road, then turn left into car park. Designated parking at rear of car park, signed.

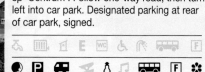

🚐 2; Max 48hrs; Max 9m None; See 54

ℹ️ Pleasant, designated, town centre parking backing onto park with hammocks and children's play area. Small town commerce adj. Convenient stop between A3, A2 and N3. Bus stop 350m on N3; take bus 317 to Leuven; 4.3km, or walk/cycle via local roads/cycle paths. Visit 4 abbeys, guidebook €1 from Leuven TO. Leuven also has 6 breweries, inc Stella Artois, and a beer festival in April, www.zbf.be www.bertem.be Inspected 2015.

AARSCHOT
E3 | 59 | N50°59.095' E004°50.354' | 3200

Demervallei. Approach on N10 from Diest. Exit to right, sp 'P Centrum', then turn left under 3.5m height restricted bridge. In 150m turn right and follow road through car parks. Turn right past Demervallei sports hall, opp row K, and Aire at end of road, signed.

8; Max 48hrs

Custom; WC emptying/drive over drain behind bollard, but key attached on chain; 8 2amp CEE elec points

Unglamorous designated parking at rear of enormous town car park adj to noisy main road with a view of a power substation. Swimming pool adj. Cycle/walking path adj along river to town centre, 230m, or all the way to Mechelen. www.aarschot.be Inspected 2015.

HERENTALS
E3 | 60 | N51°10.661' E004°51.459' | 2200

Noordervaart. Turn off N13 at roundabout onto R15 ring road, sp Noodervaat'. Turn right, sp 'Noodervaat', and follow road through industrial estate to end. Designated parking in car park on left adj to river, signed.

2

Tap at marina; Toilets at marina (Locked)

Designated parking adj to small municipal marina, pole fishing only in marina. Views across to canal with popular cycle path. Small industrial/retail park adj. Town commerce, 2km, has a pleasant central square and two historical city gates, one to the north and one to the east. www.herentals.be Inspected 2015.

VOSSELAAR 🏃 D3 | 61 | N51°18.145' E004°53.742' 2350

Diepvenneke. Exit A21 at Junction 23, sp 'Turhout-West' and 'Vosselaar', and follow sp 'Turhout'. In 400m at traffic lights turn left, sp 'Vosselaar'. Follow road for 1.6km, then turn right into sports centre car park. Designated parking on far edge, signed.

🚐 5; Max 48hrs; 6m bays plus overhang; See info
🛒 None; See | 51 |

ⓘ Designated parking at sports centre by open access sports field. Although bays are 6m, it is always likely to have space so lengthways parking poss. Distant road noise as conveniently close to Junction 23 of A21/E34.
http://toerismevosselaar.be
www.vosselaar.be Inspected 2015.

GEEL 🏛 E3 | 62 | N51°09.511' E004°59.486' 2440

Diestseweg. From south turn off R14 onto N118. At traffic lights by Texaco fuel station turn left onto N71, sp 'N142 Politie'. In 150m turn right into car park, sp 'Stedelijk Zwembad'. For parking turn 1st right, then immediately right again. For Service Point turn 1st left and it is in 150m adj to swimming pool building, signed.

🚐 3; €5/night, purchase day ticket; Max 8m
🛒 Seijsener bollard; Water €0.50; 3 16amp CEE elec points €1/kW

ⓘ Aire in town centre near swimming pool. Despite its location, surroundings mostly residential with some pleasant grass landscaping. Town commerce adj. 1944 Battle of the Geel Bridgehead saw fierce fighting between British and German troops. 130 civilians and around 1000 soldiers killed. Military cemetery to east: N51°09.869' E005°00.911'. Inspected 2015.

BELGIQUE

BELGIUM

LEOPOLDSBURG 1   E3 | 63 | N51°08.028' E005°15.390'   3970

Rode Kruisstraat. Exit town on N746, sp 'Lommel'. Turn right by bus stop towards church into Rode Kruisstraat, signed. Go straight on past church and parking is against building on right, signed.

🚐 10

🔗 None; See | 62 |

ℹ️ Sheltered designated parking beside community facilities at former school, now residential area with village hall. Recreational facilities inc plenty of green space, children's play area and open access basketball court. Ideal night halt. Day parking adj to fishing lakes applying to be Aire: N51°08.156' E005°14.521', apply here for fishing licence. Reinspected 2015.

LEOPOLDSBURG 2   E3 | 64 | N51°07.781' E005°14.914'   3970

Antwerpsesteenweg, at boat marina. Marina is parallel to N18, but on opp side of canal. Exit Leopoldsburg to northwest, sp 'Mol'. Turn right just before marina canal and follow road to left around marina. Pass restaurant and parking in concrete area on left adj to canal.

🚐 15; €10/night; Collected by Harbour Master in pm

🔗 Custom; 12 10amp CEE elec points

ℹ️ Popular Aire favoured by large motorhome users, with all but 3 bays overlooking canal terminus with moored pleasure boats. Road noise and views of N18. Bar/restaurant adj. Local commerce inc ALDI 800m, town commerce 1.7km. Reinspected 2015.

Damme

LOMMEL		E3	66	N51°14.587' E005°22.153'	3920

Boskantstraat. Exit Lommel on N715, sp 'Kolonie'. After crossing canal bridge turn left, sp 'De Meerpal Lommel Yachthaven'. Follow road to end and the parking is on the far edge, signed. The Service Point is against the building, signed.

🚐 8; €10/day; Pay at restaurant

💧 Custom; Water €0.50; Water discharge €2.50; 6 elec points €1/2kWh; Showers €1

ℹ️ Marina Aire, but no view of boats from parking. Good view of boats from adj restaurant. Washing machine/dryer €5. Town centre commerce 7km. Glass museum, €5pp, behind TO: N51°13.842' E005°18.474'; see hetglazenhuis.be and toerismelommel.be Reinspected 2015.

NEERPELT   E4 [67] N51°14.007' E005°25.933' 3910

Jaak Tassetstraat. Exit N74 at Grote Heide Junction onto N71, sp 'N71'. At end of road turn right, sp 'Neerpelt-Centrum'. Follow road across canal bridge, then to left, and to right. Turn left at roundabout into one-way street, then at end turn left. Follow road and turn right before canal (GPS taken here). Service Point on right before parking, signed.

🚐 10; €6/24hrs; €4/24hrs (overflow); Pay at machine; Max 48hrs

🔧 Custom; 5amp elec; Very heavy grid for WC emptying

ℹ️ Popular, pleasant Aire overlooking canal and moored boats. Sloping bays, levelling may be impossible. 3.5t weight restricted overflow parking with no canal views: N51°14.009' E005°25.781'. Purchase ticket at Aire, then exit to left. Turn 1st right and car park entrance in 200m. www.neerpelt.be Reinspected 2015.

BOCHOLT ✶   E4 [68] N51°10.643' E005°35.130' 3950

Schipperstraat. Turn off N73 onto N76, sp 'Bocholt'. At end of dual carriageway go straight on at roundabout. Then turn left into Sportlaan, sp 'Bocholt-Centrum'. Follow road straight on, then turn right when road bends left near De Haize supermarket. Aire in 20m adj to canal, signed.

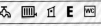

🚐 7; €6.50/24hrs inc 6amp Cont elec; Max 48hrs; 10m bays

🔧 Marycamp Flair; Water €0.50/90L

ℹ️ Pleasant, popular Aire with designated bays overlooking working waterway and boat moorings. Adj large boat is a bar selling the locally brewed Martins pils. Cycle path along canal to neighbouring towns. Supermarket 100m. Town centre with small town commerce 450m. www.bocholt.de/tourismus Reinspected 2015.

TONGERLO   E4   69   N51°07.420' E005°39.313'   3960

Keyartstraat. From Oppitter exit to north at church, sp 'Tongerlo'. Follow road and turn right directly after crossing canal bridge, signed. Follow road down slope and straight on past restaurant and parking is on left, signed.

6; Max 24hrs

Seijsener bollard; Water €1/100L; 4 CEE elec points €1/1kWh

i Designated parking overlooking canal adj to canalside cycle path, an excellent spot for watching big boats go by. Restaurant/bar adj (English spoken), can be busy/noisy at times. Metal jetty to fish off if not busy. www.toerismelimburg.be Reinspected 2015.

HELCHTEREN   E3   70   N51°03.691' E005°23.167'   3530

Bosstraat. Exit N715 at traffic lights onto N719, sp 'Meevwen-Gruitrode'. Turn left, sp 'Sporthal'. Follow sp 'Sporthal' and 'De Dool P' through residential streets. Designated parking in far side of De Dool car park, signed

5

None; See 74

i Shaded parking under oak trees adj to sports stadium. Walk for 400m past outdoor gym through avenue of trees, sp 'De Dool', to Brewery Ter Dolen. The brewery produces five outstanding beers, offers brewery tours, Sat/Sun 3pm €7pp, and has a large bar, www.terdolen.be Town centre with local commerce 600m. toerisme.houthalen-helchteren.be Reinspected 2015.

HOUTHALEN — E4 — 71 — N51°01.813' E005°26.517' — 3530

Kelchterhoefstraat. Exit A2 at Junction 30 onto N726, sp 'Kelchterhoef', and follow for 2.5km. Go straight over roundabout and follow road into parking at end. Designated parking at rear of car park, signed.

🚐 5; See info   🏕 None; See 74

ℹ Shaded parking in section of large unrestricted car park within Kelchterhoef leisure area. One lake has a swimming beach and the extensive woodlands are popular with walkers and mountain bikers. Restaurant/bar adj. Vrije Markt, indoor weekend market, 250m; €3pp. vrijemarkthouthalen.be Park hosts Extrema Outdoor festival, May 13-15, 2016, Jun 3-5, 2017; www.xofestival.be Reinspected 2015.

MEEUWEN-GRUITRODE — E4 — 72 — N51°05.367' E005°35.347' — 3670

N771/N730. Turn off at N771/N730 roundabout into the car park, signed. Parking in car park, no designated spaces.

🚐 5; Max 24hrs; See into
🏕 None; See 68

ℹ Centrally located parking adj to main routes and suffering road noise. All bays are 5m car bays and none are suited to motorhomes, although it would make an acceptable night halt. Adj local commerce includes an event hall with weekly acts including music and comedy. Green space behind event hall. www.meeuwen-gruitrode.be Inspected 2015.

STOKKEM — E4 — 73 — N51°01.426' E005°44.992' — 3650

Maascentrum de Wissen. Turn off N78 opp N771 junction by LIDL, sp 'P Negenoord'. Follow road for 1.9km, then turn left, sp 'Negenoord' and 'VVV Dilsen Stokken'. Follow road straight on and round to right, sp 'VVV' and 'De Wissen'. Go straight on into car park. Designated parking in far right corner, signed.

🚐 3; 8m bays plus 2m overhang
🚰 None; See 74
ℹ️ Designated parking within car park for lakeside recreation area with walking and cycling trails. Pleasantly located on edge of village, 30m from TO with toilets, bar/restaurant and WiFi, open Tues-Thurs 10am-6pm, Fri-Sun 10am-10pm. Local commerce 400m.
www.toerisme-dilsen-stokkem.be
Reinspected 2015.

BILZEN — E4 — 74 — N50°52.191' E005°31.332' — 3740

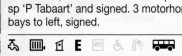

P Tabaart. Approach Bilzen on N730 from north. Follow the road straight on, sp 'De Spelver'. Turn right, sp 'P Bilzen Centrum'. At end of road turn left, then turn right, sp 'P Bilzen Centrum'. Follow road to left, then turn left into car park, sp 'P Tabaart' and signed. 3 motorhome bays to left, signed.

🚐 3; Max 24hrs
🚰 Sani Station; €2; No drive over drain; 5 unmetered CEE elec points
ℹ️ Popular Aire in small car park also used by small trucks. Overlooked by a block of flats and in residential area. Park 150m downhill by fire station. 400m downhill to pleasant town centre with jazz museum and commerce. Reinspected 2015.

GENK
 E4 | 75 | N50°57.422' E005°31.944' | 3600

Kattevennen, at stables. Approach from north on N75, then turn left at roundabout onto N750, sp 'Campos St Jan'. At traffic lights in 800m turn left, sp 'Bloso'. Follow road to left, then right, sp 'Cosmodrome'. A 2.3m height barrier may block access for 12 events per year, but there is space to turn around and additional parking. Follow road into car park at end, designated parking near entrance, signed.

7; €5/24hrs inc 16amp CEE elec and 100L water; Pay at office/café; Max 24hrs Scijsener bollard; Token; Key from office/café through trees at rear of parking (€25 deposit)

ℹ Popular Aire adj to Nationaal Park Hoge Kempen, ideal for woodland walking, dog walking, mountain biking and horse riding (stables adj). Planetarium adj with sun spotting in summer/stargazing in winter; follow sp 'Cosmodrome', see www.cosmodrome.be www.visitgenk.be Reinspected 2015.

REKEM
 E4 | 76 | N50°55.313' E005°42.283' | 3621

Kanaal. Exit A2 at Junction 33 onto N78 following sp 'Lanaken'. Go straight over 2 roundabouts, then turn left at traffic lights, sp 'Rekem - Centrum'. In 1.2km, before bridge, turn left, sp 'P Oud-Rekem'. Designated parking immediately on right, signed.

14; 8m bays plus up to 2m overhang
None; See 74

ℹ Popular, landscaped designated parking adj to and overlooking Zuid Willemsvaart canal. Road noise from and views of N78 road bridge. The charming historic town centre, 400m via road through car park, has local and tourist commerce, pleasant buildings and TO. Across N78 is Hoge Kempen National Park, www.rlkm.be/hogekempen Maasmechelen outlet village is 10km, www.maasmechelenvillage.com Inspected 2015.

HASSELT 1 🏢 E3 〔77〕 N50°56.314' E005°19.265' 3500

Herkenrodesingel. From south follow R71 ring road to west, sp 'Diest'. At the traffic lights for N2 towards Diest go straight on and then immediately right, sp 'Ring Z.9 Centrum'. Turn left at the roundabout and in 200m turn right, sp 'P+R Alverberg'. Service Point on left, signed.

🚐 10+; Unrestricted parking behind building; See 〔78〕 and 〔79〕
🚽 Sani Station; €2; Rubbish disposal €1

ℹ️ Service Point in unrestricted car park which is now P+R, adj to sports facilities just off main ring road. Parking adj to Service Point is max 30 mins. Retail park and supermarket on opp side of road which can be accessed by pedestrian underpass. Town centre 2km walk/cycle. www.hasselt.be Reinspected 2015.

HASSELT 2 🚶 E3 〔78〕 N50°56.187' E005°20.928' 3500

Elfde Liniestraat. Approach from north on N74. Turn left at traffic lights onto R71, sp 'Genk'. In 550m turn 1st right, not signed. In 350m turn left into car park by Eddy's Broodjesbar. Designated parking in far right corner, signed.

🚐 3; 6m bays plus 2m overhang
🚽 None; See 〔77〕

ℹ️ Ideal for families as designated parking overlooks children's play area with several climbing frames and a popular skateboard park. The park extends for 900m and includes a Japanese garden. Hasselt historic centre, 800m, has a Jenever (gin) museum; open Feb-Dec Tues-Sun 10am-5pm, €6pp, see www.jenevermuseum.be/en Jenever festival every 3rd weekend of Oct, see www.jeneverfeesten.be Inspected 2015.

HASSELT 3   E3   79   N50°55.278' E005°19.545'   3500

Bakkerslaan. Approach from south on N80. At traffic lights, once off of dual carriageway, go straight on towards town, sp 'Centrum'. In 350m turn left, sp 'VDAB Competentiecentrum'. Follow road for 300m and designated parking in car park on left, signed.

🚐 3; 2 bays have unlimited overhang; Reinforced grass parking

☕ None; See 77

ℹ️ Pleasant reinforced grass parking under trees in a residential area. Church adj has noisy bells which are silenced at night. Car park is deserted at weekends, but school opp could make parking busy during drop off/pick up. Bus stop adj, town centre 1km. www.hasselt.be Inspected 2015.

HERK DE STAD   E3   80   N50°56.043' E005°10.011'   3540

Pikkeleerstraat. Turn off N2 at traffic lights northeast of town, sp 'Alken'. At roundabout turn left onto N716a, sp 'Nieuwerkerken'. Go straight over 2 roundabouts, then turn left, sp 'Stadhuis' and 'VVV'. In 300m, past country house, turn left into car park, signed. Designated parking just past Service Point on left, signed.

🚐 6; Max 9m

☕ Marycamp XL; Water €1/90L; 8 CEE elec points €1/kWh; Toilets in daylight hrs

ℹ️ Popular, landscaped Aire adj to open access gardens and woodland of former manor, now council offices with TO, 200m. Service Point difficult to access, up kerb adj to entrance road. Small town commerce 500m. Annual music festival, Rock Herk, held in July adj to Aire, www.rockherk.be www.herk-de-stad.be Inspected 2015.

BOLDERBERG 🏛 E3 81 N50°59.178' E005°16.128' 3550

Galgeneinde. Turn off A2/E314 at Junction 27 and follow sp 'Hasselt' onto N729. Turn off N729 at the roundabout by the church in Bolderberg into 3.5t weight restricted road, sp 'Domein Bovy'. In 200m turn left into car park, signed. Aire at the far end of the car park, signed.

🛆 🏭 🗐 E 🚾 🔧 🍴 🚐 F

● P 🚐 ⚓ 🍼 🎵 🚌 F ✳

🚐 3

🚰 Euro Relais Junior; €2; No drive over drain

ⓘ Aire adj to large park which was a former estate. There are walking routes to follow around the park as well as leisure attractions, bars and restaurants. www.newsite.domeinbovy.eu Local commerce in village centre, 400m. Race circuit on outskirts, 1km, www.circuit-zolder.be http://toerisme.heusden-zolder.be Reinspected 2015.

SP 🌳 🏕 🧗 📷 🖥 🚶 🚴 🏄 🎿 🦢

SCHERPENHEUVEL 🏃 E3 82 N50°58.614' E004°58.562' 3270

Den Egger. Follow N10 from Diest. Turn left, then in 300m turn left again, and after 120m turn left again into car park, all sp 'Den Egger'. In car park turn right to upper terrace. Parking adj to Den Egger sport hall, signed.

🛆 🏭 🗐 E 🚾 🔧 🍴 🚐 F

● P 🚐 ⚓ 🍼 🎵 🚌 F ✳

🚐 2; Reinforced grass parking; See info

🚰 None; See 80

ⓘ 2 designated 6m bays in busiest area of car park. Signs prevent overhang, but car park is large so suggest park on opp side. The town is dominated by Basiliek van Scherpenheuvel. The elaborate basilica was commissioned in 1605 to be built on the site of a holy oak tree. Use day parking at P Mariahal: N50°58.930' E004°58.827' or walk 500m; free entry. www.scherpenheuvel.be Inspected 2015.

SP 🌳 🏕 🧗 📷 🖥 🚶 🚴 🏄 🎿 🦢

DIEST 🏃 E3 │83│ N50°59.069' E005°03.812' 3290

Leopoldvest. Approach from Hasselt on N2. At roundabout turn right onto R26 ring road, sp 'N29 Beringen'. Follow road for 1km, past car parks on right, then turn right, signed. Cross lake and turn right, signed. Aire is through barrier on left, signed. Access key from info office, 40m past Aire.

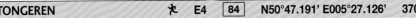

🚐 4; €15/24hrs inc service and 16amp CEE elec; Pay at office for access key
🛒 Custom; Inside barrier

ℹ️ Pleasant Aire in fenced, high security compound adj to park with fishing lakes and walking/cycling paths; no water views and distant road noise. Diest citadel is being turned into an art space, www.citadelartediest.be It is conveniently 400m from town and has unrestricted free day parking: N50°59.006' E005°02.849'. Inspected 2015.

Citadel parking

TONGEREN 🏃 E4 │84│ N50°47.191' E005°27.126' 3700

Fonteindreef, Betalend. Approach on N20 from Hasselt. Turn right before town, sp 'Rode Kruis' and signed. Aire is on left, enter through barrier.

🚐 24; €10/24hrs; CC, Max 24hrs; Reinforced grass parking
🛒 Seijsener bollard and WC sink; Water €0.50/100L; 16amp CEE elec €0.50/kWh; All inside barrier

ℹ️ Large landscaped commercial Aire with generous bays at recreation facilities on the outskirts of town. Adj to newly constructed swimming pools, children's play area and park with cycle routes to town centre, 1km. Self-service laundry 300m on N20. Inspected 2015.

RUMMEN　　🏭 E3 ｜85｜　N50°53.568' E005°09.623'　3454

Ketelstraat. From Herk-de-Stad follow N716, sp 'Nieuwerkerken'. At traffic lights turn right, sp 'Rummen-Centrum'. At Stop junction turn right, sp 'Centrum'. Designated parking 550m on left at rear of car park, signed.

🚐 2; Space for 4+

🚽 None; See ｜80｜

ℹ️ Pleasant, well located designated parking at far side of car park overlooking small park. 2 official bays and space to park adj with overhang as desired. Local commerce 300m. Cycle path from nearby Geetbets (4km) to Diest in north and Tienen and beyond in south. Inspected 2015.

DIEPENBEEK　　🚶 E4 ｜86｜　N50°54.833' E005°25.323'　3590

Stationsstraat. Turn off N76 at roundabout onto N76d (both 3.5t weight restricted), sp 'Sportcentrum'. In 1.5km turn right into car park, sp 'Sportcentrum Demerstrand'. The motorhome parking is to the right, signed.

🚐 4; Max 48hrs

🚽 Custom; Water €2/10 mins; 4 CEE elec points €2/8hrs; Max 1000w

ℹ️ Designated motorhome Aire adj to dog enclosure at sports and recreation facilities. Café adj. Small town commerce and train station 550m. www.diepenbeek.be Reinspected 2015.

BELGIQUE   BELGIUM

ALKEN   🏃 E3 [87]   N50°52.488' E005°18.791'   3570

Koutermanstraat. Turn off main route through, sp 'Recreatie De Alk'. In 100m turn right, sp 'De Alk'. Turn right into the car park, sp 'Sportshallen', and the parking is at the far end, signed.

🚐 5; Lengthways
🚰 Toilets in park; See [86]

ℹ Parking adj to cemetery within sports centre. Facilities include open access sports field, fishing lake and crazy golf all open to the public, pay as you play. Local commerce 350m. www.alken.be Reinspected 2015.

KORTESSEM   🏛 E3 [88]   N50°51.451' E005°23.484'   3720

Kapittelstraat. Turn off N20 at traffic lights onto N76, sp 'Genk'. Turn 2nd right, signed, drive past church and follow road straight on. Turn left at end of road and parking on right by the hedge and tennis courts, signed.

🚐 5; Max 48hrs
🚰 Water only; See [86]

ℹ Designated parking adj to sports facilities only 300m from centre with small town commerce. ALDI 450m. Adj sign displays mountain biking routes. Parking obstructed by fair 1st weekend of July. Other local parking available. Esso on N20 has self-service laundry inside shop. www.kortessem.be Reinspected 2015.

BLEGNY   T   E4   89   N50°41.136' E005°43.342'   4670

Rue Lambert Marlet. Exit A3 at Junction 36 onto N604 following sp 'Blégny'. At roundabout turn right, sp 'Blégny-Mine'. Follow road to Blégny, then at roundabout turn left and immediately left, sp 'Blégny-Mine'. Follow road 1.3km to Blégny Mine on left, signed. Gates locked 7pm-7am.

8; Max 24hrs; See info

Depagne for WC emptying; Custom for water; 6amp CEE elec €2/12hrs; Token; Toilets at mine

Popular, oversubscribed Aire within a large car park of a former working mine, now a UNESCO World Heritage site; 1.5hr tours, €9.60pp, and English audio tours daily Apr-Aug and at weekends Mar-Nov 11am-5pm. There is also a café and children's play area on site. www.blegnymine.be Inspected 2015.

EUPEN (Barrage de la Vesdre)   E4   90   N50°37.325' E006°05.496'   4700

Langesthal. From Eupen centre follow sp 'Weser-Vesdre' onto N67. Turn left at roundabout, sp 'Weser-Vesdre'. Follow road for 3.5km, then cross dam. Follow road to left, sp 'Parking', then immediately to right and uphill to car park.

10; 6pm-10am only

None; See 95

Parking in car park by large reservoir and dam, no views; www.eupenertalsperre.be Parc Naturel Hautes Fagnes adj with cycle/walking paths from car park, www.naturpark-eifel.de Restaurant with viewpoint 200m uphill. May feel isolated if alone. Eupen, 2km, is the capital of German-speaking Belgium and became part of Belgium after WWI. Inspected 2015.

JALHAY (Barrage de Gileppe)   F4   91   N50°35.241' E005°58.180'   4845

N629/Route de la Gileppe. In Jalhay turn off N672 onto N629, sp 'Eupen' and 'Lac de la Gileppe'. In 2.7km turn right, sp 'Lac de la Gileppe'. Follow road for 500m to car park. Motorhome parking is in the 1st 4 bays on right by observation tower, signed.

4

Seasonal daytime toilets; See 95

ℹ️ Designated parking in large car park adj to dam, no views. Visitor centre with toilets and viewpoint over 3km reservoir; free lift up to restaurant with panorama, or down to seasonal café adj to dam. Reservoir on edge of Hautes Fagnes Eifel National Park, with peat bog boardwalks and the highest point in Belgium. May feel isolated if alone. http://gileppe.com Reinspected 2015.

AYWAILLE   F4   92   N50°28.553' E005°40.681'   4920

Rue de la Heid. Exit A26 at Junction 46 and follow sp 'Aywaille' onto N633d, then onto N633. In Aywaille follow road to right onto N30, sp 'Sprimont', and cross river. Turn 1st right, sp 'Centre Sportif' and signed. In 150m turn right, sp 'Centre sportif' and signed. Designated parking on left, signed. Service Point past parking adj to swimming pool, signed.

8; €8/48hrs inc 1 token; Pay at machine, display ticket; 8m bays plus overhang
Flot Bleu Pacific; Token (FB); €5; Flot Bleu Elec; Token (FB); €2/2hrs CEE elec; Pay at machine, then show ticket at swimming pool for tokens

ℹ️ Ideal for families as designated parking overlooks excellent children's play area at sports facility with BMX track, outdoor gym and open access playing fields. Adj indoor swimming pool has a slide, sauna, hot tub and café, entry €3.10pp; open daily, various hours, closed holidays and 14 days for Christmas. www.agisca.be www.aywaille.be Inspected 2015.

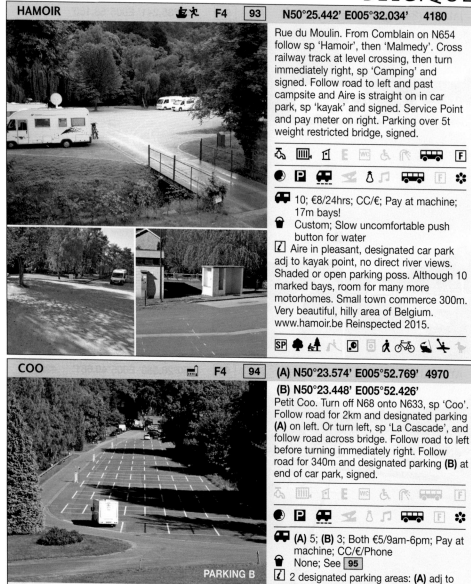

HAMOIR   F4   93   N50°25.442' E005°32.034'   4180

Rue du Moulin. From Comblain on N654 follow sp 'Hamoir', then 'Malmedy'. Cross railway track at level crossing, then turn immediately right, sp 'Camping' and signed. Follow road to left and past campsite and Aire is straight on in car park, sp 'kayak' and signed. Service Point and pay meter on right. Parking over 5t weight restricted bridge, signed.

🚐 10; €8/24hrs; CC/€; Pay at machine; 17m bays!

🚰 Custom; Slow uncomfortable push button for water

ℹ️ Aire in pleasant, designated car park adj to kayak point, no direct river views. Shaded or open parking poss. Although 10 marked bays, room for many more motorhomes. Small town commerce 300m. Very beautiful, hilly area of Belgium. www.hamoir.be Reinspected 2015.

COO   F4   94   (A) N50°23.574' E005°52.769'   4970

(B) N50°23.448' E005°52.426'
Petit Coo. Turn off N68 onto N633, sp 'Coo'. Follow road for 2km and designated parking (A) on left. Or turn left, sp 'La Cascade', and follow road across bridge. Follow road to left before turning immediately right. Follow road for 340m and designated parking (B) at end of car park, signed.

🚐 (A) 5; (B) 3; Both €5/9am-6pm; Pay at machine; CC/€/Phone

🚰 None; See 95

ℹ️ 2 designated parking areas: (A) adj to N633, some road noise, and (B) at rear of large car park. Both 300m from cascades comprising of 2 15m waterfalls. Viewpoint under bridge accessible via approx 50 uneven steps with waterfalls either side. Best view of cascades from Plopsa outdoor activity park, €15-€25pp, open Mar-Jul; www.plopsa.be Tourist commerce in village. Inspected 2015.

PARKING B

PARKING A

MALMEDY   F4   95   N50°25.372' E006°01.835'   4960

Place du Parc, Avenue de la Gare. Exit A27 at Junction 11 and follow sp 'Malmedy'. Follow N62 through town, sp 'St Vith' and signed. Turn right at roundabout, signed. Follow road for 300m, then turn right, signed. Aire in P4, a compound adj to bus station, signed.

🚿 ▥ 🏳 E WC ♿ 🚻 🚌 F

🌐 P 🚐 ⚓ 🔥 🎵 🚌 F ✳

🚐 20; €5/24hrs; €35/week; CC/€; Pay at machine

🚰 Custom; Water €0.50; 18 16amp CEE elec points €0.50/unspecified amount

ℹ️ Large, fenced parking area adj to former railway, now a cycle/walking route to St Vith via Waimes. Pleasant town commerce 550m downhill; www.malmedy.be Spa motor racing circuit 6km: N50°25.687' E005°58.914'; congestion likely late August weekend during Formula 1 race, www.F1.com Reinspected 2015.

SP 🌳 ⛺ 🎣 📷 🍴 🚶 🚲 🛶 ⛵

BARVAUX   F4   96   N50°21.142' E005°29.715'   6940

N831/Petit Barvaux. From Hamoir on N831 follow sp 'Barvaux'. As enter Barvaux turn left before river bridge, sp 'P 200 Places' and signed. Follow road past 2 height barriered car parks and Aire on left, signed.

🚿 ▥ 🏳 E WC ♿ 🚻 🚌 F

🌐 P 🚐 ⚓ 🔥 🎵 🚌 F ✳

🚐 €10/24hrs; Pay at machine, display ticket; Reinforced grass parking

🚰 Flot Bleu Pacific; Token (FB); €2; Flot Bleu Elec; Token (FB); €2/2hrs

ℹ️ Pleasant riverside Aire with both shaded and open parking adj to shallow, fishable/kayakable river; fishing restrictions on information board. Cycle/walking path along river to Durbuy. Supermarket opp, small town commerce across river, 350m. Tokens from TO at 16 Grand Rue: N50°21.028' E005°29.721'. www.ourthe-etaisne.be Inspected 2015.

SP 🌳 ⛺ 🎣 📷 🍴 🚶 🚲 🛶 ⛵

BELGIUM

BELGIQUE

SANKT VITH F4 97 N50°16.852' E006°07.336' 4780

N675/Rodter Strasse. From town centre turn off N62 onto N675, sp 'Vielsalm' and signed. Turn right at roundabout with Olympic rings, signed, then immediately right into parking. Service Point on furthest edge of car park from Olympic rings.

🚐 20; 4 large undesignated bays
Marycamp XL; Water €1/90L; No drive over drain
ℹ️ Aire in large open, unrestricted, underused car park adj to sports facilities. Large children's play area 150m towards town centre. Town centre with high street commerce 400m uphill. Cycle/walking path from town to Malmedy. St Vith forest, 5km, has large car park adj to Biermuseum/restaurant: N50°17.845' E006°03.743'. Plenty of marked walks, Nordic walks and cross country skiing in winter. Reinspected 2015.

Sankt Vith forest parking

WAIMES F4 98 N50°23.744' E006°04.191' 4950

N62. Adj to N62 5km south of Malmedy at La Faitafondue restaurant, signed.

🚐 20; €9/night inc service and elec; Free if eat in restaurant; Collected Custom; 10 4amp/900W Cont elec points
ℹ️ Large, open, well maintained commercial Aire in car park of family run fondue party restaurant, open Fri-Sun; www.lafaitafondue.com Pleasant rural views, but some road noise from adj main route. Ideal place to visit with friends on the weekend or as a rally destination, pleasant outdoor seating area and indoor BBQ to rent, €18. Baugnez museum dedicated to, and built on the site of, the WWII Malmedy massacre, www.baugnez44.be www.waimes.be Inspected 2015.

HOTTON 1   F4   99   N50°16.126' E005°26.627'   6990

Rue du Batty. From Barvaux on N86 enter Hotton and cross river, then turn immediately right into 3.5t restricted road, sp 'Sur le Batty' and signed. Follow road past church and small park and Aire on right, signed.

🚐 4; €10/24hrs inc 20 mins service; CC; Pay at Service Point; Max 8m

🚰 Flot Bleu Euro; CC; 1 CEE elec point; Only open 20 mins upon paying €10 for parking!

ℹ️ Pleasant Aire adj to, and with views of, river and small park. Slipway adj (date restrictions apply to boating), no fishing or swimming near weir. Small town commerce 250m along river. Better than 100 , but still bureaucracy before benefit. Follow sp 'Grottes de Hotton' off N66: N50°15.560' E005°27.312'. Open daily Apr-Oct 10am-5pm, Nov-Mar weekends only, €12pp www.grottesdehotton.com For other attractions see 100 . Inspected 2015.

War Cemetery Parking

HOTTON 2   F4   100   N50°16.167' E005°27.540'   6990

P En Longchamps, Haie Notre-Dame. Approach on N807 from Erezée. Turn right before town and drive through cemetery car park. If you miss this turn continue and turn right at roundabout, sp 'P En Longchamps' with motorhome symbol. Aire on right/at end of road, signed.

🚐 6; €10/24hrs inc 20 mins service; CC; Pay at Service Point; Max 8m

🚰 Flot Bleu Euro; CC; 1 CEE elec point; Only open 20 mins upon paying €10 for parking!

ℹ️ Remote Aire adj to cemetery with distant road noise. Another case of bureaucracy before benefit. The parking area is relatively narrow and may require reversing out. As well as the grottoes, see 99 , there are also WWII commonwealth war graves nearby: N50°15.751' E005°26.828', with local unrestricted parking: N50°15.696' E005°26.888'. www.hotton.be Inspected 2015.

MABOGE   F4 101 N50°10.050' E005°37.554' 6982

Maboge. Follow N860 from La Roche. At Maboge turn right, sp 'P 50 places'. Aire on right in large grass field, signed.

 50; Max 24hrs; 2 hardstanding bays
None; See 105

Pleasant designated parking in large grass field adj to river in small, charming village with local and tourist commerce. Fishing poss, but restrictions apply, see information board. Enjoy this Aire while it lasts. The area is a national park with numerous walking and cycling routes, www.pndo.be There is a hydroelectric dam nearby, follow sp 'Nisramont Dam', which has good day parking, a café/bar and kayak hire: N50°08.466' E005°40.258'. www.maboge.be Inspected 2015.

ROCHEFORT F3 102 N50°09.506' E005°13.482' 5580

Rue du Hableau. Approach from Marche-en-Famenne on N836 following sp 'Rochefort'. At roundabout turn right onto N86, sp 'Rochefort'. At next roundabout go straight on onto 3.5t restricted N86d, sp 'Hableau' and signed. Turn left before tunnel, signed. Turn immediately left into car park, signed. Best parking in parallel bays in two different places, not signed.

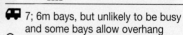

7; 6m bays, but unlikely to be busy and some bays allow overhang
Water tap by picnic table (Not working)

Undesignated car park adj to main road suffering constant road noise. Always likely to have space. Town commerce 100m via footpath. 700m uphill is Grottes de Lorette, a limestone cave: N50°09.314' E005°13.587'. Open daily Jul-Aug, weekends Apr-Oct, €8.50pp. www.rochefort.be Inspected 2015.

HAN SUR LESSE F3 103 N50°07.654' E005°11.264' 5580

Rue de la Lesse. From north on N86 enter Han-sur-Lesse and turn right, sp 'Parking' and signed. Turn right into car park, signed. Turn right again into Aire, signed.

🚐 40; €7.50/24hrs Sept-Jun; €10/24hrs Jul-Aug; Inc unmetered elec

🚰 Custom; emptying point by seasonal toilets (€0.40); CEE elec and water points in hedges

ℹ️ Designated parking in large car park on edge of village overlooking sports fields. Village centre 200m with tourist commerce. Access to Grotto de Han, €16pp, via tram, then on foot down 508 steps (dogs allowed). The cave is permanently 13°C, so take a jumper; see www.grotte-de-han.be Reinspected 2015.

FOURNEAU ST MICHEL (ST HUBERT) F3 104 N50°05.040' E005°20.408' 6870

N849. From St Hubert take N849 to Fourneau-St-Michel. Follow road past Fourneau St Michel and Aire is on left in P1, signed.

🚐 16; Max 24hrs

🚰 Custom; Both water points marked not drinking water; 4 CEE elec points €1/15 mins

ℹ️ Aire in rural woodland location between Musee du Fer, the Iron Museum, and Musee Vie Rurale, an open air museum of preserved rural buildings. Plenty of green space and woodland walks, but may feel isolated. The area is known for iron smelting, take a look at the preserved 18th century furnace in the iron museum. www.fourneausaintmichel.be Inspected 2015.

BELGIUM

BELGIQUE

ST HUBERT   🏛 F3 [105]   N50°01.630' E005°22.856'   6870

Rue du Parc. Exit N89, sp 'N848 St Hubert'. At end of road turn left, then 1st right, sp 'Piscine' and signed. Aire immediately on right, signed. Well signed through town.

🛠 🎫 🚰 E WC ♿ 📻 🚌 F

🌐 P 🚐 ⛵ 🚿 🎵 🚌 F ❋

🚐 3; Max 48hrs; 9m bays plus overhang, partly impeded by tree branches

👜 Custom

ℹ️ This Aire is conveniently close to N89 in a peaceful location with distant road noise. The Aire is landscaped, slightly sloping and adjoins a park with picnic benches. A lane behind cemetery leads to town with basilica. www.saint-hubert-tourisme.be Reinspected 2015.

BASTOGNE   🏛 F4 [106]   N49°59.907' E005°42.885'   6600

Place du Général Patton, N30. Enter Bastogne on N84 from Luxembourg. At the roundabout go straight over, sp 'Centre' and signed. In 150m turn left into car park, sp 'P Gratuit' and signed. Aire at far side of car park adj to memorial to General Patton, signed.

🛠 🎫 🚰 E WC ♿ 📻 🚌 F

🌐 P 🚐 ⛵ 🚿 🎵 🚌 F ❋

🚐 15; Along far edge

👜 Custom; Damaged/unusable tap behind drive over drain; See [107]

ℹ️ Only 100m from town centre commerce and TO, which is adj to American WWII tank. Strategic town in WWII during the Battle of the Bulge. Follow the numbered info panels around town to understand the events. Also visit the American memorial and Bastogne War Museum, open Tues-Sun 9.30am-6pm; www.bastognewarmuseum.be Reinspected 2015.

ARLON   G4   107   N49°41.414' E005°49.129'   6700

Caserne Callemeyn. Turn off N4 at roundabout onto N882, sp 'Redange'. At next roundabout turn left, sp 'Pompiers', then take 2nd right, signed.

5; Max 48hrs

Custom; See info; 4 unmetered Cont elec points on wall; No drive over drain

ℹ️ Oversubscribed, landscaped Aire with free electric and well designed parking in an industrial area. The lift up drains by each tap are also for WC emptying and you will need at least a bucket of water to flush them effectively. Noise from main road and occasionally from fire station. Motorhomes are banned from all other parking. www.arlon.be Reinspected 2015.

Leopoldsburg fishing lakes

GPS Co-ordinates for SatNav

The GPS Co-ordinates published in this guide were taken onsite by our inspectors. We consider them a valuable and unique asset and at the time of publishing have decided not to publish them as electronic files for use on navigation devices. You have permission to type in the co-ordinates of an Aire you intend to visit but not to store or share them. For the security of our copyright:

- **Do not compile them into lists**
- **Do not publish, share or reproduce them anywhere in any format**

HERBEUMONT
G3 109 N49°46.630' E005°14.226' 6887

N884. Approach Herbeumont from south on N884. Before the village, after a zebra crossing, turn left, not signed. Drive down an avenue of trees and the Aire is on the right, signed.

🚐 30+; Unrestricted parking

🪣 Custom; In 2 places; No drive over drain

ℹ️ Pleasant large open car park on edge of village adj to walking/cycling path on former railway. The charming village centre, 550m, has tourist commerce and an open access ruined castle, 650m uphill. In addition there are 95km of walking trails through the Ardennes forest. www.herbeumont-tourisme.be Inspected 2015.

BOUILLON
G3 110 N49°47.441' E005°03.485' 6830

Route de Bouillon. From N89 turn off onto N828, sp 'Bouillon-Centre'. Turn left, sp 'Corbon', and go through tunnel, then turn right into Blvd Vauban, sp 'Abbaye de Cordemois'. Follow road along river, then turn 1st left and cross river, sp 'Cordemois' and signed. Follow road for 600m, then turn left into car park, not signed. Designated parking on one-way road to rear of car park at sports facilities, signed.

🚐 10; Max 24hrs

🪣 Custom; 4 metered CEE elec points in metal box; Token (2/1); 1 Token/kWh; If numbers showing, unused power avail

ℹ️ Popular Aire surrounded by sports facilities in a tranquil location near river, no views. 10 designated gravel bays in the sun and plenty of paved parking under trees. May feel isolated if alone. Fort de Bouillon, visible from parking, €7pp, open daily Feb-Dec, weekends only Jan. Town centre 1km. Inspected 2015.

POUPEHAN ★ 🛥 G3 111 N49°48.543' E005°00.240' 6830

Rue du Pont. From Rochehaut, which has a lovely viewpoint, take N893 following sp 'Poupehan'. Follow the road, which is an easy drive, into Poupehan. In Poupehan turn right immediately before river bridge, sp 'Vieux Molin' and signed. Follow road to river, then turn right. Aire 90m on right, signed.

🛌 ▥ 🛗 E 🚻 ♿ 🚰 🚌 F

⚫ P 🚐 🏊 ⛺ 🎵 🚌 F ❄

🚐 20; Max 24hrs

🛗 Custom; 4 metered CEE elec points in metal box; Token (2/1); 1 Token/kWh; If numbers showing, unused power avail; Slow water

ℹ A pleasant riverside Aire adj to the Semois river, no real view but plenty of riverside picnic space. The river is slow moving and mostly shallow so perfect for paddling in. The Aire is surrounded by open access sports fields. Slipway opp and seasonal kayak hire. The village has limited tourist commerce. Inspected 2015.

SP 🌳 🏕 🏞 📷 🗑 🚶 🚲 🛶 🛝

BOHAN 🏛 G3 112 N49°52.234' E004°53.102' 5550

Rue de Mont les Champs. In Bohan turn off N914 behind the church, sp 'Mont les Champs' and 'Centre Recreatif la Mairie'. Turn immediately right, sp 'P Mobilhomes'. Follow road past Camping les Bouleaux and designated parking is on the left and right by communal space, signed.

🛌 ▥ 🛗 E 🚻 ♿ 🚰 🚌 F

⚫ P 🚐 🏊 ⛺ 🎵 🚌 F ❄

🚐 3 🛗 Water tap in hedge

ℹ Designated roadside parking surrounded by campsites, most without touring pitches. Open access community ground adj and opp inc small football pitch. River La Semois accessible on foot, no views. Pleasant village centre 650m with tourist commerce and kayak hire in season. Camping les Bouleaux: N49°52.155' E004°53.188', has 4 fully serviced 8m motorhome pitches outside the barrier and is signed as an Aire, but charges campsite prices, www.camping-des-bouleaux.be http://bohan.be Inspected 2015.

SP 🌳 🏕 🛝 📷 🗑 🚶 🚲 🛶 🛝 🏇

TREIGNES | T | F3 | 113 | N50°05.457' E004°40.916' | 5670

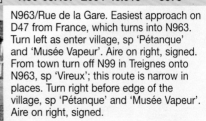

N963/Rue de la Gare. Easiest approach on D47 from France, which turns into N963. Turn left as enter village, sp 'Pétanque' and 'Musée Vapeur'. Aire on right, signed. From town turn off N99 in Treignes onto N963, sp 'Vireux'; this route is narrow in places. Turn right before edge of the village, sp 'Pétanque' and 'Musée Vapeur'. Aire on right, signed.

🚐 7   🚰 Euro Relais Junior; Token

ℹ️ Designated parking adj to Musée du Chemin de Fer a Vapeur, a train museum, a café in a former buffet carriage and a pétanque club. Steam and diesel trains to Mariembourg run daily Jul-Aug, 10am-6.30pm, and weekends Apr-Oct, 10am-5pm. The 14km journey takes 2hrs, €12.50pp return. Railway station behind parking is disused and advertised as for sale. www.treignes.info Inspected 2015.

NISMES | | F3 | 114 | N50°04.408' E004°32.892' | 5670

Place de Chatillon. Exit N5, sp 'Nismes', and follow sp 'Nismes' under 3.3m height restricted bridge. At end of road turn right. At roundabout turn right, sp 'Givet' and 'Nismes Centre'. At next roundabout turn left, sp 'Givet' and 'Nismes Centre'. In 150m cross river bridge and turn right. In 200m turn right, sp 'P Centre', and cross back over river. Turn 1st right and the Service Point is on the right, signed.

🚐 15   🚰 Euro Relais Junior; Token (ER)

ℹ️ Aire in large, undesignated car park in a pleasant village adj to river. Local and tourist commerce adj inc small motorboats for hire. Mariembourg, 5km, is the starting point of a 14km steam train track that runs near Nismes to Treignes; it is possible to cycle alongside the railway line from Nismes to Mariembourg. Reinspected 2015.

BELGIQUE

BELGIUM

ERPION/CERFONTAINE   F2   115   N50°11.565' E004°22.784'   6441

Off N589 adj to Barages de l'Eau d'Heure. From north at Walcourt follow N978 south, sp 'Cerfontaine'. Turn right onto N907, sp 'Beaumant' and 'Aqua Centre'. Follow road 1.9km, past several unrestricted car parks, then turn left onto N589, sp 'Aqua Centre'. Service Point in 3.3km on left: N50°11.550' E004°22.966'. For parking turn right just before Service Point, sp 'Aqua Centre'. Turn left into car park and use parking to right.

🚐 20

Custom; Access via attendant; €5

ℹ️ Parking adj to 3km long reservoir with plenty of parking; high banks obscure views and waterside parking has height barriers. Seasonal café with viewing terrace and toilets, €0.30. Adj visitor centre for dam open Wed/Sat/Sun 11am-3.30pm for tours, €7.50pp, not in English. As Service Point has been constructed in different location, expect change. Reinspected 2015.

PERUWELZ ★   F2   116   N50°31.107' E003°36.573'   7600

Rue de la Boiterie. Turn off N50 in Basècles, sp 'Peruwetz 4'. In 2.2km, after road bends to left, turn left before river bridge, sp 'Port de Plaisance'. Follow road straight on, past Capitainerie building on left. Park in car park at end, not signed.

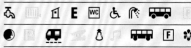

🚐 15

Custom; In various places; 5amp CEE elec and water €5/night or €25/7 days; Showers €1.80; No drive over drain

ℹ️ Undesignated parking in large car park at marina. Choose either to overlook navigable river or pleasure boat marina. The onsite bar looks like the inside of a barge. Distant road noise and some train noise. Popular with fishermen. Riverside cycle/walking paths adj. www.peruwelz.be Inspected 2015.

THIEU T ☼ F2 117 N50°28.599' E004°06.336' 7070

N552. Travelling eastbound on A7 exit at Junction 21a into service station. Turn 1st right and in 100m turn left to exit service station. Follow road 1.4km to Thieu, then turn left and follow sp 'Ascenseur' 1km to car park.

🚐 5; Tolerated overnight, ask in visitor centre

🚰 None; See 118

ℹ️ Car park overlooking Canal du Centre Ascenseur Funiculaire de Strépy-Thieu, claimed to be the biggest boat lift in the world when it was finished in 2002. 900m along the canal at the other end of Thieu are the preceding hydraulic lifts, now a UNESCO World Heritage site. Day parking: N50°28.284' E004°05.363'. www.canal-du-centre.be Inspected 2015.

Photo: Sue Moore

UNESCO Lifts

BOUFFIOULX 🏛 F3 118 N50°23.422' E004°30.853' 6200

Rue Général Jacques. Exit R3 at Junction 10, sp 'Châtelet', and follow sp 'Châtelet'. At roundabout turn right, sp 'Bouffioulx'. In Bouffioulx turn right across railway track, sp 'Maison de la Poterie'. Follow road uphill and Aire is in car park next to Maison de la Poterie.

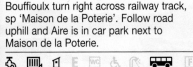

🚐 3; Car park could take more depending on local events

🚰 Raclet; Token (2/1)

ℹ️ Aire in car park adj to Maison de la Poterie, a small museum dedicated to the local pottery industry. Exhibits include a small section of historic town photos, and an exhibition space, €2.50pp. Some sports facilities adj with a small amount of grass to one side. A few artisan potters around town including Poterie Dubois 200m: N50°23.395' E004°30.984', www.poteriedubois.be Reinspected 2015.

NAMUR F3 119 N50°28.068' E004°51.004' 5000

Place André Ryckmans. From south on N92 turn left at citadel, sp 'Citadelle'. Follow road for 1.5km, then at next roundabout turn right, sp 'Namur Expo'. At next roundabout turn left and follow one-way street 450m along river edge. Turn left at end. Aire on left, signed.

8; 8m bays plus 2m overhang

Flot Bleu Euro; CC; €7.50

Designated parking in oversubscribed local parking backing onto sports centre gym with constant daytime music. The bays are wide, but slope front to rear. Patrons of the bar opp and sports centre park in camper bays late into the evening. Local commerce nearby, town commerce 900m. Citadel 1.8km, open daily Apr-Sept, €11pp; www.citadelle.namur.be www.namur.be Inspected 2015.

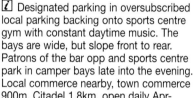

HUY 1 F3 120 N50°30.996' E005°14.089' 4500

N90/Chaussée de Napoléon. Follow N90 from Namur. Aire adj to N90 on lower parking, opp Hotel du Fort. Entrance at both ends.

2; 9m bays plus overhang

Portable toilets; Adj tap turned off; See 121 info or 118

2 designated riverside bays, 1 slightly impeded by willows, in car park slightly lower than main road. Although the N90 is noisy, there is a lovely view of the river Meuse and passing barges. Unrestricted slipway adj. Fort de Huy, which overlooks the Aire, was a WWII detention centre; open daily Apr-Oct 10am-5pm. www.huy.be Reinspected 2015.

Avenue Godin-Parnajon. From 120 go straight over roundabout. Fork right and go straight over the next roundabout with monument into the car park. Parking on right by park entrance, behind bus stop!

🚐 1; Max 6m

🚻 None; See info or 118

ℹ️ 1 impractical designated bay under trees beside bus stop, busses may impede access. Entrance to public park adj. Use if 120 full. Dilapidated Service Point at former campsite in Tihange: N50°31.981' E005°15.568'; still has WC emptying point, but no water. Reinspected 2015.

Tihange Service Point

Roeselare

Beaufort

Redange

LUXEMBOURG

Dudelange

Schengen

WILTZ G4 1 N49°58.306' E005°56.068' 9550

Rue Joseph Simon. Exit 15 onto 26 and follow sp 'Wiltz', then at Wiltz follow road to left onto 26a, sp 'Clervaux'. In 1.5km turn left, sp 'Kaul 300m' and 'Camping'. Turn immediately right, sp 'Kaul'. Follow road and Aire is on left opp bike jumps, before swimming pool, signed.

3; 7m bays; See info

Flot Bleu Pacific; €1

Landscaped Aire with 3 designated bays, but adj undesignated parking big enough for another 7 motorhomes or one large motorhome. Located in community recreation area which includes mountain bike course, outdoor swimming pool, restaurant and campsite. Town 500m. Inspected 2015.

HEIDERSCHEID G4 2 N49°52.674' E005°59.641' 9157

15, opposite Fuussekaul Camping. Turn left off 15 as exit Heiderscheid towards Ettelbruck just after camper sales, signed. Aire beside and behind Fox Burger, a small fast food restaurant.

34; €10/night Sept-Jun; €15/night Jul-Aug; Inc service and 16amp CEE elec; Pay at reception

Seijsener WC sink; Can use campsite toilets and showers €1/5 mins

This nicely landscaped Aire is managed by the campsite on the other side of the main road, accessible via underpass. Further parking for large motorhomes uphill behind supermarket, signed. Adj facilities inc fast food restaurant, restaurant, motorhome dealer and supermarket, making it a convenient stop. Some road noise. www.fuussekaul.lu Reinspected 2015.

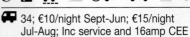

GRAND DUCHY   LUXEMBOURG

 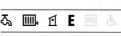
Route de Gilsdorf. Follow sp 'Camping de la Sûre' through town to campsite. Aire before campsite entrance, signed.

🚐 8; €7/24hrs Nov-Mar; €12/24hrs Apr-Oct; Pay at machine

🚰 Holiday Clean; 8 4amp CEE elec points

ℹ️ Aire located outside a small community campsite; English spoken. The Service Point is always accessible. Diekirch, 500m, has city status and town commerce. The excellent WWII museum is 900m away on north edge of town: N49°52.259' E006°09.532'. www.mnhm.net www.camping.diekirch.lu Reinspected 2015.

BEAUFORT ☀️ △ G4 4 N49°50.368' E006°17.293' 6310

Grand Rue. From Echternach head west on 10. Turn left off N10 onto 364, sp 'Beaufort'. Follow 364 for 12km, then at roundabout turn right, sp 'Château'. In 750m turn left, sp 'Camping'. Follow road past grass parking. Service Point on right outside TO and Camping Plage, signed.

🚐 5; Daytime only; See 5

🚰 Seijsener bollard; Water €0.50

ℹ️ Service Point only. To visit the impressive Medieval and adjoining Renaissance châteaux, follow sp 'Château' to adj parking: N49°49.989' E006°17.278'. Open Easter-Oct 9am-5.30pm, €5pp inc taste of local cassis (blackcurrant) liqueur. www.castle-beaufort.lu Reinspected 2015.

ECHTERNACH   🏛 G5   5   N49°48.574' E006°25.714'   6414

Rue des Bénédictins. Turn off 10 onto 11, sp 'Luxembourg'. Turn immediately right into Rue des Bénédictins, sp 'P'. Car park at end of road, large bays in middle. 3.5t weight restriction for commercial vehicles.

🏕 5; Large bays in middle of parking

🛍 Holiday Cleany (Under construction in photo); Near entrance

ℹ Large car park on edge of town, adj to 10 so suffers road noise. Old walled town with commerce and stunning Benedictine abbey 800m via footpath. Large lake and Roman villa southwest of town. Capital of area known as Little Switzerland, which has lots of cycle and walking paths, see the Mullerthal Trail Pocket Guide. www.echternachtourist.lu Inspected 2015.

LAROCHETTE   ⛺ G4   6   N49°47.109' E006°12.626'   7620

Rue de la Piscine, off Rue de Mersch. At Larochette follow sp 'Camping Birkelt' onto 118. Turn left, sp 'Camping Birkelt'. Aire on right outside campsite before reception, signed.

🏕 8; 4pm-10am only; 50% off campsite + ecotax; Pay at reception; Mar-Oct

🛍 Custom; Service and use of showers/toilets inc; 10amp CEE elec; All inside campsite

ℹ This Quick Stop Aire has large hedged bays with elec points to rear of the middle bays. Aire users are excluded from using the swimming pool. Full campsite prices range from €20 low season to €37 high season, however the site is listed in discount schemes. www.irisparc.co.uk Reinspected 2015.

Arrivée à partir de 16h00
Départ avant 10h00
Enregistrement à la réception
ou au restaurant
50 % du tarif camping + ecotax
Pas d'accès à la piscine

Check-in after 4.00 pm
Check out before 10.00 am
Check-in at reception or restaurant
½ price campsite + full price ecotax
No free swimming pool

NOMMERN ⛺ G4 7 N49°47.156' E006°10.046' 7465

Rue Nommerlayen. Follow sp 'Camping Nommerlayen'. Bays between Service Point and campsite reception.

🚐 17; €10/24hrs; Pay at reception; Mar-Oct excl Jul-Aug; Grass parking

🛒 Seijsener WC sink; €2; 10amp CEE elec €2; Water on pitch at elec bollards

ℹ️ Peaceful Aire outside campsite overlooking nice countryside. Water at Service Point €2, but free on electric bollards. No use of showers or toilets. Campsite listed in several discount schemes; English spoken. A 4.3km wellbeing trail departs here. www.nommerlayen-ec.lu Reinspected 2015.

REDANGE 🏃 G4 8 N49°46.141' E005°53.704' 8510

Rue de la Piscine. From Belgium follow 22 through town towards Ettelbruck. In Redange follow sp '12 Wiltz' and 'Medicin'. Turn left, sp 'Centre Médical' and signed. Turn right at far end of sports field and before the swimming pool, signed. Designated parking in section adj to Service Point, signed.

🚐 6; Max 48hrs

🛒 Custom; 6 16amp Cont elec points opp

ℹ️ The Aire is in a sloping car park on the edge of town adj to bus stop/parking, open access sports fields and swimming pool complex with café/bar. Town centre with local commerce 700m downhill. Reinspected 2015.

SCHWEBSANGE 🏕 ⛴ G4 9 N49°30.500' E006°21.924' 5447

10/Quai de la Moselle. Turn off 10 into campsite, sp 'Port de Plaisance'. If space, park before barrier and report to reception. Once through barrier follow road to far end and the motorhome parking is along the outside edge.

🛁 ▥ 🔟 E wc ♿ 🐾 🚌 F

● P 🚐 ◁ ⚱ 🎵 🚐 F ❄

🚐 €10/night; Pay at reception; Apr-Oct;
🚰 Seijsener bollard and WC sink; In entrance to campsite; Inc; 10amp Cont elec €2.50, long cable needed
ℹ Overlooking marina and 5 bays have river views. Motorhomers can use this community-run campsite's facilities, there is also a bar/restaurant and fresh bread available. The 10 is a very pleasant, scenic drive/cycle along the Moselle with riverside car parks and picnic areas. National river fishing license available in town. www.camping-port.lu Reinspected 2015.

SP 🌳 🍴 🧗 📷 🚻 🚶 🚴 🛋 🪝 🦢

MONDORF LES BAINS 🏛 G4 10 N49°30.337' E006°16.697' 5627

Avenue Frères Wiesenbach. Approaching on 152 from Schengen, turn left at the roundabout, sp '16 Frisange'. Follow road for 500m, then turn right, sp for MATCH supermarket and signed. Turn 1st right, signed. Aire in car park on right at end of road, signed.

🛁 ▥ 🔟 E wc ♿ 🐾 🚌 F

● P 🚐 ◁ ⚱ 🎵 🚐 F ❄

🚐 10; See info
🚰 Holiday Cleany; No drive over drain
ℹ Aire in car park with car-sized bays, often filled with local vehicles and partially obstructed by trees. Suggest park in roadside bays, max 2hrs Mon-Sat 8am-6pm, and assess Aire on foot. Hotel with restaurant and interesting architecture adj. Small town commerce 150m. Luxembourg's only thermal spa is 600m, open daily; www.mondorf.lu Inspected 2015.

SP 🌳 🍴 🧗 📷 🚻 🚴 🛋 🪝

DUDELANGE   G4   11   N49°28.283' E006°04.707'   3481

Rue Gare Usines. Exit A3 at Junction 3 and follow sp 'Dudelange', then 'Centre'. Turn right, sp 'Toutes Directions', then in 80m turn left in front of church, sp 'France'. Turn right past bandstand, signed. Then follow signs. After underpass take 1st left, signed. Follow road uphill and Aire is on left, signed.

🚐 7; Max 48hrs

🚰 Holiday Clean

ℹ️ This small Aire has 7 marked bays. It is adj to a noisy main road, railway line and small Park & Ride. The area feels urban/industrial and there is a large skateboard park over the bridge. The pleasant town centre is 1.5km walk or catch bus from adj stop. Reinspected 2015.

LUXEMBOURG CITY   G4   12   N49°36.005' E006°06.290'   1248

Rue de Bouillon. Turn off A6 onto A4, sp 'Hollerich' and 'Luxembourg'. Turn off A4, sp 'Merl' and 'P&R'. Then turn off, sp 'P&R Bouillon'. Service Point located at Autocars bus parking. There is no parking.

🚐 None

🚰 Custom; Water €1/100L

ℹ️ This Service Point is located in a tourist coach parking area and bus waiting area for the adj Park and Ride. There is no parking for motorhomes here or nearby. www.vdl.lu Reinspected 2015.

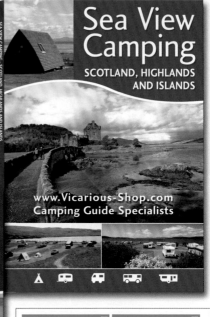
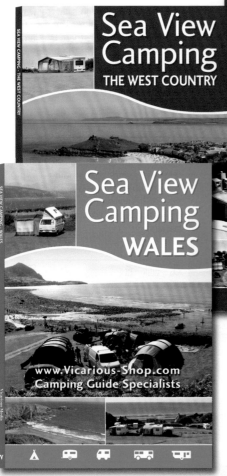

Gouda

Sas van Gent

THE NETHERLANDS

Arnhem

Westendorp

SAS VAN GENT ★   E2   1   N51°13.552' E003°48.139'   4551

Oostkade, adj to canal by marina. Turn off N62 at traffic lights, sp 'Sas van Gent'. Follow road straight over roundabout and cross lift bridge. At roundabout turn left, sp 'Havens 4000-4500'. Turn 1st left, signed, then 1st right, signed. Follow road to grass parking at end, signed. Well signed in town and visible from main road.

2; Max 24hrs; Grass parking; See info
None; See 13

ℹ️ Popular designated parking in a large grass area that can take 50 motorhomes. Oversubscription at this excellent spot is currently being tolerated, but this may change. Moored pleasure boats adj. Pretty town 350m. Enjoy it while you can! Reinspected 2015.

WESTDORPE   E2   2   N51°13.748' E003°49.284'   4554

Bernhardstraat. Turn off N62 at traffic lights, sp 'Westdorpe'. Follow road and turn right at roundabout, sp 'Westdorpe'. In 230m turn right into parking, signed.

2; Reinforced grass parking
None; See 13

ℹ️ This Aire is located at the village boundary in a small parking area adj to a wood that leads through to a long lake. 350m from the local commerce and mini market. This is a pleasant spot, ideal if 1 is unavailable. Reinspected 2015.

AXEL

D2 | 3 | N51°15.567' E003°54.624' | 4571

Kinderdijk. Exit N258 at roundabout, sp 'Axel'. Aire 750m on right opposite water tower, signed. Large motorhomes could access the small car park but may not be able to turn around to exit.

🚐 2; Max 8m

🛏 None; See **13**

ℹ Shaded parking at the end of a tiny roadside car park overlooking fishing pond with nature walks. Water tower opp is open Apr-Sept Wed-Fri 1.30-5pm, Sat 1-4.30pm; walk through the botanical gardens surrounding the water tower and you might catch sight of a peregrine falcon, www.hetwarenhuis.nl Town commerce 700m; Saturday market. Reinspected 2015.

TERNEUZEN

D2 | 4 | N51°20.114' E003°49.276' | 4531

Binnenvaartweg. From centre follow sp 'Sas Van Gent'. Aire in car park adj to Sas Van Gent turning, just before lift bridge over lock.

🚐 4; Max 24hrs; Motorhome parking free, pay meter is for cars only; Reinforced grass parking

🛏 None; See **13**

ℹ Despite being located between the sea, a double lock, a marina and the town centre, none of these are visible from the Aire. The busy road is the dominant feature, but this does not put motorhomers off from parking overnight. The seaside resort centre with high street commerce is 300m. www.terneuzen.nl Reinspected 2015.

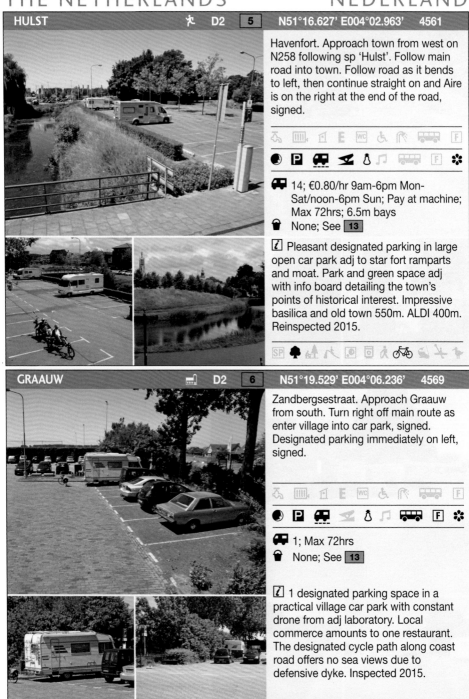

HULST   🏃 **D2**   **5**   **N51°16.627' E004°02.963'**   **4561**

Havenfort. Approach town from west on N258 following sp 'Hulst'. Follow main road into town. Follow road as it bends to left, then continue straight on and Aire is on the right at the end of the road, signed.

🚐 14; €0.80/hr 9am-6pm Mon-Sat/noon-6pm Sun; Pay at machine; Max 72hrs; 6.5m bays
🛒 None; See **13**

ℹ️ Pleasant designated parking in large open car park adj to star fort ramparts and moat. Park and green space adj with info board detailing the town's points of historical interest. Impressive basilica and old town 550m. ALDI 400m. Reinspected 2015.

GRAAUW   **D2**   **6**   **N51°19.529' E004°06.236'**   **4569**

Zandbergsestraat. Approach Graauw from south. Turn right off main route as enter village into car park, signed. Designated parking immediately on left, signed.

🚐 1; Max 72hrs
🛒 None; See **13**

ℹ️ 1 designated parking space in a practical village car park with constant drone from adj laboratory. Local commerce amounts to one restaurant. The designated cycle path along coast road offers no sea views due to defensive dyke. Inspected 2015.

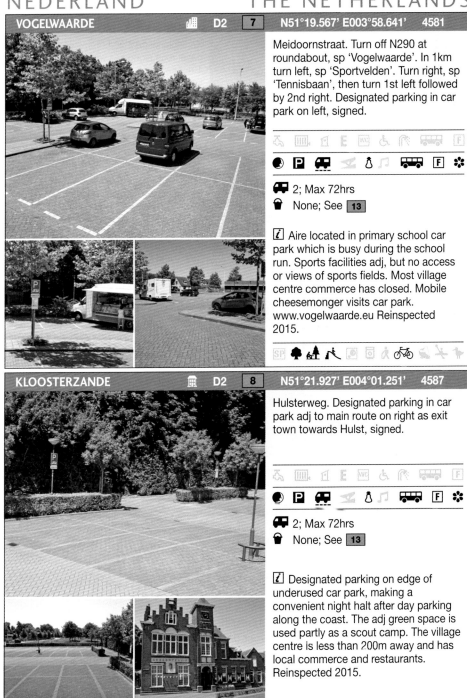

VOGELWAARDE — D2 — 7 — N51°19.567' E003°58.641' — 4581

Meidoornstraat. Turn off N290 at roundabout, sp 'Vogelwaarde'. In 1km turn left, sp 'Sportvelden'. Turn right, sp 'Tennisbaan', then turn 1st left followed by 2nd right. Designated parking in car park on left, signed.

🚐 2; Max 72hrs
🚻 None; See 13

ℹ️ Aire located in primary school car park which is busy during the school run. Sports facilities adj, but no access or views of sports fields. Most village centre commerce has closed. Mobile cheesemonger visits car park. www.vogelwaarde.eu Reinspected 2015.

KLOOSTERZANDE — D2 — 8 — N51°21.927' E004°01.251' — 4587

Hulsterweg. Designated parking in car park adj to main route on right as exit town towards Hulst, signed.

🚐 2; Max 72hrs
🚻 None; See 13

ℹ️ Designated parking on edge of underused car park, making a convenient night halt after day parking along the coast. The adj green space is used partly as a scout camp. The village centre is less than 200m away and has local commerce and restaurants. Reinspected 2015.

EMMADORP   ⚓ D2   9   N51°19.690' E004°08.939'   4568

Koninginnestraat and Emmaweg. Follow coast road along sea wall to Emmadorp. The Aire is outside café Het Verdronken Land, signed.

🚐 1; Max 72hrs; Motorhomes banned from adj car park

🚰 None; See 13

ℹ️ Only 1 designated space on roadside verge, but room for more. Aire situated by the sea wall, a café, and the Verdronken Land (the 'drowned land') visitor centre, entry €2pp unless part of tour. Adj marshland is largest brackish marsh in Europe; no view due to the sea wall, but this fascinating area can be walked through on boardwalks. Guided tours available from visitor centre, €8pp; open May-Sept Tues-Sun 1-5pm, Apr/Oct weekends only 1-5pm. www.saeftinghe.eu Reinspected 2015.

Sas van Gent

HAVE YOU VISITED AN AIRE?

Take at least 5 digital photos showing
• Signs
• Service Point
• Parking
• Overview
• Amenities

Visit www.all-the-aires.co.uk/submissions.shtml
to upload your updates and photos.

ℹ️ Submit updates
• Amendments
• New Aires
• Not changed

| PAAL | ⚓ D2 | 11 | N51°21.196' E004°06.561' | 4569 |

Havenstraat. Designated parking adj to road opposite the sea wall, signed.

🌐 P 🚐 ⛵ ♨ ♪ 🚌 F ❀

🚐 1; Max 72hrs; Max 8m

🚰 None; See 13

ℹ️ Designated roadside parking adj to sea and small marina, but neither are visible due to the large sea wall. There is a lively looking café/restaurant/bar adj and another in the small boat marina. Reinspected 2015.

SP 🌳 🏕 🎿 📷 🏊 🚶 🚴 🛶 🎣 🦆

| HOOGERHEIDE 1 | 🏭 D2 | 12 | N51°25.392' E004°20.119' | 4631 |

Huijbergseweg. Turn off N289 at roundabout, sp 'Hoogerheide'. Just before 30kph restriction signs turn left, signed, then immediately right. Designated parking on left, signed.

🌐 P 🚐 ⛵ ♨ ♪ 🚌 F ❀

🚐 6; Max 48hrs

🚰 None; See 13

ℹ️ Shaded designated parking in large car park on edge of town. The car park can take any sized motorhome and there is always likely to be space. The parking is adj to main route in a residential area close to the sports facilities. Small town commerce 850m. Inspected 2015.

SP 🌳 🏕 🎿 📷 🏊 🚶 🚴 🛶 🎣 🦆

HOOGERHEIDE 2   D2   13   N51°25.513' E004°20.824'   4631

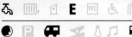
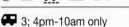

Buitendreef. Turn off N289 at roundabout, sp 'Huijbergen' and 'De Kooi. Turn 1st left, sp 'De Kooi'. Turn 1st right and the Service Point is on the right just past Peter Broos Ford, signed.

🚐 3; 4pm-10am only

🚻 Custom; Water tap; 3 CEE elec points

ℹ️ The Aire is located in an industrial area on a garage forecourt. The mechanics will work on any vehicle including motorhomes and tractors, so if you need something unusual fixed this is a good place to go. Tel: 0164 673358 www.peterbroos.nl Reinspected 2015.

BERGEN OP ZOOM   D2   14   (A) N51°29.046' E004°16.806'   4617

Parking B

(B) N51°29.234' E004°16.621'
Binnenschelde, De Boulevard Noord. Exit A4 at Junction 29 and follow sp 'Bergen op Zoom'. At roundabout turn left, sp 'Binnenschelde'. At traffic lights go straight on, then right at next lights. Follow road going straight over roundabout, then turn left, sp 'Binnenschelde'. Turn 1st left towards seafront, then turn left to **(A)** or turn right to **(B)**. Route signed entire way.

🚐 **(A)** 8; Max 72hrs **(B)** 5; Max 72hrs

🚻 None; See 16

ℹ️ **(A)** In residential area overlooking leisure lake, waterside cafés adj. **(B)** In busy area by numerous indoor sports facilities including a swimming pool and overlooking a sandy swimming beach; no dogs. WiFi at McDonald's. Thursday market in town centre 9am-3.30pm. www.bergenopzoom.nl Reinspected 2015.

Parking A

HANSWEERT ✳   ⚓ D2   15   N51°26.708' E004°00.365'   4417

Westhavendijk. Exit A58 at Junction 33 and follow sp 'Hansweert' onto N289. Follow sp 'Hansweert' for 5.2km, across canal, then left along canal. In Hansweert turn left at road marked roundabout, sp 'Amos'. Follow road straight on, past SPAR minimarket on left, then turn left up hill. Aire on right just over crest of hill, signed.

🛐 P 🚐   🚌 F ✿

🚐 5   🛢 None; See 16

ⓘ Popular designated parking in an unusual area adj to entrance of Kanaal door Zuid-Beveland. Barges negotiating the entrance can be seen from the Aire; check which ship it is on www.fleetmon.com/en/ports/Hansweert_5814 Info panels dotted around area behind parking show photos of the old abandoned lock/basin network. Village with local commerce 300m. Seasonal pedestrian ferry adj. Service Point at De Plantage farm shop: N51°28.121' E004°02.676', €12.50/night. Reinspected 2015.

MIDDELBURG 1   T D2   16   N51°30.043' E003°37.712'   4332

Oude Veerseweg. Exit A58 at Junction 38 onto N57, sp 'Middelburg-Oost'. Follow sp 'Middelburg', then exit, sp 'Ramsburg' and 'Middelburg-Centrum'. Turn right at 1st roundabout and left at 2nd roundabout, sp 'Ramsburg' and 'Centrum'. Follow road straight on over roundabout, then turn left, sp 'P Oude Veerseweg'. Designated parking on left in car park, signed.

🛐 P 🚐 🍽 🛢 🎵 🚌 F ✿

🚐 5; 8m bays + 2m overhang; See info
🛢 Seijsener bollard; Water €1; 4 16amp CEE elec points €1

ⓘ This popular Aire occupies a small part of a large car park on the outskirts of town. Oversubscription currently tolerated overnight, but car park very busy during the day. The centre of this star fort city is a 1km waterside walk and has a Medieval abbey, €8.50pp, www.visitmiddelburg.nl Toll tunnel to Terneuzen, €5; www.westerscheldetunnel.nl Reinspected 2015.

MIDDELBURG 2   ⚓ 🏢 D2 17   N51°29.670' E003°36.937'   4337

Kanaalweg. Exit A58 at Junction 39 onto N245, sp 'Middelburg-Centrum'. Follow N245 to town centre, going straight over 1 roundabout and 3 sets of traffic lights, all sp 'Centrum'. At 4th set of traffic lights cross level crossing and turn immediately right alongside canal, sp 'Station'. Parking 100m on right, 150m before railway station, signed.

3; €1.60/hr or €10/day Mon-Sat 8am-8pm; Free 8pm-8am and all day Sun; CC/€; Pay at machine; Max 48hrs; 6m bays + 3m overhang; Soft ground

None; See 16

Designated parking sandwiched between main road and railway line, adj to train station car park. The parking offers views of both a swing and lift bridge, which brings the traffic to a standstill every time boats go through. Very convenient day parking for visiting the star fort town, which is just over the bridges. Inspected 2015.

MIDDELBURG 3   🏢 D2 18   N51°29.793' E003°36.275'   3313

Hof van Tange. From 17 go back to lights and turn right to cross bridge, sp 'P Centrum'. At next traffic lights turn left, then turn right at following set, sp 'Veere'. Follow road, sp 'Veere', for 500m, then turn left, sp 'Parking Van Tange'. Designated parking on left as enter car park, signed.

5; €1.80/hr or €10/day Mon-Sat 8am-8pm; Free 8pm-8am and all day Sun; CC/€; Pay at machine; Max 6m

Pay toilet; See 16

Designated parking in car park near town centre, accessible via underpass. This is likely to be more peaceful at night than 17 . The car park is located on one of the triangles of the defences, which form about 2km of pleasant waterside parklands around the town. Roads cut the parks into sections, but all are linked with a foot and cycle path. Inspected 2015.

ROOSENDAAL   D3   19   N51°33.827' E004°27.754'   4751

Mobiledrôme, Argon. Exit A17 at Junction 20, sp 'Borchwerf'. Follow sp 'Borchwerf 2000-2300'. At roundabout turn right, sp '2000-2049'. Turn right into industrial park, sp '2100-2299'. Aire at far end of motorhome dealer Mobiledrôme & Partners on right, signed.

8; Max 48hrs; At both ends of parking Holiday Cleany; Water €0.50; No drive over drain; 12 16amp CEE elec points €0.50/metered amount

i The parking is located outside a motorhome dealer in an industrial park close to a busy road, so expect some noise. The dealership retails many brands and will work on most motorhomes; open Tues-Fri 9am-5.30pm, Sat 10am-5pm. www.mobiledrome.nl Reinspected 2015.

DORDRECHT 1   D3   20   N51°48.552' E004°39.166'   3314

Weeskinderendijk. Exit A16 at Junction 21 and follow sp 'Dordrecht Centrum'. Follow sp 'Centrum' for 1.5km, then turn right before and opposite BP fuel station. Parking on left under flyover, signed.

2; 24hrs free, then €1/4hrs; Max 72hrs; 6m bays; Poss need to get ticket even in free period
None; See 21

i Designated parking under flyover beside a railway siding and large, popular height-barriered car park. You could park here overnight, but you probably would not want to. Bus stop adj. River, 200m, has 800m walk/cycle path to town. The 3km Rondje Dordt walk and 1hr Waterrondje boat trip combined claim to pass almost 1000 sights, including monuments, museums and all the town quirks. www.vvvdordrecht.nl Reinspected 2015.

DORDRECHT 2   D3   21   N51°49.095' E004°41.255'   3313

Maasstraat. Turn off N3, sp 'Wijk 13' and 'De Staart', then turn left at traffic lights, sp 'Staart-West'. Follow road for 1.3km and Aire in car park on right, before Noah's Ark, sp 'Parkeerterrein Ark van Noach'. Service Point on right in entrance, signed. Designated parking to rear, closest to river, signed. Actual GPS: N51°49.155' E004°41.192'.

12; €0.50/hr 9am-10pm; Free 10pm-9am and all day Sun; Pay at machine; Max 72hrs

Custom; Water €1

ℹ️ Designated parking on far side of large, open car park adj to water taxi. Views of navigation from 2 end bays. A full scale replica of Noah's Ark is currently moored adj and opens daily, €12.50pp. www.arcofnoah.org Town centre is 1 stop on the water taxi or a 2km walk/cycle. Inspected 2015.

GEERTRUIDENBERG 1   D3   22   N51°42.212' E004°51.792'   4931

Statenlaan. From Raamsdonksveer follow sp 'Geertruidenberg'. Cross river bridge, then turn right at roundabout with cannon in centre after bridge. Follow road straight on and designated parking is in the car park on right, adj to Jachthaven Geertruidenberg entrance, signed.

2; Max 8m; See info

None; See 21

ℹ️ Small popular designated parking in car park. Adj marina now has motorhome parking, see 23, so this Aire may change. Views across star fort defences to power station. Pretty town, high street and central square 350m; weekly market Friday 1-4pm. Reinspected 2015.

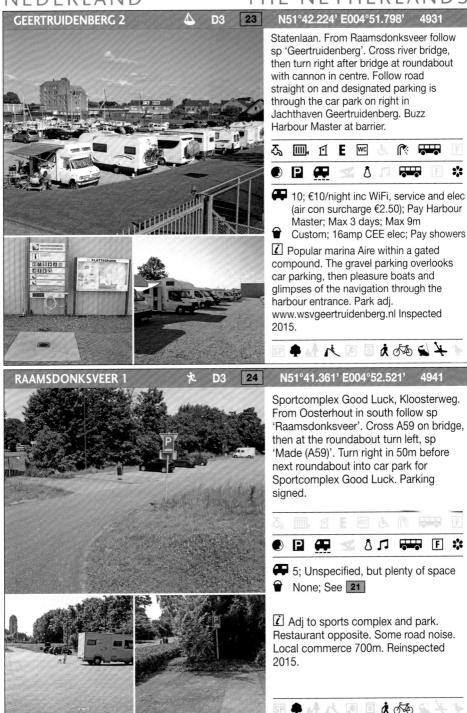

GEERTRUIDENBERG 2 ⚓ D3 **23** N51°42.224' E004°51.798' **4931**

Statenlaan. From Raamsdonksveer follow sp 'Geertruidenberg'. Cross river bridge, then turn right after bridge at roundabout with cannon in centre. Follow road straight on and designated parking is through the car park on right in Jachthaven Geertruidenberg. Buzz Harbour Master at barrier.

🚐 10; €10/night inc WiFi, service and elec (air con surcharge €2.50); Pay Harbour Master; Max 3 days; Max 9m
🚰 Custom; 16amp CEE elec; Pay showers

ℹ️ Popular marina Aire within a gated compound. The gravel parking overlooks car parking, then pleasure boats and glimpses of the navigation through the harbour entrance. Park adj. www.wsvgeertruidenberg.nl Inspected 2015.

RAAMSDONKSVEER 1 🏃 D3 **24** N51°41.361' E004°52.521' **4941**

Sportcomplex Good Luck, Kloosterweg. From Oosterhout in south follow sp 'Raamsdonksveer'. Cross A59 on bridge, then at the roundabout turn left, sp 'Made (A59)'. Turn right in 50m before next roundabout into car park for Sportcomplex Good Luck. Parking signed.

🚐 5; Unspecified, but plenty of space
🚰 None; See **21**

ℹ️ Adj to sports complex and park. Restaurant opposite. Some road noise. Local commerce 700m. Reinspected 2015.

RAAMSDONKSVEER 2   ⚓ D3 25   N51°41.570' E004°51.623'   4941

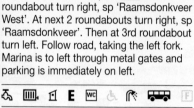
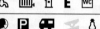

Kartuizertsraat. Drive past 24 and at roundabout turn right, sp 'Raamsdonkveer West'. At next 2 roundabouts turn right, sp 'Raamsdonkveer'. Then at 3rd roundabout turn left. Follow road, taking the left fork. Marina is to left through metal gates and parking is immediately on left.

🏕 🎹 ⛽ E 🚻 ♿ 🚿 🚌 F

● P 🚐 ⛵ ⛲ 🎵 🚌 F ❄

🚐 6; €8/night inc service, showers and WiFi

🚽 Custom; In multiple places; Seijsener WC sink; 16amp CEE elec €2

ℹ Small, cramped and basic, but pleasant marina Aire. Expect to be close to your neighbour. Views over marina towards power station. Café on site, town centre 1km. www.jachthavendok12.nl Star fortified Geertruidenberg town centre and TO 1.5km: N51°42.051' E004°51.594'. Inspected 2015.

SP 🌳 🏕 🛝 📷 ⑥ 🚶 🚴 🚣 🤾 🎣

RAAMSDONK   🏃 D3 26   N51°41.118' E004°54.815'   4944

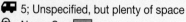

Lageweg. Exit A59 at Junction 35 and follow sp 'Raamsdonk'. Go straight over roundabout, then turn right, sp 'Raamsdonk'. Follow road to Raamsdonk. 1.3km after entering Raamsdonk turn left, sp 'Sportpark'. Take next left, then turn right before dead end sign. Parking in 300m on right, signed.

🏕 🎹 ⛽ E 🚻 ♿ 🚿 🚌 F

● P 🚐 ⛵ ⛲ 🎵 🚌 F ❄

🚐 5; Unspecified, but plenty of space

🚽 None; See 21

ℹ Designated parking adj to sports fields on the outskirts of the village. The car park is empty outside of sporting events. The large St Bavo catholic church, 700m, was designed by Carl Weber and is a national monument. Reinspected 2015.

SP 🌳 🏕 🛝 📷 ⑥ 🚶 🚴 🚣 🤾 🎣

GORINCHEM   ⛵ D3   27   N51°49.592' E004°58.030'   4201

De Punt. Exit A27 at Junction 24, sp 'Avelingen'. Follow sp 'Gorinchem', then sp 'Centrum' over lift bridge. Follow narrow one-way system through town, past church (max 9m), and turn right, sp 'Woudrichem'. Turn right into car park by river, signed. Drive along dyke to end, park at barrier and report to restaurant on right. Access between 8am-10pm.

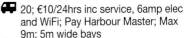

🚐 20; €10/24hrs inc service, 6amp elec and WiFi; Pay Harbour Master; Max 9m; 5m wide bays

🛠 Custom; Seijsener WC sink; Showers €0.50

ℹ Very popular marina Aire. Dedicated parking at tip of spit of land alongside marina and 4 bays also overlook the river. Leisure beach, restaurants and start of town 600m through park. www.vvvgorinchem.nl. Reinspected 2015.

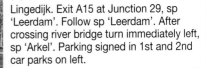

LEERDAM 1   🚢 C3   28   (A) N51°53.220' E005°05.227'   4142

(B) N51°52.979' E005°05.216'

Lingedijk. Exit A15 at Junction 29, sp 'Leerdam'. Follow sp 'Leerdam'. After crossing river bridge turn immediately left, sp 'Arkel'. Parking signed in 1st and 2nd car parks on left.

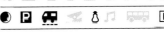
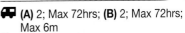

Parking A

🚐 (A) 2; Max 72hrs; (B) 2; Max 72hrs; Max 6m

🛠 None; See 33

ℹ Designated parking in 2 car parks overlooking river, both located near the National Glass Museum, www.nationaalglasmuseum.nl (A) is a larger car park, but is close to the Royal Leerdam Crystal factory, which hums throughout the night; factory tours 1pm Tues/Fri, http://royalleerdamcrystal.nl (B) is a small car park overlooked by residential flats. Reinspected 2015.

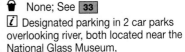

Parking B

LEERDAM 2 — C3 — 29 — N51°53.387' E005°05.690' — 4141

Zuidwal. Exit A15 at Junction 29 and follow sp 'Leerdam' onto N848. In 6.3km cross river and go straight on at traffic lights, sp 'Utrecht'. Cross railway line, then turn right at traffic lights, sp 'Utrecht'. At roundabout turn right, sp 'Centrum'. Follow road left, then turn 1st right before thatched house. Follow road over hill to very end. Turn right and follow road to right into car park. Designated parking at rear, signed.

3; Max 72hrs; Max 9m

Poss; See Harbour Master

i Small, shaded area that feels jammed in at remote corner of car park. Adj marina is fenced off, but partial views of pleasure boats. National Glass Museum studio adj, open Tues-Sat 10am-5pm, €8pp. www.nationaalglasmuseum.nl Adj pedestrian bridge leads to pleasant town. www.vvvleerdam.nl Inspected 2015.

OOSTERWIJK (LEERDAM) ★ — C3 — 30 — N51°52.470' E005°04.384' — 4163

Lingedijk. Exit A15 at Junction 29, sp 'Leerdam'. Follow sp 'Leerdam'. After crossing river bridge turn immediately left, sp 'Arkel'. Follow road along dyke and after 2km turn left. Drive through gate and parking adj to water, signed. Gate open 8am-10pm.

3; €8/night; Pay Harbour Master at café; Max 48hrs; Hardstanding; Additional grass parking when dry; Apr-Sept

Custom; WC emptying in toilet; 16amp CEE elec €2

i Charming marina Aire with parking adj to river and moored pleasure boats. Area is part of recreation network along the river Linge with pedestrian ferries, canoes, walking and cycling trails; see www.uiterwaarde.nl Unique little café and park adj. Pedestrian ferry, €1pp, to Heukelum with local commerce and castle. www.kasteelheukelum.nl Reinspected 2015.

VIANEN   🏛 ⚓ C3 31   N51°59.710' E005°05.776'   4132

Sluiseiland. Exit A27 at Junction 27 and follow sp 'Centrum'. After crossing lift bridge turn right at roundabout, sp 'P1' and 'P3'. The motorhome parking is in car park on right, sp 'P1' and signed.

🚐 4; Max 72hrs

🏠 None; See 33

ℹ Oversubscribed motorhome parking in large, open car park. Fortified town 650m across pedestrian bridge by library. Lock for large canal adj, but no view as up bank. Annual horse fair held for the past 744 years around the 2nd Thurs in Oct with parades, activities and fireworks; http://paardenmarktvianen.nl www.vvv-vianen.nl Reinspected 2015.

GELDERMALSEN   ⚓ D3 32   N51°53.092' E005°17.410'   4191

P Centrum, Kostverlorenkade. At Geldermalsen turn off N327, sp 'Centrum'. Follow road through town centre to roundabout by LIDL and turn right, sp 'P Centrum'. Turn immediately left into car park, sp 'P Centrum'. Parking on left, signed.

🚐 1; Max 8m

🏠 None; See 33

ℹ This is a busy tree-lined, riverside car park just off the high street with 1 dedicated motorhome bay. At times motorhomes overflow into parking with overhang adj to water and moored boats. Town centre commerce and LIDL 160m. www.geldermalsen.nl Reinspected 2015.

ALBLASSERDAM   D3   33   N51°51.670' E004°39.440'   2951

P Landvast, at ferry port. Exit A15 at Junction 22, sp 'Alblasserdam'. Follow sp 'Alblasserdam Oost'. At roundabout turn left, sp 'Vinkenwaard' and 'Kinderdijk'. Follow road and turn right, sp 'Kinderdijk'. Follow sp 'Kinderdijk' for 800m. Turn left, signed, and immediately left again, both sp 'P Landvast'. Aire on right, signed.

14; Free day parking until 3pm; €10/night; Collected by Harbour Master Custom; Water €0.50

ℹ️ Popular parking adj to marina and cinema. Town with high street commerce opp. Kinderdijk, 4km, is a collection of 19 windmills with UNESCO status: N51°53.362' E004°38.155'; entry €7.50pp. Suggest walk, cycle, bus or waterbus to the windmills from this Aire. www.kinderdijk.com www.alblasserdam.nl Reinspected 2015.

STRIJENSAS   D3   34   N51°42.883' E004°35.284'   3929

Sassedijk. Turn off N491, main route through Strijen, sp 'Strinjensas'. 250m after exiting Strijen turn right, sp 'Jachthaven'. Follow road for 3km to end, then turn left and follow road up and over dyke into marina, sp 'Jachthaven Strinjensas'. Report to Harbour Master, or restaurant after 6pm. Drive through gate, pass grey drain and follow to parking on right, signed.

10; €7/24hrs; Pay Harbour Master; Max 72hrs
 Custom; Water in parking area €0.50/100L; 6amp CEE elec €2.50/night; Shower €1/7 mins; Seijsener WC sink by gate; Toilets/showers closed 11pm-7am

ℹ️ The marina is adj to a large estuary, but no views. The summer parking overlooks an offshoot with moored pleasure boats barely visible through the long grass. In winter motorhomes park adj to the restaurant overlooking the marina. Free WiFi. Village with local commerce adj. www.jachthavenstrijensas.nl Inspected 2015.

OUD BEIJERLAND   D3   35   N51°49.771' E004°23.750'   3207

Oude Tol. Exit A29 at Junction 21 and follow sp 'Oud Beijerland' onto N217. Go straight across 1st roundabout, then turn left at next, sp 'Nieuw-Beijerland'. Go straight over 3 roundabouts and at 4th turn right, sp 'Zuid Beijerland'. Turn left after horse riding stables, sp 'Oude Tol', and designated parking in car park at end of road, signed.

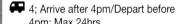

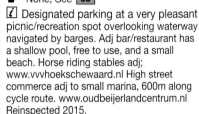

🚐 4; Arrive after 4pm/Depart before 4pm; Max 24hrs

None; See 33

ℹ️ Designated parking at a very pleasant picnic/recreation spot overlooking waterway navigated by barges. Adj bar/restaurant has a shallow pool, free to use, and a small beach. Horse riding stables adj; www.vvvhoekschewaard.nl High street commerce adj to small marina, 600m along cycle route. www.oudbeijerlandcentrum.nl Reinspected 2015.

SPIJKENISSE   D2   36   N51°50.715' E004°19.431'   3201

De Ritte. Exit A15 at Junction 16 and follow sp 'Spijkenisse'. At traffic lights turn left, sp 'Spijkenisse'. At traffic-lighted roundabout turn left, sp 'Centrum'. At next traffic lights turn right, sp 'P Route'. At roundabout turn left, then follow road straight on for 550m before turning right into car park adj to Penta College. Designated parking on left, signed.

🚐 2; Max 72hrs; Max 7m

None; See 33

ℹ️ 2 small bays in car park adj to college. The area has a slightly remote feel and the parking is deserted at weekends, but busy during college hours. Road noise from main route. If you appreciate modern architecture, check out the library in the town centre, 650m: N51°50.989' E004°19.508'. Inspected 2015.

VLAARDINGEN   C2   37   N51°54.215' E004°20.850'   3134

Oosthavenkade. Exit A4 at Junction 16 and follow sp 'Vlaardingen'. Follow road along railway line and parking is at end of road in car park adj to lock.

🚐 4; Max 48hrs
👕 None; See 33

ℹ️ Adj to lock (no view), railway line, main road and docks. Partial view of pleasure boats. Very noisy, unlevel parking suitable as a night halt en route to Hoek van Holland port. Town centre with high street commerce 500m. www.vvvvlaardingen.nl Reinspected 2015.

MAASSLUIS ★   C2   38   N51°54.983' E004°14.713'   3144

Scheldeweg. Exit A20 at Junction 7, sp 'Maasluis', and follow sp 'Maasluis' straight on for 1.8km. After road bends to right, cross lift bridge and turn 1st left, sp 'Nieuwe Waterweg'. Cross railway line, then follow road to waterside. Turn left and designated parking on right, signed.

🚐 3; Max 48hrs   👕 3 CEE elec points

ℹ️ Waterside parking overlooking the estuary and the ships coming and going to Rotterdam, so expect noise at night. Promenade/cycle path follows water's edge to park with benches and fishing spots. Chain ferry across waterway adj. Small town commerce 800m. Train station, 1km, has trains to Schiedam, home of jenever (gin), and Rotterdam. www.maassluispunt.nl Inspected 2015.

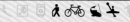

SCHIEDAM 1	C3	39	N51°55.161' E004°23.635'	3119

Noordvest. Exit A20 at Junction 11 and follow sp 'Centrum' and 'H Vlietland'. Turn right after train track, sp 'Centrum'. Follow road, then turn left, sp 'Molen'. Follow road straight on, then turn right immediately after crossing canal. Designated parking in 300m, just past windmill adj to canal, signed.

6; €1.80/hr or €6.60/day Mon-Fri 9am-9pm/Sat 9am-5pm; Free 9pm-9am and all day Sunday; CC; Pay at machine; Max 72hrs; 8m bays; See info

None; See 41

8m designated parking, but overhang the canal as much as you dare! Schiedam is a charming old town and the adj windmills are the tallest of their kind in the world. The town is famous for gin production, known as jenever. Jenever museum 900m. www.jenevermuseum.nl Inspected 2015.

SCHIEDAM 2	C3	40	N51°55.174' E004°24.059'	3111

Officierenpad 3. Exit A20 at Junction 11 and follow sp 'Centrum' and 'H Vlietland'. Turn right after train track, sp 'Centrum'. Follow road, then turn left, sp 'Molen'. Follow road straight on, then turn left after crossing canal. Follow road along canal, past car park on right and straight on. Designated parking opp windmill No. 6, signed.

2; €1.80/hr or €6.60/day Mon-Fri 9am-9pm/Sat 9am-5pm; Free 9pm-9am and all day Sunday; CC; Pay at machine; 8m bays

None; See 41

Roadside parking on a little used street near the old jenever warehouses. Small green space adj. Views of navigation and lift bridge. Windmill No. 6 300m: N51°55.239' E004°23.934'. Open Easter-Oct Tues-Sat, Nov-Easter weekends only 11.30am-5pm; €4.50pp. www.schiedamsemolens.nl Inspected 2015.

DISTILLEERDERIJ
M.DIRKZWAGER B.V.
FLORYN

GOUDA
T 🏢 C3 **41** N52°00.713' E004°42.938' 2806

P Klein Amerika. Exit A12 at Junction 11 and follow sp 'Gouda'. At traffic lights turn left, sp 'H Groene Hart'. Follow road turning right past train station and travelling under 3.8m underpass. Then turn left at traffic lights, sp 'Oudewater'. In 600m turn left, sp 'P Klein Amerika'. Enter through ticket barrier, designated parking at far end of car park.

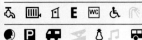

🚐 30; €1/40 mins; €8/9am-9pm Mon-Sat; Free Sun; Take ticket and pay at machine; Max 72hrs

🛒 Custom; Inside barrier; Seijsener WC sink; 12 16amp CEE elec points

ℹ️ The Service Point is inside the barrier, but is free to use. The car park is just 300m from historic Gouda centre. There's no whey you can miss the Cheese Weighing House museum or the famous Gouda Cheese Market, held every Thurs morning Apr-Sept. www.welkomingouda.nl Reinspected 2015.

BLEISWIJK
🏢 C3 **42** N52°00.851' E004°32.034' 2665

Jan van der Heydenstraat. Exit A12 at Junction 8 and follow sp 'Bleiswijk' onto N209. Turn left off N209 at traffic lights, sp 'Centrum'. Turn 1st right, sp 'Centrum'. Follow road and after passing church turn left. Turn left again, then drive through parking area. Designated parking at end on right, signed.

🚐 2; Max 48hrs

🛒 None; See **41**

ℹ️ Unglamorous parking adj to fire station in truck and car parking area that could be noisy in the early morning. Town centre with high street commerce 500m. There is a pleasant cycle path along the nearby De Rotte river which can be followed for 13km into central Rotterdam. Reinspected 2015.

OUDEWATER — C3 — 43 — N52°01.118' E004°52.296' — 3421

Molenwal. Turn off N228 in Oudewater by bus stops, sp 'Skeelerbaan'. Turn immediately right, sp 'Skeelerbaan', and follow road through car park to end. Designated parking at end. Actual GPS: N52°01.056' E004°52.412'.

🚐 5; Max 72hrs; Grass parking

🚰 None; Standpipe tap removed; Toilets at sports facilities locked; See 41

ℹ️ Popular, pleasant grass camping field located between main route through and raised canal, could take 10+ motorhomes. Oudewater, 650m, has a small, pleasant, touristy centre. For 15 mins of fun visit the witches museum. Witches (camperettes) are weighed as they were in the 1600s, only you now have to pay €5pp, but they won't be killed; open Apr-Oct Fri-Sun 11am-5pm. www.heksenwaag.nl Inspected 2015.

BODEGRAVEN — C3 — 44 — N52°05.303' E004°44.823' — 2411

Sportlaan. Turn off N458 ring road at roundabout, sp 'P Centrum Noord'. In 250m turn right, sp 'De Kuil'. Turn right again into car park, sp 'De Kuil'. Designated parking bay immediately on left, signed.

🚐 1; Max 72hrs; Max 6m

🚰 None; See 41

ℹ️ Adj to road in sports centre and swimming pool car park. 1 designated, car-sized bay only and overhanging is not possible due to cyclists going to and from the adj bike storage. Swimming pool is very popular on weekends, hot days and holidays and the car park, inc the motorhome bay, are likely to be full. Town commerce 400m in a modern development. Inspected 2015.

DRIEBRUGGEN | C3 | 45 | N52°02.617' E004°47.741' | 3465

Kerkweg. Exit A12 at Junction 13 and follow sp 'Driebruggen'. At end of road, turn right then immediately left into car park. Designated parking on left, signed.

🚐 1; 5m bay; Max 72hrs; See info

🛒 None; See **41**

ℹ 1 designated space in village car park adj to café. The bay is 5m deep, so parallel parking is required subject to space. The village is pretty due to numerous waterways. Take the cycle path on the opp side of the restaurant 2km to Reeuwijkse Plassen, a lake district formed by peat excavation and an excellent area to explore by bike. Inspected 2015.

ABBENES (Het Groene Hart) | C3 | 46 | N52°13.567' E004°37.150' | 2157

Kaagweg. From south on A44 exit at Junction 1, sp 'Oude Wetering'. At T-junction at end of slip road turn right into Kaagweg, sp 'Easypark2fly'. In 650m turn left into farm, signed. Reception immediately on right. Parking past reception on right. Be aware this is a working farm, other vehicles may appear within the farm yard.

🚐 17; €10/night Mar/Jun-Oct; €12/night Apr/May; Inc service and WiFi; Pay at reception; Mid Mar-Oct

🛒 Seijsener bollard and WC sink; Elec €2; Showers €1

ℹ Pleasant, landscaped, commercial Aire at a working farm in the heart of bulb country; an ideal place to experience the bulbs between mid Apr- end May. Some airplane noise. Bike hire, €7.50/9am-9pm. Motorhome accessory and repair shop 2km: N52°13.426' E004°38.576'. Laundry €5. www.camperplaatshetgroenehart.nl Reinspected 2015.

MIJDRECHT   C3   47   N52°12.537' E004°52.182'   3641

Rondweg. Turn off N201 at traffic lights on bend, sp 'Mijdrecht'. At roundabout turn left, sp 'Centrum'. Turn left in 400m into car park, signed. Designated parking to left at end of car park, signed.

🚐 4; Max 48hrs

🚻 None; See 41

ℹ️ Located in car park on edge of retail estate adj to main road; little traffic at night. Cafés adj. Town centre with high street commerce 350m across lift bridge, www.shoppingmijdrecht.nl Reinspected 2015.

AMSTERDAM CITY CAMP   C3   48   N52°23.899' E004°54.087'   1032

Papaverweg 55. From southwest on A10 or A5 pass through tunnel and exit at Junction 18 following sp 'S118' and 'Tuindorp Oostzaan'. Follow S118 across 2 roundabouts, sp 'Noord 150-499'. 1.9km after 2nd roundabout turn right at traffic lights, sp 'Noord 216-249'. Turn 1st right, sp 'Amsterdam City Camp' on fence. Aire on left, signed. Enter through CC-operated barrier.

🚐 96; €15/night; CC; Pay at barrier; Max 7 nights

🚻 Seijsener bollard and WC sink; Inside barrier; 48 bays with 6amp elec €4; Select at barrier upon entry

ℹ️ Large, commercial, unmanned Aire with CCTV and security fencing. www.amsterdamcitycamp.nl Area receiving trendy regeneration of docks. Free water taxi to city centre, 800m: N52°24.059' E004°53.509'. www.gvb.nl Inspected 2015.

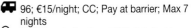
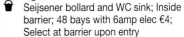

ALMERE POORT   ⛵ C3 [49]   N52°20.524' E005°08.111'   1361

Marina Muiderzand, IJmeerdijk. Travelling towards Amsterdam on A6 exit at Junction 2, sp 'Almere Poort'. At traffic lights turn left, then right. Turn left, sp 'Marina Muiderzand' and follow signs through development. Turn left into car park and report to reception/Harbour Master. Designated parking through barrier, signed: N52°20.331' E005°07.996'. Directions may change with development.

🚐 10; €13.50/night inc 16amp elec; Pay Harbour Master; May-Sept
🚰 Custom; Seijsener WC sink; Toilet block opp parking; All inside barrier
ℹ️ Designated parking in isolated marina surrounded by large development that has been 'in progress' for many years. Parking adj to pleasure boat marina and a swimming beach, partial boat and water views. The marina has a restaurant and shop. Some airplane and construction noise. www.marinamuiderzand.nl www.vvvalmere.nl Reinspected 2015.

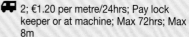

ALMERE HAVEN 1 ✱   ⛵ C3 [50]   N52°20.020' E005°13.292'   1357

Sluis. Exit A6 at Junction 4 and follow S102, sp 'Almere Haven'. Follow S102 straight across all roundabouts and junctions, sp 'Havenkom'. Parking on left, just past lift bridge and adj to marina, signed. Access is very restricted due to design; max 8m.

🚐 2; €1.20 per metre/24hrs; Pay lock keeper or at machine; Max 72hrs; Max 8m
🚰 Custom; Seijsener WC sink down steps by café; Water tap by office; Showers €0.50
ℹ️ A great marina Aire for smaller motorhomes adj to lift bridge/lock which takes boats a long way up and down from marina to navigation. Electricity is to be installed at a charge of €0.50/kW. Waterside views, cafés and restaurants adj. Riverside park and path adj. www.vvvalmere.nl Reinspected 2015.

ALMERE HAVEN 2 C3 [51]   N52°19.920' E005°13.016'   1353

Jachthaven Almere Haven. Exit A6 at Junction 4 and follow S102, sp 'Almere Haven'. Follow S102 straight across all roundabouts and junctions, sp 'Havenkom'. Drive past and follow road around marina. Aire through gate on left, sp 'Jachthaven Almere Haven'. At barrier press button for entry. Harbour Master's office adj to barrier and up stairs. Must arrive by 5.30pm.

🚐 26; €13.50/night; Pay Harbour Master; Grass parking; Mar-Nov

🚰 Custom; 6amp elec €2/night; Toilet and showers accessible by pass (€10 returnable deposit); All inside barrier

ℹ️ Spacious marina Aire with grass parking adj to and overlooking pleasure boats. Café onsite, more restaurants 350m at main harbour side. Harbour Master open 9am-5.30pm (until 8.30pm Jul-Aug). Swimming beach 350m across road. www.vvvalmere.nl Reinspected 2015.

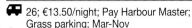

HUIZEN C3 [52]   N52°18.514' E005°14.393'   1271

IJsselmeerstraat. Exit A1 at Junction 8 and follow sp 'Huizen' onto N527. In Huizen by LIDL turn left at roundabout with green buoy, sp 'Oude Haven'. Follow road 400m to parking on left, signed. From Aire drive back to roundabout and turn left. Take the 2nd left and follow road. Service Point is just past a portable cabin on the left, marked 'Energieweg 3' and signed: N52°18.473' E005°14.613'.

🚐 8; Max 48hrs; Reinforced grass parking

🚰 Custom; Water to left by boat mooring; No drive over drain

ℹ️ Popular, pleasant parking by sports facilities adj to large green park with a 2km path through woods alongside a river. The 4 lime kilns of de Kalkovens Hotel restaurant set the scene at this now quaint part of a large marina area. www.huizen.nl Reinspected 2015.

Service Point

LAREN C3 53 N52°15.434' E005°14.367' 1251

Schapendrift, at sports centre. Exit A27 at Junction 34 and follow sp 'Laren'. Turn right in Laren, sp 'Zwembad' and 'Tennishal' on small yellow signs. Drive past sports centre marked 'Family Fitness'. Designated parking at far end of car park, signed.

2; Max 24hrs None; See 52

ℹ️ Located at a large multi sport complex in a peaceful and shaded section of a large parking area which may be full of cars during matches. High street commerce 1km. Singer Laren, a modern art museum and theatre, in centre with parking: N52°15.538' E005°13.262'. www.singerlaren.nl Good alternative when 52 full. Reinspected 2015.

PURMEREND C3 54 N52°30.420' E004°57.009' 1441

Nieuwstraat. Exit A7/E22 at Junction 5 and turn left, sp 'Purmerend'. Follow road for 1.2km and turn right at traffic lights, sp 'P Eggert' and 'P 't Lammetje'. Aire 200m on left opp 't Lammetje multi-storey car park.

5; €2/hr or €6.90/day Mon-Sat 9am-9pm; Free 9pm-9am and all day Sun; CC (except MasterCard); Pay at machine; Max 72hrs; 9m bays, some overhang

Seijsener bollard; Water €1; 5 16amp elec points €1

ℹ️ Well located, pleasant Aire overlooking river adj to waterside park. Beware: the cobbled parking has sagged in places. Cemetery adj, but not dead quiet as some road noise. Just 240m from high street commerce. www.purmerend.nl Inspected 2015.

OOSTHUIZEN — B3 — 55 — N52°34.538' E004°59.859' — 1474

Hoornse Jaagweg. Exit town on N247 to the north. Turn off N247 at roundabout, sp 'Beets'. Designated parking in car park on left, signed. Be careful to avoid concrete bollards at entrance.

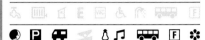

🌐 P 🚐 🛶 🛢 🎵 🚌 F ✽

🚐 2; Max 48hrs

⛺ None; See 56

ℹ️ Adj to narrow waterway with some moored pleasure boats and a slipway. As the parking is located just off the main road, expect some road noise. Local commerce is across roundabout and 1st right into Raadhuisstraat. At the end of this street is the church with 15th century organ. www.laagholland.com Reinspected 2015.

SCHAGEN — B3 — 56 — N52°47.452' E004°47.258' — 1742

Lagedijkerweg, at marina. Turn off N248 at roundabout onto N245, sp 'Schagen'. At 2nd traffic lights turn right, sp 'Sint Maarten' and 'Lagedijk'. At roundabout turn right. The parking and Harbour Master's office is on right, signed. Other parking on opp side of marina: N52°47.508' E004°47.327'.

🚐 14; €7/24hrs +€0.98pp inc elec; >8m +€4/night; Pay Harbour Master; Max 72hrs

⛺ Custom; Seijsener WC sink outside Harbour Master's office; Water €0.50/100L; No drive over drain

ℹ️ Parking in 2 areas at dead end marina. 8 places by Harbour Master's office have elec, but suffer industrial estate noise. 6 places on opp side of marina are sloping and adj to busy main road. Card for showers, €15 returnable deposit plus €0.05/min. WiFi €1/24hrs. Laundry €4. Large annual street market in town last Sun of Aug. www.vvvtopvanholland.nl Reinspected 2015.

DEN HELDER ★   T   B3   57   N52°57.726' E004°46.196'   1781

Willemsoord. Follow N250 into Den Helder, sp 'Texel'. Pass Reddingmuseum across water on right, then turn right at traffic lights, sp 'N250' and 'Texel'. Turn 1st right over lift bridge, sp 'Willemsoord', then turn left, signed. Turn last right to designated parking at far corner of car park, signed. Service Point: N52°57.717' E004°46.249'. From parking drive towards marina and turn right along quay. Service Point on right, signed.

🚐 14; €10/night; Max 48hrs; Pay at TO or Harbour Master in pm

🪣 Custom; 5* sanitation; Access via pin code; Inc showers and Seijsener WC sink; Water €0.50; 16amp CEE elec €1/12hrs; Token

ℹ️ Very pleasant, popular Aire within an old naval shipyard, now a naval museum; oversubscription tolerated. Attractions inc a submarine and a defence museum; free to wander around the docks reading the 20 interpretation panels in English. TO adj. www.willemsoordbv.nl Reinspected 2015.

MIDDENMEER   ⚓   B3   58   N52°48.724' E004°59.475'   1775

Zuiderzeeweg, adj to canal by swing bridge. Turn off A7 at Junction 12 and follow sp 'Middenmeer'. At roundabout turn right, sp 'Middenmeer'. Follow road for 1.1km, crossing lift bridge, then at roundabout go right around roundabout, sp 'Middenmeer'. Parking on right just past/at end of Texaco fuel station before crossing back over lift bridge, signed.

🚐 7; €10/night inc service and 16amp elec; Pay Harbour Master; Max 48hrs

🪣 Custom; Seijsener WC sink; No drive over drain; Toilets/showers accessible via pin code from Harbour Master

ℹ️ Designated parking at small, open access riverside marina; views of river and boat moorings depending on parked cars. Adj green space has dog exclusion. Pleasant town 200m with small town commerce. Reinspected 2015.

NEDERLAND

HOORN ⛵ B3 59 N52°38.080' E005°03.407' 1621

Visserseiland. Exit A7 at Junction 8. At 1st roundabout follow sp 'Hoorn', then at 2nd follow sp 'Centrum'. At traffic lights turn right, sp 'Centrum'. Go straight at next 2 traffic-lighted crossroads. Follow road to left into residential area, then to right and along water's edge. Turn right, keeping to water's edge, and follow road passing several dead end signs. Gated entrance is on left before car park; press button on intercom for access. No access 8pm-8am.

🚐 27; €14.60 inc water, 16amp elec and WiFi (get code on arrival); Pay Harbour Master

🪣 Custom; Near Harbour Master's office; Toilets and showers open all night, €1

ℹ️ Designated marina Aire with moored boats to one side and Markermeer inland lake to other, no view of either. Lakeside park adj. Only 500m from historic town with high street commerce. www.hoorn.nl Reinspected 2015.

ENKHUIZEN T ⛵ B3 60 N52°41.901' E005°17.420' 1601

Dirck Chinaplein. From Hoorn on N506 turn right at traffic lights onto N302, sp 'Lelystad'. Turn left at traffic lights, sp 'Enkhuizen'. Follow road and turn right into harbour, signed. Designated parking at rear of car park, signed. To pay walk 200m towards town and turn right past the tourist information and go to the left of the building. Pay at machine adj to showers: N52°41.989' E005°17.414'.

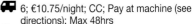

🚐 6; €10.75/night; CC; Pay at machine (see directions); Max 48hrs

🪣 Toilets and showers €1; Open 7am-11pm Apr-Oct; 300m adj to ticket machine

ℹ️ Parking adj to active harbour with views of tall ships crewed by enthusiastic groups. Many pleasure cruises leave from harbour, inc ferry to the excellent Zuiderzee Museum; €16pp, www.zuiderzeemuseum.nl TO next to pay point/toilets. Historic town 500m. www.vvvenkhuizen.nl Reinspected 2015.

Zuiderzee Museum

MEDEMBLIK ⚠ B3 61   N52°46.304' E005°06.815' 1671

Oudevaartsgat. From east on N239 follow sp 'Medemblik' onto N240. When N240 goes left, carry straight on across lift bridge. At 1st roundabout follow sp 'Centrum', then go straight over 2nd. In 350m turn left on right-hand bend by canal, sp 'P Centrum'. In 30m turn 1st right into marina, sp 'P Centrum' and signed. Follow road straight on for 300m and Aire in car park on right, signed.

🚐 5; €8/night inc elec; Pay Harbour Master; Max 48hrs
🔧 Seijesner WC sink; No drive over drain; 5 10amp CEE elec points

ℹ️ Open access marina Aire surrounded by water and adj to pleasant harbour, no views. Showers, toilets and café at Harbour Master's office. Kasteel Radboud, 100m, is surrounded by a pleasant park. Entry to castle/museum €6pp; www.kasteelradboud.nl Old town centre with high street commerce 850m on other side of marina. Reinspected 2015.

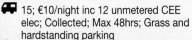

DEN OEVER ⚓ B3 62   N52°56.070' E005°02.378' 1779

Sluismeester A, Oostkade. Exit A7 at Junction 14 onto N99, sp 'Den Oever'. Turn right at roundabout, sp 'Den Oever P&R'. Follow road to right, sp 'i 300m', then follow road straight on, parallel to A7. Aire in car park at end of road.

🚐 15; €10/night inc 12 unmetered CEE elec; Collected; Max 48hrs; Grass and hardstanding parking
🔧 Seijsener bollard; Other side of office: N52°56.078' E005°02.357'

ℹ️ Marina Aire at southwest end of 30km A7 road viaduct/dyke which protects the Netherlands from the North Sea. Exposed spot with road noise by harbour. Seasonal seal watching trips and other boat trips possible. Small seasonal café adj. Local commerce 650m on other side of harbour. www.vvvtopvanholland.nl Reinspected 2015.

MAKKUM | B4 | 63 | N53°03.199' E005°24.186' | 8754

Workumerdijk. Exit A7 at Junction 16 and follow sp 'Makkum' for 4.3km. Go straight over 2 roundabouts, 1st sp 'Makkum' and 2nd sp 'Strand'. Cross lift bridge, then turn right at roundabout, sp 'Centrum P'. In 300m turn left before lift bridge and opp Harbour Master, sp 'Recreatieatra'. Drive down slope and designated parking on left past facilities block.

🚐 2; €10/night; Pay Harbour Master; Max 72hrs

🚰 Custom; Toilets and WC emptying in adj facilities block; No drive over drain

ⓘ 2 marked bays overlooking parking, fishing fleet, commercial boats and waterway to industrial building. All this activity makes it an interesting spot. Quaint Makkum centre, across lift bridge, has its fair share of tourist commerce. www.makkum.nl Inspected 2015.

ZURICH | B3 | 64 | N53°06.742' E005°23.599' | 8751

Schoolstraat. From Den Oever on A7 cross Afsluitdijk and exit at Junction 15, sp 'Zurich'. Exit right again, sp 'Zurich', then at end of road turn left, sp 'Zurich'. Follow road straight on into Zurich. Aire on left opp gift shop called 'Zuricher Bank', signed.

🚐 2 (space for 5); €3/night + €1pp tax; Pay at Zurich Bank opp; Max 72hrs; Large motorhomes poss with creative parking, subject to other vehicles

🚰 None; See 62

ⓘ Aire located in a charming village that appears to be in miniature, but is full scale. Adj fishing tackle shop provides 5 mins of fun as it plays on the link with Zurich in Switzerland, due to having received 100 items of misdirected post. In addition, the shop has its own money and stamps. No sea views. Restaurant/bar 100m. Inspected 2015.

HARLINGEN ⚓ A4 **65** N53°10.751' E005°25.040' 8861

Nieuwe Vissershaven. Exit A31 at Junction 19 and follow N390, sp 'Harlingen-Havens'. Follow road and turn right, sp 'Vissershaven' and signed. Turn 1st left into car park. Designated parking is along the water's edge, signed.

🛒 10; €7.50/24hrs; CC/€; Pay at machine; Max 3 days

💧 Custom; Water €1/100L; 30 sec WC rinse free; 16amp CEE elec €1/2kWh

ℹ This Aire is adj to a sea lock with lift bridge and temporary moorings for waiting boats. Commercial fishing fleet dock behind, no views. Pleasant historic port town with town commerce 800m; walk towards church spire. Free day parking on other side of town: N53°10.099' E005°25.056'. www.harlingen-friesland.nl Reinspected 2015.

JIRNSUM ⛵ B4 **66** N53°04.327' E005°48.194' 9011

It String 9. Exit A32 at Junction 14 and follow sp 'Jirnsum'. At end of road turn left, sp 'Akkrum'. After leaving Jirnsum turn left at roundabout, sp 'Akkrum'. Follow road, then at end of industrial estate turn left, sp 'Sneekerhof', then immediately turn left. Turn right into harbour, sp 'RFU Jachtspecialist' and signed. Harbour Master adj to marina on left.

🛒 5; €8/night inc unmetered CEE elec, WiFi and showers; Pay at Harbour Master

💧 Custom; WC emptying down toilet; No drive over drain

ℹ Marina advertising camper parking, but not designating any. Views of pleasure boats and a working boatyard. Some noise from adj industrial units involved in boat building. Nearby day parking ideal for fishermen: N53°04.006' E005°48.437'. www.rfu-jachtspecialist.nl Inspected 2015.

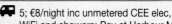

IJLST   🏭   **B4**   **67**   **N53°00.507' E005°37.647'**   **8651**

De Tsjalk. Turn off N354, sp 'Ijlst', and follow road straight on to village. 450m after entering village, before dead end sign where road goes to right, turn left into De Tsjalk. Turn right past dead end sign and Aire is on right, signed.

🚐 4; €7.50/night + €1.50 tax; Collected; Max 72hrs; Max 7m

🚰 CEE elec; Toilet, shower, WiFi and kitchen in adj sports building

ℹ️ Aire adj to a Fierljeppen (dyke jumping) beach and pond. Contestants pole vault over the water from June to mid-September, see www.fierljeppenijlst.nl Events are well attended, so arrive several days before. The pretty village centre has waterside restaurants. From the train station you can sneak off to Sneek, 3.5km. Reinspected 2015.

Musselkanaal

LANGWEER
B4 | 69 | N52°57.612' E005°43.144' | 8525

Pontdyk. From Sneek exit A7 at Junction 23 and follow sp 'Joure'. At end of road turn right, sp 'Joure'. Go straight over 1st roundabout, then turn right at 2nd, both sp 'Langweer'. In 4km turn right, sp 'Langweer'. Follow road for 4km and just before exit village turn left into car park, sp 'P'. Designated parking to right, signed. The other approach involves a 16t weight restricted car ferry.

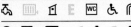 

🚐 4; Max 72hrs

Poss in marina; See Harbour Master for WC emptying, adj to toilets; Water available, container needed; Toilets/showers open access; Showers €0.50

ℹ️ Aire located in car park with free WiFi opposite a marina. Adj to pleasant village and recreation area with local and tourist commerce 350m. This area is famed for its lakes, where skûtsje, old fashioned flat bottomed barges, are raced every August; see www.skutsjesilen.nl www.langweer.nl Reinspected 2015.

MOLKWERUM
B3 | 70 | N52°54.262' E005°23.632' | 8722

't Slúske. Exit N359 at roundabout, sp 'Molkwerum'. At Y-junction in Koudum turn left, sp 'Molkwerum'. Follow road to left at fuel station/garage. In 4km in Molkwerum turn right, sp 'Hindeloopen' and ''t Séleantsje'. 2.2m width restriction in 500m sign relates to the bridge just past the Aire, so do not approach from Hindeloopen. Aire on left 50m past Camping 't Séleantsje.

🚐 16; €10/night + €1pp tax inc elec; Collected; Max 48hrs

Water and 16amp elec; At parking; WC emptying; Free; Showers €0.50; Both at campsite

ℹ️ Very pleasant Aire overlooking canal. IJsselmeer lake adj, but no view due to defensive bank which is used by sunbathers watching kite surfers, weather permitting. Camping 't Séleantsje adj with a bar/small restaurant. Small town commerce 600m. Reinspected 2015.

HEERENVEEN 1 🏃 B4 71 N52°56.302' E005°56.707' 8443

Heremaweg. Exit A32 at Junction 10 and follow sp 'Heerenveen Zuid'. Follow road for 1.7km and, as it bends left, turn right before crossing railway track, sp 'Thialf'. In 150m turn left into large car park, sp 'Thialf'. Aire on right in far corner of car park, signed.

🚐 4; Max 72hrs 🚰 None; See 72

ℹ️ Aire in car park of internationally renowned indoor ice rink. The ice rink houses both speed skating and ice hockey events. Up to 17,000 spectators can attend events which are held between Oct-Mar, see www.thialf.nl for fixtures list. Ongoing building works are due to be finished late 2016. Some train noise. Reinspected 2015.

HEERENVEEN 2 🏢 B4 72 N52°58.062' E005°56.386' 8443

Venus. Exit A32 at Junction 12 and follow sp 'Tjalleberd'. At traffic lights turn left, then turn 1st right into industrial estate, sp 'Venus'. Turn right as road bends to left. Service Point through gate on right, signed.

🚐 None; See 71

🚰 Drain only; Mon-Fri 8am-4pm; See info

ℹ️ Heavy manhole cover over drain, take caution very deep hole. Hook to lift cover hangs on Service Point sign. Professional truck wash also suitable for motorhomes, 100m. Reinspected 2015.

LEEUWARDEN 1   A4   73   N53°12.322' E005°47.809'   8911

Wissesdwinger. Exit A32 at Junction 17 and follow sp 'Leeuwarden Zuid'. At roundabout turn left, sp 'Leeuwarden'. Follow road straight on through numerous traffic lights. After crossing lift bridge turn left at traffic lights, sp 'Casino' and 'Ring'. Cross numerous roundabouts to large one with fountain and turn right, sp 'P Centrum'. At next roundabout, with cow, turn right. Go straight over 1 roundabout, then left at next, sp 'P Route'. In 600m turn left into Aire, not signed, just before next roundabout.

🚐 2; €6.50/night; Pay at machine; Max 48hrs; Max 8m

🛢 Seijsener CEE elec €1; Daytime toilets 250m in park

ℹ️ 2 designated bays in small city centre car park; 4 motorhomes were parked and 4 elec points provided. For 5 mins of fun visit Oldehove tower, 500m, which leans ominously; climb up to the top and enjoy the views, €3.50. www.oldehove.eu Inspected 2015.

LEEUWARDEN 2   A4   74   N53°11.906' E005°46.239'   8914

Harlingertrekweg. Exit A32 at Junction 17 and follow sp 'Leeuwarden Zuid'. At roundabout turn left, sp 'Leeuwarden'. Follow road straight on through numerous traffic lights. After crossing lift bridge turn left at traffic lights, sp 'Casino' and 'Ring'. Straight over several roundabouts, cross canal and turn left at roundabout, sp 'Casino'. Follow road left of casino entrance, turn right and then left in car park. At canal edge turn right to designated parking along canal.

🚐 5; Max 72hrs   🛢 None; See 65

ℹ️ Designated parking behind casino adj to canal and moored boats; ideal if you fancy a flutter. Large exhibition centre adj. Walk or cycle 2km along canal into the large town with several museums dedicated to Friesland history and culture. www.vvvleeuwarden.nl Inspected 2015.

NEDERLAND THE NETHERLANDS

SUWALD ⚓ A4 `75` N53°10.293' E005°55.976' 9265

Zuiderend. Exit N356 at traffic lights in Burgum, sp 'Suwâld'. Follow road and, just after it bends to the right, turn left, sp 'Suwâld'. Follow road 4.2km, then turn right. Aire on left just past marina, signed.

🚐 5 hardstanding; 12 grass parking; €8/night +€2 tax; Collected

🔧 Seijsener bollard and WC sink; 16amp CEE elec €1; Showers €1 (honesty box)

ℹ️ Pleasant marina Aire adj to small volunteer-run community marina. The parking and Service Point are open access. There is year round hardstanding parking, but the grass parking is closest to the navigation and the best place to watch the barges go by. Solar-powered pedestrian/cycle ferry connects Suwâld to Garyp and links footpaths on both sides of the canal, €1pp each way. www.suwald.nl Inspected 2015.

HEGEBEINTUM T A4 `76` N53°20.178' E005°51.155' 9173

Pypkedyk. Turn off N357 near Ferwert, sp 'Ferwert Industrial' and follow sp 'Hegebentum'. Follow road, then turn left, sp 'Bezoekerscentrum'. Turn 1st left into car park, sp 'Campers Welkom'.

🚐 6; Max 24hrs

🔧 None; See `65`

ℹ️ Parking possible outside TO, open Mon-Sat 10am-5pm, closed Mon Nov-Mar. Local area dotted with terps, manmade hills accommodating farmsteads. The church (€2.50pp) is perched on a 9m terp, the highest in the Netherlands. Exit car park left, in 1 min you can see it, in 3 mins you are at the top! N53°20.217' E005°51.020'. Also follow the terps driving route east to Dokkum `85` or south to Leeuwarden `133` and `134`. Inspected 2015.

EARNEWALD   B4   77   N53°07.761' E005°56.160'   9264

Eilansgrien. Exit N31 at roundabout, sp 'Earnewâld'. At end of road turn left, sp 'Earnewâld'. When road bends to left, turn right, sp 'Earnewâld'. At end of road go straight on into residential street, sp 'Camperplaats'. The Aire is in the 1st car park on the right, signed.

🚐 7; Max 72hrs

🛏 None; See Harbour Master

ℹ️ Aire was under renovation at time of inspection and could change.
Hotel/restaurant and large marina 400m with departure point for daily pleasure cruises or trips to watch the skûtsjesilen sailing competitions, from €10pp see www.rondvaardij-princenhof.nl Town within De Alde Feanen national park, a large area of peat bog wetland ideal for birdwatching or canoeing; boat hire poss. www.dealdefeanen.nl www.earnewald.nl Reinspected 2015.

OUDEGA   B4   78   N53°07.393' E005°59.980'   9216

Slotsingel. In Oudega turn off main route by SPAR convenience store. Follow road and turn left before road narrows, then right, signed. Aire at marina, signed.

🚐 3; €8/night; Pay Harbour Master; Max 72hrs; Grass parking (Apr-Nov)

🛏 Seijsener bollard; Water €1/100L; 4 16amp metered elec points €1; Shower €1

ℹ️ This marina Aire is in a pleasant location adj to and overlooking a small number of moored pleasure boats. Local commerce and SPAR convenience store 200m. 4km from De Alde Feanen national park, boat and bicycle rental available; www.dealdefeanen.nl Reinspected 2015.

DRACHTEN   B4   79   N53°06.171' E006°05.285'   9203

Gauke Boelensstraat. Exit N31 onto N369 and follow sp 'De Haven' and 'Drachten Noord'. Go straight over 5 roundabouts through industrial area, sp 'Centrum'. At 2nd traffic lights by BP fuel station turn left, sp 'Centrum'. In 200m turn right into car park, signed. Designated parking along the back of the car park, signed.

🚐 5; Max 72hrs   🏠 None; See 87

i Located alongside a residential, but busy, road near an industrial area. However, the parking is acceptable and backs onto sports facilities. The tree-lined high street is 800m. Markets are held in the central square every Thurs and Sat, 9am-5pm. All shops are closed on Sundays. www.uitindrachten.nl Reinspected 2015.

EASTERMAR   A4   80   N53°10.538' E006°03.307'   9261

Snakkerbuorren. Turn off N356 at Sumar and follow sp 'Eastermar'. Cross lift bridge, then turn left and immediately right. Turn 1st left, and left at end of road. Turn immediately right, sp 'P', drive past parking and follow road to left. Turn left and through barrier to Aire immediately on right.

🚐 15; €10/night inc service and WiFi; Pay Harbour Master

🏠 Custom; 16amp CEE elec €2/night; Toilets and showers accessible via card

i Marina Aire with parking overlooking pleasure boats and the navigation in the distance. The area is sensibly landscaped and gravel bays space the motorhomes nicely. Pleasant village centre with café/restaurants 200m. Large lakes in both directions along the navigation. www.tip-eastermar.nl Inspected 2015.

SURHUISTERVEEN 1   A4   81   N53°10.118' E006°07.198'   9233

Langewyk. Turn off N369 at roundabout, sp 'Surhuisterveen'. Turn 1st right, then 1st left. Aire at bar immediately on right, signed.

🚐 12; €10/night inc elec; Pay at bar

🚰 Custom; 16amp CEE elec

i Pleasantly landscaped commercial Aire adj to, and run by, a traditional bar. The Aire is just off a main road and suffers road noise. The mobile facilities block is good but not as swanky as expected in the Netherlands. The nearest town commerce is 3.3km. www.camperplaatshetjachtveld.nl Inspected 2015.

SURHUISTERVEEN 2   A4   82   N53°10.770' E006°09.644'   9231

Badlaan, at Zwembad Wettervlecke. Turn off main route through in middle of town into tree-lined car park. In 200m turn right into swimming pool car park, signed. Enter through gates and designated parking at rear. Gates locked outside business hours.

🚐 5; €5; Pay at swimming pool; Grass parking; May-Sept

🚰 Water €1; Elec €1

i Designated parking in pleasant car park of privately owned outdoor swimming pool. Although parking could be noisy during the day, it is deserted at night and during cold weather. If you wish to stay out of season call: 0512-361507/364484 or 0653816590. Town centre with high street commerce and Saturday market 200m. www.wettervlecke.nl www.surhuisterveen.com Reinspected 2015.

LUTJEGAST   A4   83   N53°14.129' E006°15.579'   9866

Abel Tasmanweg. At roundabout in village centre turn opposite direction to church, signed. Aire is 200m from church in car park behind the community building, signed.

🚐 2; 8m bays + 1m overhang
🚰 None; See 87

ℹ️ Designated parking in small car park in small village. There is a walk around the village described on the front of community building. Children's play area beside church. Former village resident, Abel Janszoon Tasman, charted the coast of New Zealand in 1642. Reinspected 2015.

KUKHERNE (FEANWALDEN)   A4   84   N53°14.471' E006°01.136'   9271

Camperpark Kuikhorne/Jachthaven 't Eibertsnêst. Exit N356 at traffic lights, sp 'De Zwette', into Feanwâlden. Take 1st right, sp 'Kukherne' and signed. Follow road through Kûkherne. There is a new road coming through here; directions will change. Turn left before bridge into Jachthaven 't Eibertsnêst and Camperpark Kuikhorne, signed. Wait at barrier for assistance.

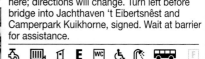

🚐 25; €10/night; Collected; Max 72hrs
🚰 Seijsenser bollard and WC sink; Water €0.50/100L; 6amp elec; Showers €0.50

ℹ️ Family run marina Aire with a pleasant feel and an excellent facilities block. Grass parking area offers some views over pleasure boats. Service Point and 2 bays adj to quayside; boat hire poss. www.camperparkkuikhorne.nl Vogelzang, 2km, has small supermarkets. Feanwâlden, 2.5km in the opposite direction, has local commerce. Both have train stations on the Leeuwarden and Groningen line. Reinspected 2015.

DOKKUM | 🏛 A4 | 85 | N53°19.587' E006°00.576' | 9101

Harddraversdijk. From south turn off N356 onto N361, sp 'Lauwersoog' and 'Dokkum Oost'. Follow N361 and after crossing lift bridge turn left, sp 'Dokkum Oost'. Follow road straight on along water's edge, sp 'P Centrum'. Turn right into car park, signed. Designated parking on right, signed.

🚐 3; €5/6pm-9am + tax; Collected; Max 24hrs

🛒 None; See 87

ℹ️ Designated parking in large car park adj to library with café; near a canal, but no views. 500m along the canal is the charming, fortified old town with water defences and town commerce. The Renaissance Admiralty house contains the TO and a museum; €5pp, Mon-Sat 10am-5pm. www.museumdokkum.nl www.dokkum.nl Reinspected 2015.

ONDERDENDAM | ⚐ A5 | 86 | N53°20.206' E006°35.227' | 9959

Warffumerweg. Exit village to north towards Warffum and the Aire is on the left before the village boundary, signed.

🚐 5; In marina car park; €6 + €1pp; Pay Harbour Master; Reinforced grass parking; 8m designated parking, but Harbour Master will accommodate anything

🛒 Seijsener bollard; 4amp elec €2.50/night; Shower €0.50; May-Sept

ℹ️ Small marina Aire with a nostalgic feel. Café Friday evenings. Attractive village adj with windmill, which is a restaurant on the ground floor, serving 4-8 course daily specials, and a B&B on the upper floors. 5.4km cycle path along the waterway to Winsum with town commerce and a train station. Reinspected 2015.

APPINGEDAM   🏢 A5   87   N53°19.229' E006°52.034'   9900

Farmsumerweg. From Groningen follow N360. Turn off N360 at roundabout in Appingedam, sp 'Centrum' and 'Woldweg'. Follow road straight over roundabout and lift bridge, then at roundabout turn right, sp 'Centrum' and 'Woldweg'. Turn immediately right into bus station; GPS taken here. Designated parking in far right corner adj to lift bridge, signed. Service Point at end adj to water, signed. Actual GPS: N53°19.286' E006°52.074'.

🚐 9; Max 72hrs

💧 Custom; Water adj to service building entrance; 16amp CEE Seijsener elec €1

ℹ️ Designated Aire in bus station; noise from buses at times. Compact town centre is on an island: Exit Aire to right and in 350m turn right across lift bridge. ALDI with parking: Exit Aire to right and follow road for 600m. Inspected 2015.

DELFZIJL   ⚓ A5   88   N53°20.161' E006°55.595'   9933

Zeebadweg. From Groningen on N360 turn left at roundabout, sp 'Delfzijl'. At end of road turn left, sp 'Centrum' and 'AquariOm'. Turn next left, sp 'AquariOm'. Cross over the railway track and turn immediately right. Follow road around aquarium and the designated parking is on the left, signed.

🚐 8; Max 48hrs

💧 Seijsener bollard; 8 10amp CEE elec points €1; Drive over drain difficult

ℹ️ Popular Aire in car park adj to aquarium and overlooking sea defence, which protects the town from the tidal estuary. Although the notice allows 8 motorhomes, there is room for 16. This is an interesting area and from the top of the sea wall you can see Germany. Town with high street commerce 500m to right along sea wall. www.delfzijl.nl Reinspected 2015.

| GRONINGEN | 🚶 A5 | 89 | N53°14.401' E006°35.846' | 9735 |

Off N46 ring road. Exit N46 ring road, sp 'TransFerium' and 'P&R Kardinge'. Follow sp 'Kardinge'. Parking on left on 2nd row across, signed.

🚐 12; Reinforced grass parking; Hardstanding poss

🚻 Toilets near lake; See 87

ℹ️ Popular motorhome parking in large car park provided for recreational facilities and Park & Ride. P&R costs €5 for up to 5 people to the centre of Groningen, which is a pretty, historic town known as the 'Metropolis of the North'. Recreational facilities include an extreme climbing wall, swimming pool and manmade hill for mountain for biking. Reinspected 2015.

| HAREN ⭐ | 🛶 B5 | 90 | N53°09.828' E006°34.712' | 9752 |

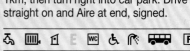

N861/Meerweg. From Groningen exit A28 at Junction 38, sp 'Haren'. At roundabout turn right onto N861, sp 'Eelde- Paterswolde'. Follow road for 1km, then turn right into car park. Drive straight on and Aire at end, signed.

🚐 6; Max 72hrs

🚻 Custom; Water, toilets and showers locked

ℹ️ Aire located in farthest parking area at pleasant recreation space. The designated parking has views across a picnic area to swimming beach and Paterswoldsemeer lake; slipway adj. Adj public toilets and showers locked, but drive over drain accessible. Restaurants and boat club cafés 500m. Inspected 2015.

ZUIDBROEK   B5 91   N53°09.689' E006°51.638'   9636

Scholtenweg. Exit A7 at Junction 43 and follow sp 'Zuidbroek'. Go over lift bridge and follow road straight on for 230m, then to right. Turn 1st right, sp 'Sappemeer' and signed. Follow road to left past marina and Aire is 150m on right after bend, signed.

2; Apr-Sept 🪣 None; See 87

ℹ️ This Aire is located in a small car park adj to canal and pleasure boat marina, no views. The small town, 200m, has local commerce, trains to Groningen and a train and tram museum; €5pp, open weekends. www.nnttm.nl A large indoor bazaar, new and second hand items, is held every Sunday by the A7 at Eurohal; 10am-4pm, €3pp. www.eurohalzuidbroek.eu Reinspected 2015.

VEENDAM   B5 92   N53°06.367' E006°50.900'   9642

Flora, near Borgerswold. Exit N33 at Junction 38 onto N366 and follow sp 'Veendam'. After lift bridge turn left at roundabout. In 1.8km turn left at roundabout. Turn 2nd right. All sp 'Borgerswoldhoeve'. Follow road for 1.2km. Aire on left at end of road.

60; €5/night + €2.50pp inc 6amp elec and service; Collected; Grass parking
🪣 Custom; Toilets in temporary cabin

ℹ️ Campsite style Aire in wooded area adj to large leisure lake with beach, no views. Old and basic, but clean, mobile facilities block; may be leftover from an earlier campsite here. Café, water ski drag and water sports at opp end of beach; https://borgerswoldhoeve.nl Large park with numerous trails beyond the lake. May feel isolated if alone. Reinspected 2015.

STADSKANAAL B5 93 N53°02.200' E006°52.467' 9503

De Roo Campers, Unikenkade. Exit N33 at Junction 36, sp 'Bareveld'. At roundabouts follow sp 'Stadskanaal'. Follow road along canal, then in 2.5km turn 1st right over 8t weight and 3.25m width restricted bridge. Turn right and follow road through gateways to motorhome dealer at end. Drive through dealer into compound. Arrive during day as compound locked at night. Actual GPS: N53°02.166' E006°52.404'.

🚐 10; Max 24hrs
Custom; 2 elec points on Service Point
ℹ Private Aire at Adria motorhome dealer with accessory shop and workshops, open Mon-Sat 9am-6pm, Sun noon-5pm. Aire is nicely constructed and well serviced making it a comfortable stop whilst having work done or awaiting delivery of parts or accessories. High fences surround the area and the gates are locked at night. www.deroocampers.nl Inspected 2015.

ASSEN B5 94 N53°00.017' E006°34.303' 9403

Van Hobokenstraat, beside canal basin and adj to industrial area. From south on A28 exit at Junction 32, sp 'Assen'. Follow sp 'Centrum'. At traffic lights turn right, sp 'Centrum'. Follow road for around 3.5km, then turn right at roundabout and immediately right again. In 300m turn left and the Aire is on the right, signed.

🚐 5, Max 72hrs; See info
Seijsener bollard and WC sink; Water €0.50; Elec €1; No drive over drain
ℹ Aire overlooking canal basin in commercial area. Plenty of unrestricted parking locally. Café adj, supermarket opp to left. The Assen TT motorcycle race is held on the last Saturday in June. Over 100,000 spectators enjoy the spectacle and preparations begin a week in advance; see www.ttcircuit.com www.vvvassen.nl Reinspected 2015.

MUSSELKANAAL ✱　　🛥 B5　95　　N52°55.667' E007°00.793'　9581

Dreef. Exit N366, sp 'Musselkanaal' and 'Open Einde', and follow these sp. Before lift bridge turn right into Marktstraat. Follow road along canal, then turn left across 1st lift bridge, sp 'STAR'. Follow road round to left, signed, then right, signed, and back around to left to Aire. WARNING: GPS will try to navigate a different route across a narrow swing bridge.

🚐 40; €8.50/night + €0.75pp tax inc service and 16amp CEE elec; Collected; Max 72hrs; Apr-Oct; Grass and hardstanding
🚰 Custom; Adj to toilet block
ℹ️ Popular commercial Aire in a pleasant and peaceful location almost on its own island. Town commerce including LIDL and ALDI 100m. www.musselkanaal.info Reinspected 2015.

TER APEL　　⛵ B5　96　　N52°52.282' E007°04.329'　9561

De Runde. From north on N366 turn left, sp 'Ter Apel'. At roundabout turn right. In 1.7km follow road to left. Follow road along canal for 1km, then turn right across lift bridge. Turn immediately left and continue down canal. In 600m turn right into Jachthaven De Runde. Camper parking at end on right.

🚐 6; €9 inc elec and WiFi; Grass parking, Hardstanding in winter
🚰 Custom; 6 10amp CEE elec points; Showers €0.50/5 mins
ℹ️ Marina Aire offering grass parking under trees with views across to the boats, but no view of the canal. Café at marina. www.jachthaventerapel.nl Local commerce 600m along Ter Apel canal. Visit Klooster Ter Apel, 550m: N52°52.556 E007°04.529, €7.50pp, monastery open Tues-Sat 10am-5pm, Sun 1-5pm. www.kloosterterapel.nl Inspected 2015.

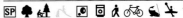

APPELSCHA 1   🏛 B4 97   N52°57.153' E006°21.801'   8426

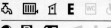

Vaart Noordzijde. Turn off N371, sp 'Appelscha', and follow waterway for 4.7km. After entering Appelscha turn 1st right across lift bridge, then turn immediately left and follow road on other side of waterway. In 250m turn right opp pedestrian lift bridge, signed. Drive into yard and Aire on left.

🚐 10; €8/night; Collected; Reinforced grass parking

🚰 Custom; 4amp CEE elec €1.50/night; No drive over drain; See 98

ℹ️ Privately run Aire on grass parking behind restaurant. Free WiFi. Pretty waterside village with local commerce and moored boats adj, but no view. Motorhome accessory shop 50m. Local area offers plenty of fun for the family with a children's theme park, outdoor activity centre and petting zoo all within 5km, see www.appelscha.nl Reinspected 2015.

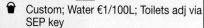

APPELSCHA 2   🏢 B4 98   N52°57.211' E006°21.444'   8426

Vaart Zuidzijde. Turn off N371, sp 'Appelscha', and follow waterway for 5.3km passing lift bridge and turning to 97 . Service Point in the car park of Vers Centrum shop on left, signed.

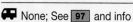

🚐 None; See 97 and info

🚰 Custom; Water €1/100L; Toilets adj via SEP key

ℹ️ Service Point only in pretty village. Washing machine accessible via SEP key. Nationaal Park Drents-Friese Wold, 2km, known for its shifting sands. Exit Service Point to left, then turn 1st left, sp 'Boerestreek', and car park on right before roundabout, cafés and TO. Keep driving through car park for additional parking: N52°57.262' E006°20.509'. www.np-drentsfriesewold.nl Reinspected 2015.

EMMEN   B5   99   N52°46.872' E006°54.168'   7813

Van Schaikweg. Turn off N391, sp 'Angelslo'. After 2.7km turn right at roundabout, sp 'P Oost'. Turn left past the fuel station, then left and immediately right to Aire under trees, signed.

🚐 18; In 2 adj parking areas

🏠 None; See 94

ℹ️ Pleasant, popular designated parking in shady area on edge of large car park on the outskirts of town. Town commerce 550m northwest of Aire. The Wildlands Adventure Zoo, 900m, has been completely redeveloped and reopened in 2016, www.wildlands.nl LPG at fuel station at entrance. www.energiekemmen.nl Reinspected 2015.

BARGER COMPASCUUM   B5   100   N52°45.305' E007°01.420'   7884

Veenpark, Berkenrode. Exit village towards Emmen following sp 'Veenpark'. Turn right, sp 'Veenpark', then turn left into car park, signed. Motorhome parking to rear and right of car park, signed.

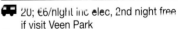

🚐 20; €6/night inc elec, 2nd night free if visit Veen Park

🏠 2 CEE elec points

ℹ️ Commercial Aire in museum car park. The facilities have seen better days and were locked. May feel isolated and will be alone. Adj open air museum depicts the history of the local peat industry. Walk around the 400m^2 park or hop on one of the narrow gauge steam railways previously used to transport the peat. Museum open daily 10am-5pm, €15pp. SPAR convenience store in village. www.veenpark.nl Reinspected 2015.

GIETHOORN 1   B4   101   N52°43.696' E006°04.528'   8355

Haamstede, Kanaaldijk. Turn off N334 south of Giethoorn, sp 'Dwarsgracht'. Cross lift bridge and turn immediately right. Follow road along canal and Aire on left, signed.

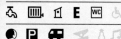

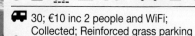

🚐 30; €10 inc 2 people and WiFi; Collected; Reinforced grass parking
🛠 Seijsener bollard; Water €0.50; 6amp elec €3; Showers €0.50/5 mins

ℹ️ Private Aire at farmhouse with enthusiastic and friendly owners. The parking is well laid out and there are excellent facilities making this a popular Aire. Local produce is available. www.haamstedegiethoorn.nl Canal adj, some views. Giethoorn is known as the Venice of the Netherlands as it is only fully accessible by waterways that link to large lakes. http://giethoorntourism.com Reinspected 2015.

GIETHOORN 2   B4   102   N52°43.299' E006°04.404'   8355

Zuiderkluft. Turn off N334 south of Giethoorn, sp 'Dwarsgracht'. Cross lift bridge and turn left. Turn next left and cross 30t weight restricted lift bridge. Follow road to right, then turn left, sp 'Zuiderkluft' and signed. Entrance immediately on left, signed.

🚐 35; €10/night + €1pp tax
🛠 Custom; Water €0.50; 16amp elec €1
ℹ️ Pleasant parking at marina Aire that feels more like a campsite. 10 bays overlook pleasure boat marina. Onsite boat hire makes it easy to explore the canals of Giethoorn and the Weerribben-Wieden wetland area; www.np-weerribbenwieden.nl Local commerce in Giethoorn village over canal. Reinspected 2015.

GIETHOORN 3 — B4 — 103 — N52°42.978' E006°04.557' — 8355

Vosjacht. South of Giethoorn turn off N334 across lift bridge, sp 'Dwarsgracht'. Follow road to left, and turn 1st left. Cross 30t weight restricted lift bridge and follow road to right, before turning 1st left. Follow road along waterway and around marina, then turn right into Aire, signed. Entrance via barrier, pay at adj kiosk.

99; €10/24hrs inc 2 people; CC; Pay at kiosk; Max 14 days; Reinforced grass parking

Seijsener bollard and WC sink; Inside barrier; Water €0.50/100L; 16amp CEE elec €3/24hrs; Card needed for toilet access

Aire in an open area surrounded by water giving three views: overlooking green space to the navigation, overlooking the birds in the wetland area or overlooking one of the two swimming beaches. Some road noise. Cafés and commerce on opp side of water. Inspected 2015.

HOOGEVEEN — B5 — 104 — N52°43.583' E006°30.064' — 7902

Exit A37 at Junction 1, sp 'Hoogeveen Oost', and follow sp 'Centrum'. Follow road over 1st roundabout, sp 'Centrum', then turn right at 2nd, sp 'Hoogeveen' and 'P&R'. At next roundabout turn left, then in 150m turn right into 'MAXX' parking. Designated parking in car park, signed.

3; Max 72hrs

None; See 94

Designated shaded parking under deciduous trees by sports facilities with indoor tennis courts and bar. Billiards club in small building near parking. Some green space adj. Town centre commerce and TO 1.7km. The water feature in the middle of the high street is claimed to be the longest in the Netherlands and it's not a canal! http://dehoofdletterh.nl Reinspected 2015.

MEPPEL   B4 [105]   N52°41.764' E006°10.866'   7941

Westeinde. Exit N375 at roundabout by VW showroom, sp 'Meppel-Zuid' and 'Oevers/Haven'. Follow road through industrial estate, crossing lift bridge, then turn left, sp 'Oevers A'. At end of road turn left, sp 'Stichting Welzijn' and 'Meppel'. Follow road past windmill, over lift bridge, and turn immediately left into narrow, but passable, one-way street. Follow road for 400m keeping water on left, signed. Aire on right at end of road. Not recommended for large or wide motorhomes.

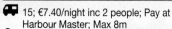

🚐 15; €7.40/night inc 2 people; Pay at Harbour Master; Max 8m
Custom; Water €0.50; Elec €2.50/day
ℹ️ Feels like a campsite and has a proper toilet block; shower block automatically locks at 9pm, don't get locked in! Boatyard nearby. Pleasant town with many bars/restaurants 200m. www.meppelstadmetstijl.nl Reinspected 2015.

HASSELT   B4 [106]   N52°35.581' E006°05.233'   8061

Jachthaven de Molenwaard. Turn off N331 into 9m length restricted road, sp 'Centrum'. Go straight on, then before church turn right, signed. Turn right taking road along river, signed, and under bridge, sp 'Jachthaven'. Follow road to right and barriered entrance on left, signed. Because the parking is right next to the main road, GPS might literally take you round in circles. Enter through barrier; token required.

 9; €8.50/night + €0.70pp tax
Custom; Seijsener WC sink; 16amp elec €2/night; Showers inc
ℹ️ Marina Aire with parking overlooking pleasure boats. Pleasant old town with high street commerce 400m. www.ontdekdeijsseldelta.nl Reinspected 2015.

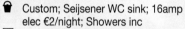

NIEUWLEUSEN   🏛 B4 107   N52°34.904' E006°16.861'   7711

Prinses Beatrixlaan. Turn off N377 at Nieuwleusen, sp 'Centrum'. Follow cobbled road through high street to roundabout, then turn right, sp 'Sportpark'. Follow road to left, then turn left, sp 'Sportpark'. Designated parking in car park on right, signed.

🚐 3; Max 48hrs

🚰 None; See 108

ℹ️ Designated parking in large, unobstructed car park adj to sports facilities and school. Ideal as a night halt as always likely to have space. Small town commerce 1km towards N377. Inspected 2015.

HARDENBURG   🧍 B5 108   N52°34.645' E006°37.752'   7772

Parkweg. From north on N34 turn left at traffic lights, sp 'Hardenburg'. At next traffic lights turn right, sp 'Centrum'. In 250m turn right into car park, signed. Aire at far end of car park, signed.

🚐 4; €10/24hrs; CC/€; Pay at machine; Max 72hrs; Reinforced grass parking

🚰 Seijsener bollard; Water €0.50; 4 CEE elec points €1/kW

ℹ️ Designated parking adj to pleasant park with small lake, gardens, aviary, play and skateboard areas. Service Point open access, but awkward to use. Parking is possible for large motorhomes, subject to other parked motorhomes. Town commerce 700m. www.hardenberg.nl Inspected 2015.

DALFSEN   C4   109   N52°29.942' E006°15.569'   7722

Stationsweg. Turn off N340 at traffic lights, sp 'Dalfsen'. Follow road straight on and across lift bridge, sp 'Hoonhorst'. At roundabout go straight on, then turn 1st right and right again into Aire, signed.

🚐 5; Max 48hrs; Reinforced grass parking

⛽ None; Poss at Avia garage: N52°30.594' E006°15.897'

ℹ️ Designated parking between the road and the train station, with a bar. 5 designated spaces, but there is room for more. Dalfsen centre 450m across river bridge. www.dalfsen.nl Adj land is owned by Havezate Den Burg country estate, some of the grounds are accessible to the public. www.havezatedenberg.nl Adj info board shows cycling/walking routes from the station. www.vechtdaloverijssel.nl Inspected 2015.

TUBBERGEN   C5   110   N52°24.634' E006°46.973'   7650

Sportlaan. Travelling southwest on N343 turn left, sp 'Tubbergen'. At crossroads turn left, sp 'P route'. Turn 1st left by round building, sp 'P' and 'TVC'. Parking 100m on left opposite swimming pool.

🚐 2; Max 72hrs; Reinforced grass parking

⛽ None; See 108

ℹ️ The official bays are impractically located in the busiest area of the swimming pool car park. There is much better parking with overhang at the back of the car park where local caravans are stored. Town centre with TO 400m. www.vvvtubbergen.nl Inspected 2015.

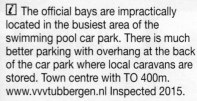

ZWOLLE 1   C4   **111**   N52°31.846' E006°04.486'   8031

Holtenbroekerdijk. Exit A28 at Junction 20 onto N35 Ring noord, sp 'Voorst'. In 2.6km turn right at crossroads, sp 'Holtenbroek' and 'Deltion College'. Drive through college and straight on at roundabout. At Holtenbroek retail outlet turn left and keep left. Turn right at crossroad before lift bridge. At T-junction turn left, sp 'Holtenbroekerdijk', onto dead end road, signed. Turn right, signed, and follow road into marina. Service Point and facilities to left, parking straight on, signed. Gates locked 10.30pm-8am.

🚐 15; €9/night inc tax; Pay Harbour Master; Grass parking; Max 8m

🛠 Custom; Seijsener CEE elec €1/2kW; Showers €1

ℹ️ Pleasant marina Aire offering grass parking alongside a boatshed overlooking the pleasure boat marina and boatyard overlooked by flats. Book swap box onsite, but curiously no telephone directory. Zwolle 3km. Bus stop 600m. Inspected 2015.

ZWOLLE 2   C4   **112**   N52°30.799' E006°06.224'   8021

Turfmarkt. On N35 travel north following sp 'Ring Oost'. Turn left at traffic lights, sp 'Wipstrik', then turn right at traffic lights, sp 'Wipstrik'. Turn left at roundabout into Hanekamp, then turn right before barriered lift bridge, sp 'P Turfmarkt'. Follow road straight on, turning right at the end of the car park towards church, then right again. Designated parking is on the right, signed.

🚐 4; Poss €4/day; CC; Pay at machine; Max 72hrs; See info

🛠 None; See **108**

ℹ️ Parallel parking on no-through road adj to school and outside pay car park, however no signs suggest payment for motorhome parking. Historic centre 900m within star fort. TO in central square has city maps in English. www.zwolletouristinfo.nl Reinspected 2015.

KAMPEN   B4   113   N52°33.174' E005°54.774'   8261

Broedersingel. From Zwolle exit N50 at Junction 31, sp 'Kampen Zuid', and turn right, sp 'Kampen'. Go straight over 1st roundabout, then turn left at 2nd roundabout, sp 'Centrum'. Follow road crossing 4 roundabouts. At 5th roundabout turn right, sp 'Stadhaus'. Turn 1st left into car park, signed. Drive to rear of car park to Aire, signed.

🚐 30; €7.50/24hrs; CC/€; Pay at machine; Max 72hrs

🛎 Custom; Inside building, get code from town hall opp (Mon-Fri 8.30am-4pm); Seijsener WC sink; Hot water €0.50

ℹ️ Aire in designated part of town hall car park, surrounded by park. Digital tourist info centre adj that also prints off maps. Interesting town with high street commerce 200m through arch. TO 950m at Oudestraat 41-43. https://stad.kampen.nl Reinspected 2015.

URK   B4   114   N52°39.602' E005°35.950'   8321

Klifweg. Exit A6 at Junction 13, sp 'Urk'. Follow N352, sp 'Urk'. Cross bridge, then at roundabout turn left, sp 'Centrum' and 'Havens'. Follow road left, then to end. Designated parking is at the marina/boatyard/fishing port, signed.

🚐 20; €15/night inc 16amp elec, WiFi and all facilities; Collected

🛎 Custom; Seijsener WC sink, water and showers all in adj toilet block by pleasure boats, open access and free; No drive over drain

ℹ️ An interesting harbour Aire located right in the thick of things. There are pleasure boats one side and everything from the fishing fleet to super cruisers on the other. Walk around the harbour to the old town with lighthouse and tourist and town commerce. www.touristinfourk.nl Reinspected 2015.

DRONTEN — C4 — 115 — N52°31.766' E005°42.798' — 8251

Havenkade. Turn off N307 at roundabout, sp 'Dronten' and 'De Noord'. Follow road straight on across 3 roundabouts, then at 4th roundabout turn right, sp 'Centrum'. Turn right, signed, immediately left into Havenweg, signed, then immediately left again down to quay. Designated parking on quay to right, signed.

🚐 5; €7.50/night; Pay Harbour Master; Max 48hrs
🪣 None; See 114

ℹ️ An unusual marina Aire providing designated parking overlooking pleasure boats and navigation. No facilities and some way from Harbour Master. Building plot adj being developed which may impact parking. Do not attempt to drive to Harbour Master in search of facilities as the route and the harbour is not suitable for motorhomes. Town commerce 700m. Inspected 2015.

ELBURG — C4 — 116 — N52°27.044' E005°49.798' — 8081

Havenkade, off N309. On N309 turn off at the roundabout with Esso fuel station, sp 'Elburg-Vesting'. Turn immediately left into car park, signed. 8 designated parking spaces on left and 10 further around on left, clearly marked.

🚐 8; €7.95/night +€1.10pp tax; Pay Harbour Master; Max 72hrs
🪣 Seijsener WC sink and bollard; Water €0.50/100L; No drive over drain; 10amp elec €0.50; Showers €0.50

ℹ️ Popular marina Aire adj to and overlooking boats. Arrival before 3.30pm recommended. 1st parking area reinforced grass parking, 2nd parking area hardstanding. 300m to Elburg's Medieval old town, which is on a fortified island with 1.3km of paths around the moat. The centre of the island has a pedestrianised high street. www.vvvelburg.nl Reinspected 2015.

EPE · C4 · 117 · N52°20.989' E005°58.992' · 8161

Pastoor Somstraat. Follow sp 'VVV' through town on the one-way 'Ring'. Turn into parking, sp 'VVV'. Aire at the back of the parking on left of the VVV building, which is the TO, signed.

3; Max 48hrs; Max 6m

None; See 127

ℹ️ Inadequate designated parking in standard car bays; beware of kerbs and bushes. TO adj and high street commerce just 90m. Morning market on Wednesdays and Saturday until 4pm. The large wood and moorlands adj cover thousands of acres from Epe past Apeldoorn. Roadside parking just off N795 has several cycle routes: N52°21.415' E005°52.486'. www.vvvepe.nl Inspected 2015.

HARDERWIJK 1 · C4 · 118 · N52°19.679' E005°36.747' · 3845

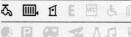

Stijkel Campers, Noorderbreedte. Exit A28 at Junction 12, sp 'Harderwijk-West', and follow sp 'Putten' onto N303. At roundabout turn right, sp 'Ermelo-West'. At next roundabout turn right towards industrial park, sp 'Tonsel', then turn left and follow road. Service Point in car park of motorhome dealer just before end of road. WC emptying point on edge of building to right, drive over drain on edge of building to left.

None; See 119   Custom

ℹ️ Service Point at motorhome dealer specialising in Adria and Cathargo, but will service all motorhomes. Service Point accessible Mon-Fri 8.30am-5.30pm, Sat 9.30am-4pm. www.stijkelcampers.nl Reinspected 2015.

HARDERWIJK 2   C4   119   N52°20.453' E005°37.785'   3842

Hoofdweg. Exit A28 at Junction 13, sp 'Harderwijk'. Follow sp 'N302 Harderwijk' onto N302 heading north. Turn right off N302, sp 'Harderwijk', then turn left at traffic lights, sp 'Centrum'. Go straight over 1st roundabout, then turn left at 2nd. Drive past BP fuel station, then at roundabout turn right, sp 'De Sypel'. Turn left and drive through car park, turning right past skate park, signed.

 3; Max 48hrs   None; See 118

ℹ Parking adj to sports facilities inc skate park. Some road/train noise. Old waterside town centre with quaint narrow streets and high street commerce 1.3km. Dolfinarium has dolphins, sea lions and walruses, €27.50pp. www.dolfinarium.nl Nearby pay day parking for Dolfinarium and town in P Boulevard: N52°21.087' E005°36.973'. www.vvvharderwijk.nl Reinspected 2015.

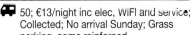

NUNSPEET   C4   120   N52°22.777' E005°45.189'   8071

Camperplaats De Zwaan, Hardenbrinkweg. Enter on N310 from Elburg and follow road straight on, sp 'Hulshorst'. At roundabout turn right, sp 'Veluwemeer' and signed 'De Zwaan'. Turn right, sp 'De Zwaan' and signed. Aire on left, signed.

50; €13/night inc elec, WiFi and service; Collected; No arrival Sunday; Grass parking, some reinforced

Custom; Seijsener WC sink; 4amp CEE elec €2/night

ℹ Well maintained commercial Aire located at rural farm. 30 pitches are on reinforced grass in a landscaped area. In addition there is a 20 pitch rally field with meeting and dining hall/room. Strong WiFi available. Modern mobile toilet and shower block. Bike garage with elec. Petanque piste. www.camperplaatsdezwaan.com Nunspeet high street 2.5km. www.vvvnunspeet.nl Inspected 2015.

THE NETHERLANDS — NEDERLAND

PUTTEN — C4 121 — N52°15.745' E005°36.460' — 3881

Fontanusplein. Approach town from north on N303. Turn left off N303 at traffic lights, sp 'Putten'. Follow road for 1km, then turn right, sp 'P Gemeentehuis'. In 200m turn left into Kelnarijstraat. Turn immediately right into car park. Designated parking is immediately on right, signed.

🚐 2; Max 48hrs 🚮 None; See 118

ℹ️ Popular central car park. Cars may be parked in, or obstruct, motorhome bays. There are two small parks adj. Town centre with high street commerce is 220m down Kelnarijstraat. 1km away is a WWII memorial walk named Oktober 44. There is parking onsite: N52°15.573' E005°35.864', free entry; www.oktober44.nl www.vvvputten.nl Reinspected 2015.

NIJKERK — C4 122 — N52°13.578' E005°28.603' — 3861

Watergoorweg. From Putten on N798 go straight over roundabout, sp 'Nijkerk Centrum'. Go straight over 2nd roundabout, then turn right at 3rd, sp 'VVV' and 'De Havenaer'. Turn right, then left, then right, following sp 'De Havenaer'. Turn left into car park, sp 'Watergoor', then turn left and drive through car park to designated parking on left, signed.

🚐 4; Max 48hrs 🚮 None; See 118

ℹ️ Pleasant designated parking on edge of large car park. Some road noise. LIDL and retail park 100m. Town centre commerce 750m. Hertog Reijnout pumping station nearby: N52°15.148' E005°26.312'. Take N301 towards Almere, then follow sp 'Stoomgemaal Hertog Reijnout'. Open Tues-Fri 10am-4pm, Sat 10am-1pm. www.nijkerk.eu Inspected 2015.

Hertog Reijnout

LELYSTAD — B4 · 123 · N52°32.783' E005°27.342' · 8221

De Aalscholver, N302. Exit A6 at Junction 11 and follow sp 'Lelystad-Noord' onto N302. Follow N302, sp 'Enkhuizen'. In 5km at roundabout turn immediately right, sp 'P Strand Houtribhoek' and 'P Max 48hrs' with motorhome symbol. Designated parking at far end of car park, signed. Actual GPS: N52°32.916' E005°27.455'.

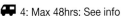

🚐 4; Max 48hrs; See info

🚽 Seasonal toilets; See 133

ℹ️ Popular, oversubscribed Aire in a car park that could easily take 50 motorhomes. Aire in isolated spot between golf course and marina. Markermeer inland sea adj, but defensive bank prevents views. Sandy swimming beach and outdoor gym over defence. Outlet village with parking 2km at other end of golf course. www.vvvlelystad.nl Reinspected 2015.

AMERSFOORT — C3 · 124 · N52°09.721' E005°22.704' · 3811

Kleine Koppel. Exit A1 Junction 12 onto N199, following sp 'Amersfoort' and 'Dierenpark'. Follow N199 over 2 roundabouts. At 2nd traffic lights turn left, sp 'A'foort Oost'. At traffic lights go straight on, then at next set turn right, sp 'Isselt'. Cross lift bridge, then at traffic lights turn left, sp 'Isselt E'. Turn left, sp 'Kleine Koppel'. Aire on left before crossroads and adj to navigation and lift bridge, signed.

🚐 3; Max 7m; €0.55 per metre/24hrs Oct-Mar; €1.10 per metre/24hrs Apr-Sept; Inc 16amp CEE elec, water, showers and toilets; CC; Pay at machine; Max 72hrs

🚽 Seijsener bollard; Access toilets and showers via pin code

ℹ️ Marina Aire with designated parking in roadside lay-by adj to boat/barge moorings. For showers cross lift bridge and turn right along towpath: N52°09.706' E005°22.846'. Follow navigation 800m to medieval centre and town commerce. www.visitamersfoort.com Inspected 2015.

APELDOORN   🏃 C4 | 125 | N52°10.984' E005°57.998'   7333

Dubbelbeek. Exit A1 at Junction 20, sp 'Apeldoorn-Zuid'. Turn left, sp 'Apeldoorn', then at traffic lights turn left, sp 'Centrum' and 'Beekbergen'. In 1.4km turn right at 2nd set of traffic lights, sp 'Centrum'. In 600m turn right at traffic lights into Dubbelbeek. Follow road through car park, then turn right. Designated parking at far end of parking, signed.

🚐 4; Max 72hrs   🛒 None; See | 127 |

i Designated parking at the furthest point from the sports facilities giving it a remote feel that attracts youths in cars during the evenings, but this is normal across the country. Facilities include swimming pools and a Kid's Paradise activity area with restaurant. Town centre 4km. Former royal palace 6.5km, www.paleishetloo.nl Inspected 2015.

VAASSEN   T C4 | 126 | N52°17.406' E005°57.929'   8171

Julianalaan. Exit A50 at Junction 26, sp 'Vaassen'. Follow sp 'Vaassen'. Go straight over 1st roundabout and turn left at next roundabout, both sp 'Vaassen'. Turn right at next roundabout, sp 'Centrum'. Follow road for 400m straight across traffic lights and Aire is in car park on left before exiting town.

🚐 4; Max 24hrs
🛒 Water only; See | 127 |

i Aire located in a car park opposite Cannenburch, a 16th century country house/castle tourist attraction; open Tues-Thurs/Sat-Sun 12-5pm, €9.50pp. There is an audio tour around the gardens and a café. www.glk.nl/cannenburch 4.8km walking route around castle and town on information board. Town centre commerce 200m. Reinspected 2015.

WIJHE　　　🚢 C4 〔127〕 N52°23.196' E006°07.687'　8131

N337, near ferry crossing point. Turn off N337 at roundabout, sp 'Heerde 9', then turn left, sp 'Camperterrein'.

🚐 10; €7/night; Collected; Max 48hrs; May-Oct

🪣 Custom; May-Oct; Open access

ℹ️ Small marina Aire with wide views of adj river navigation. River ferry adj, vehicle crossing €4.80 up to 7000kg. Café, additional parking and plenty of green space and river walks adj. Small town commerce 1km, parking: N52°23.389' E006°08.106'. Reinspected 2015.

NIJVERDAL　　　🚶 C5 〔128〕 N52°22.285' E006°27.880'　7443

Sportlaan. Turn off N35, sp 'Nijverdal' and 'Centrum'. In 1.7km turn left, sp 'Hulsen'. Go straight over roundabout, then turn immediately left, signed. Designated parking on far edge, signed.

🚐 3; €5/night + €0.65pp tax; Pay at Wilgenweard reception (9am-5pm); Max 48hrs; May-Oct

🪣 Drive over drain only; Open access; Toilets/showers at Wilgenweard

ℹ️ Designated parking under trees adj to sports facilities and Wilgenweard activity centre and high wire course; www.wilgenweard.nl Town centre with high street commerce 750m. Nationaal Park De Sallandse Heuvelrug, 1.8km on western edge of town. www.sallandseheuvelrug.nl Reinspected 2015.

LOSSER
C5 — 129 — N52°16.172' E007°00.832' — 7581

From west on N732 turn off at roundabout, sp 'Centrum'. At next roundabout follow sp 'Centrum'. Turn 1st left opp church and past supermarket. Then follow sp 'Sportspark' and 'Camperplaats' to parking.

🚐 2; Max 72hrs   🛒 None; See 133

ℹ Peaceful parking area at sports facilities 650m from town. Town has high street commerce and a good liquor shop next to supermarket. The local Losser beer is worth a try. 1.5km from Losser is a picnic area adj to water-filled gravel pits. Walking trails through the woods lead to sand dune and viewing tower offering views of Losser and Germany: N52°15.798' E007°01.812'. Reinspected 2015.

ENSCHEDE
C5 — 130 — N52°12.326' E006°54.113' — 7541

JJ van Deinselaan. Exit A35 at Junction 25, sp 'Enschede'. Then follow sp 'Centrum'. At traffic lights turn right towards McDonald's and KFC. Follow road and at traffic lights go straight on. Turn right into sports facility car park, sp 'Sportspark Het Diekman'. Follow road through car park and designated parking is outside Star World, signed.

🚐 5; Max 48hrs   🛒 None; See 133

ℹ Designated parking on edge of sports facilities adj to activity outlets such as snooker, bowling and swimming pool. This is an unusually large parking area and there is plenty of green space linking the various sports facilities. Town commerce is in the historic town centre, 2km. www.visitenschede.nl Inspected 2015.

HAAKSBERGEN 1   ⛺   C5   131   N52°08.862' E006°43.496'   7481

Scholtenhagenweg. Turn off N18 at traffic lights, sp 'De Wilder'. Follow road, then turn right, sp 'P1' and signed. Aire on left before campsite entrance.

🚐 24; €10/night inc 2 people, unmetered CEE elec and service; Max 72hrs
🪣 Custom; Water on every pitch; Shower €1

ℹ Campsite-run commercial Aire providing designated, hedged, grass pitches. The campsite facilities include a café and children's play area and there is another café at the adj public swimming pool. Town centre commerce 2km across N18. Steam trains chug to Boekelo from the Museum Buurtspoorweg: N52°09.464' E006°44.159' www.museumbuurtspoorweg.nl Inspected 2015.

HAAKSBERGEN 2   🏢   C5   132   N52°08.941' E006°42.741'   7481

Henk Pen Caravans. Turn off N18 at traffic lights, sp 'N347' and 'Goor'. Follow road around Henk Pen dealers and turn 1st right, sp 'West' and 'Oost'. Turn immediately right and follow road, then turn left, sp 'Showroom'. Parking signed outside megastore entrance.

🚐 2; Non-customers must arrive after 5pm and depart before 9.30am; Max 8m
🪣 2 CEE elec points; Water avail when store open

ℹ Outside caravan and motorhome dealer with well stocked accessory shop. Busy area during day and noisy all the time. Reinspected 2015.

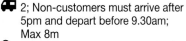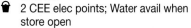

NEEDE — C5 — 133 — N52°08.510' E006°36.642' — 7161

N824. At roundabout north of town turn off N315 ring road, sp 'Goor'. In 200m turn left just past café at base of windmill, signed. Parking behind windmill, signed; Service Point to left. Signage in is confusing; if you drive through picnic area turn left back onto road to windmill parking on left.

4; €10/24hrs inc 6amp CEE elec; Pay at Service Point; Grass and hardstanding

Holiday Cleany; Water €1/80L; No drive over drain

ℹ️ Private Aire in car park of restaurant. Parking in large gravel car park in winter; grass parking subject to weather. Some noise from nearby main roads. De Olde Mölle café/restaurant open Mon-Fri from 11.30am, Sat-Sun from 10am, www.deoldemolle.nl TOP point details local walks and cycle routes. Adj windmill is privately owned and occasionally opens to the public. Inspected 2015.

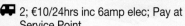

RUURLO 1 — C5 — 134 — N52°06.142' E006°26.557' — 7261

Wildpad. Exit Ruurlo heading north on N312. 550m after town boundary turn left, sp 'Camping Tamaring'. Aire on right in verge as approach campsite, signed.

2; €10/24hrs inc 6amp elec; Pay at Service Point

Holiday Cleany; Water €1/80L; WC emptying inside campsite

ℹ️ Pleasant shaded parking on a hardstanding area in the verge outside the campsite. Wood adj with walking/cycling paths through wood and to town, 1.9km. Town has commerce and a windmill which is a working sawmill; open to the public Saturdays 9am-4pm in summer, 9am-1pm in winter, see http://agneta.info Reinspected 2015.

RUURLO 2 — C5 — 135 — N52°04.065' E006°30.260' — 7261

Bekkenwal, adj to Camping De Meibeek. Turn off N315 at roundabout onto N319, sp 'Groenlo' and 'De Meibeek'. In 2.2km turn left, then immediately right, sp 'De Meibeek'. In 800m turn 1st right into Branderveenweg, sp 'De Meibeek'. Follow road, then turn left, sp 'Camping'. Follow road and Aire is on left, signed.

🚐 4; €10/24hrs inc 6amp elec; Pay at Service Point

💧 Holiday Cleany; Water €1/80L; No drive over drain

ℹ Very small Aire adj to campsite and small pond. 4 motorhomes could park here, but 2 would have to be blocked in. The location is very rural with town commerce 5km away. Advisable to check campsite prices as may be comparable to Aire. www.campingdemeibeek.nl Reinspected 2015.

BORCULO — C5 — 136 — N52°07.364' E006°31.624' — 7271

Kamerlingh Onnesstraat, outside motorhome dealer Bruggink Caravan and Campers. Exit N315 at traffic lights, sp 'Lochem'. In 550m turn left, sp 'Borculo'. Follow road to right, then left, then turn right, sp 'Bruggink Caravans'. Parking 230m at motorhome dealer, park outside display barn.

🚐 2; Arrive after 6pm and depart before 9am

💧 Unmetered CEE elec available 6pm-9am; See 133

ℹ This large, open, municipally owned, grass camping field is popular with motorhomers. Located adj to swimming beach at lake, no views. Suitable for all motorhomes, subject to weather conditions. Very basic facilities at adj campsite/leisure beach, follow sp 'Toiletten'. Reinspected 2015.

Grave

HAVE YOU VISITED AN AIRE?   GPS co-ordinates in this guide are protected by copyright law

Take at least 5 digital photos showing
- Signs
- Service Point
- Parking
- Overview
- Amenities

Visit www.all-the-aires.co.uk/submissions.shtml
to upload your updates and photos.

i Submit updates
- Amendments
- New Aires
- Not changed

HENGELO-GLD   C4   138   N52°02.668' E006°18.214'   7255

Elderinkweg. Approach Hengelo on N316 from south. At roundabout turn left into Elderinkweg, sp 'Het Elderink'. Turn 1st left into the car park and the Aire is on the right, signed.

🚐 2; Max 24hrs

🛁 None; See 133

i Aire located in the car park of sports facilities, including a swimming pool, and opp municipal offices. The car park is busy on hot summer days, at weekends and during school holidays, but empty at night. Town commerce, 800m. Cross roundabout and follow Hummeloseweg towards church to end. www.vvvbronckhorst.nl Reinspected 2015.

BATHMEN   C4   139   N52°15.026' E006°17.958'   7411

Prinses Margrietlaan. Exit A1 at Junction 25 and follow sp 'Bathmen'. Turn right, sp 'Bathmen'. Turn right at end of road, sp 'Sportpark' and 'Sporthal'. Turn right 3 times following sp 'Sportpark' and 'Sporthal'. Designated parking in sports hall car park, signed.

2; Max 48hrs; 8m bays; See info

None; See 133

ℹ️ Shaded and peaceful parking at sports facilities. Although there are 2 designated spaces, there is room for many more motorhomes of all sizes. According to www.bathmen.nl 'there are no major attractions'. Town 800m with small town commerce and a bus to nearby town of Deventer. Reinspected 2015.

ENTER   B4   140   N52°17.882' E006°34.957'   7468

Werfstraat. Exit N347, sp 'Enter'. Follow road into town. Turn left, sp 'Borne' and signed, then immediately right, signed. In 350m turn left, sp 'Sportspark de Werf', just before exit Enter. Turn 1st right and Aire on left, signed.

3; Max 72hrs; Max 8m subject to bushes

None; See 127

ℹ️ Designated parking alongside a country lane under deciduous trees between 2 sports fields. 50m to café adj to a former boathouse, and turnaround basin that has been partially regenerated. River cruises in Jul-Aug; hourly departures Tues-Sat, €4.50pp. www.entersezomp.nl A map details 3 circular walk/cycle routes, www.wierden-enterinfo.nl Village centre with local commerce 200m. Inspected 2015.

THE NETHERLANDS NEDERLAND

ALMEN ⚓ C4 `141` N52°09.981' E006°17.850' 7218

Scheggertdijk. Exit Zutphen on N346, sp
'Almen'. Turn left into Kapperallee before fuel
station, sp 'Eefde'. Follow road to right, sp
'Almen'. At end of road turn left, sp
'Scheggertdijk'. Cross bridge, then turn 1st
right. Turn right again and drive past café to
water's edge. Designated parking on left,
signed.

🚐 10; €10/night inc WiFi and 16amp CEE
elec
🚽 Custom; Seijsener WC sink; Water
€0.75/100L; Showers €0.75; Pay at café
ℹ️ Pleasant, landscaped marina Aire with 5
bays overlooking a grass verge to the
Twenthe Canal, a 65km long navigation used
by large working barges. This small, neat
marina accommodates only 12 boats. Ample
parking unless café is full, it opens from
11am daily. www.nieuwe-aanleg.nl Almen
centre with local commerce 1.5km.
Inspected 2015.

TERWOLDE C4 `142` N52°16.892' E006°05.977' 7396

N792. Exit A50 at Junction 26 and follow
sp 'Terwolde' onto N792. In Terwolde
follow sp 'Twello'. Turn right into the car
park adj to Kriebelz Brasserie.
Designated parking at far end of car
park, signed.

🚐 2; Max 24hrs 🚽 None; See `127`
ℹ️ Designated parking adj to restaurant
on edge of village. The parking is
municipal and it is free to park here, but
the restaurant has an interesting menu
and good coffee and beer, so is easy to
support. www.brasserie-kriebelz.nl
Village church 200m. Working windmill
milling flour open Thurs-Sat with shop:
N52°16.291' E006°06.341'. Parking
outside, or alternatively it is a pleasant,
short cycle. Inspected 2015.

TWELLO | C4 | 143 | N52°14.069' E006°05.900' | 7391

Jachtlustplein, at the sports facilities in the centre of town. Exit A1 at Junction 22 and follow sp 'Twello'. In Twello follow sp 'Sporthal Jachtlust'. Designated parking outside entrance.

🚐 1; Max 6m

🚰 None; See 144

i Impractical designated parking at sports hall entrance, which is unfortunate as the car park has much more suitable parking opportunities. In residential area in centre of town. Bar, sports facility, skateboard, basketball and table tennis adj. High street commerce 500m. Reinspected 2015.

ZUTPHEN 1 ★ | C4 | 144 | N52°08.212' E006°11.918' | 7201

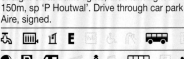

Houtwal. Approach town on N346 from Lochem. At traffic lights go straight on, sp 'Zutphen Centrum'. Go straight over roundabout, then at traffic lights turn left, sp 'Ring Centrum'. Follow road, which weaves 1st right, then left, then right, then left, then right, mostly one-way and sp 'Ring Centrum'. Go straight on at traffic lights, then turn right in 150m, sp 'P Houtwal'. Drive through car park to Aire, signed.

🚐 8; €0.50/hr or €2/day 8am-6pm; Free 6pm-8am; Pay at machine; 7m bays plus overhang

🚰 Holiday Cleany x 2; Water €1; 8 CEE elec points €10/24hrs; No drive over drain

i Popular Aire overlooking the grassy banks of the former star fort defensive water and town. Medieval centre 550m. Sir Philip Sidney, an Elizabethan poet, diplomat and soldier, was fatally wounded here; memorial at: N52°08.540' E006°12.761'; on street parking nearby. Reinspected 2015.

ZUTPHEN 2 C4 145 N52°08.399' E006°11.496' 7204

IJsselkade. From 144 exit and turn right. Follow road then turn left into riverside car park, signed. Parking to right, signed. Best to reverse in.

2; €1.30/hr or €7.80/day Mon-Thurs/Sat 8am-6pm, Fri 8am-9pm; Free 6pm/9pm-8am and all day Sun; Pay at machine; Max 48hrs; Max 8-9m in end bay

Toilet only; See 144

i Designated parking in roadside car park that overlooks the navigable IJssel river. Road noise and rushing water sound from the adj storm water outlet. This parking is not as popular as 144, but it is more interesting if you like to watch the world go by. Historic centre and town commerce 200m. www.zutphen.nl Inspected 2015.

GENDRINGEN 1 D4 146 N51°52.464' E006°23.233' 7081

Ulftseweg 4. Follow N317 towards Germany. When road bends left, just after Ulft boundary sign, follow road to right. Follow road for 2.4km, over roundabout, then turn left into stables and petting farm, sp 'Diekshuus Paardensportcentrum'. Drive to rear of car park, signed.

4; €10/night inc 6amp elec; Pay at machine; Grass parking

Holiday Cleany; Water €1/80L; No WC rinse tap; No drive over drain

i Aire in large gravel car park adj to riding stables and behind a small petting farm that is free to enter. Livestock includes sheep, chickens and ponies, www.kinderboerderij-engbergen.nl The adj café/restaurant overlooks the indoor and outdoor riding sand schools. www.diekshuus.nl Large public park opp. Town commerce 650m. Inspected 2015.

GENDRINGEN 2   D4   147   N51°52.193' E006°22.797'   7081

Julianastraat. Follow N317 towards Germany. When road bends left, just after Ulft boundary sign, follow road to right. In 2.8km, when road bends to left, take 2nd right immediately after small roundabout. Avoid 1st right, sp 'Centrum'. Aire in 10m in car park on left, signed.

🚐 3; Max 72hrs

🚰 None; See 146

ℹ️ Designated parking in town car park also marked as bus and truck parking, just off main route. At time of inspection the motorhome parking sign had been removed during maintenance. Please let us know if it is missing or reinstalled; we will post updates online on our updates page. Bar adj. Local commerce 400m. German border 750m. Reinspected 2015.

WESTENDORP   C5   148   N51°57.006' E006°25.252'   7054

Recreatieoord Hippique, Doetinchemseweg. Turn off main route through town, sp 'Recreatieoord Hippique' and signed. Follow driveway through automatic gateway and straight on past house and stables to the motorhome parking at the end on the left.

🚐 4; €10/night inc 6amp elec and WiFi; Arrive between 9am-8pm

🚰 Holiday Cleany; Water €1/80L; Use of toilets/showers €2.50pppn

ℹ️ Pleasant commercial Aire at exceptionally clean and tidy holiday centre where people bring their own horses. Lovely facilities block opposite house. This Aire is comparable to an exceptionally good certificated site (CL/CS) in the UK. Distant road noise. Local commerce 450m. www.recreatieoordhippique.nl Inspected 2015.

AALTEN 1 ⛺ C5 149 N51°55.559' E006°36.295' 7121

Eskesweg, at Camping Lansbulten. Turn off N318 and follow sp 'Camping'. Aire is in the car park of the campsite, signed. Difficult to find without GPS.

🚿 ⬛ 📶 E 🚾 ♿ 📡 🚌 F
⚫ P 🚐 ⛴ 🍼 🎵 🚌 F ✳️

🚐 4; €10 inc 6amp elec; Pay at Service Point
💧 Holiday Cleany; Water €1/80L; No drive over drain

ℹ️ The Aire is in the corner of a campsite car park; in the summer it is shaded by large deciduous trees. There is a lakeside café nearby and town centre is 2km. www.vvvaalten-bredevoort-dinxperlo.nl Reinspected 2015.

SP 🌳🏕️🏃📷🔲🚶🚴🛶🤸

AALTEN 2 🏛️ C5 150 N51°56.020' E006°34.929' 7121

Lichtenvoordsestraatweg. Turn off N313 at traffic lights onto N318, sp 'Aalten'. In 1.2km turn right at roundabout, sp 'Lichtenvoordsestraatweg'. Turn next left opp 't Noorden bar/restaurant and Aire is in car park on left, signed.

🚿 ⬛ 📶 E 🚾 ♿ 📡 🚌 F
⚫ P 🚐 ⛴ 🍼 🎵 🚌 F ✳️

🚐 4; €10/24hrs inc 6amp elec; Pay at Service Point
💧 Holiday Cleany; Water €1/80L; No drive over drain

ℹ️ This Aire is in a large car park opposite a railway-themed pancake restaurant with children's play area, open 11am-10pm. This is the best Aire for visiting town, 700m, straight across roundabout down Lichtenvoordsestraatweg. The town hid huge numbers of people during WWII, the museum in the TO details this time; €5pp, open Tues-Sat 10am-5pm, Sun 1-5pm. www.aaltensemusea.nl Reinspected 2015.

SP 🌳🏕️🏃📷🔲🚶🚴🛶🤸

AALTEN 3 ⛺ C5 151 N51°56.693' E006°32.656' 7122

Boterdijk, at Campsite Goorzicht. Turn off N318 at roundabout onto Aladnaweg. Then follow sp 'Goorzicht Camping' to campsite. Aire at far end of car park outside campsite, signed.

🚐 4; €10 inc 6amp elec; Pay at Service Point

🚰 Holiday Cleany; Water €1; No drive over drain; Showers €0.50

ℹ️ Designated parking outside campsite in far corner of car park. Use of facilities including swimming pool and play area included. WiFi €2.50/hr or €5/day. The campsite also has a bar. This is a remote, rural campsite and is the furthest Aire from Aalten centre, 4.3km; also see 149 and 150. www.goorzicht.nl Reinspected 2015.

LICHTENVOORDE 🚶 C5 152 N51°59.450' E006°33.614' 7131

Raadhuisstraat. Turn off N18 at traffic lights at Lichtenvoorde border. Follow road straight on, signed, then turn left opp De Schatberg restaurant and immediately right into car park, sp 'P'. The Aire is on the left, signed.

🚐 4; €10 inc 6amp elec; Pay at Service Point

🚰 Holiday Cleany; Water €1

ℹ️ Designated parking in subsection of large car park adj to sports ground. There are 2 restaurants opp and town centre with high street commerce 750m. Every September there is a flower parade where fantastic floats decorated with flowers parade through the streets and are then exhibited for 2 days. https://bloemencorso.com www.lichtenvoorde.nl Reinspected 2015.

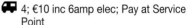

BREDEVOORT　　C5　153　　N51°56.854' E006°37.415'　7126

Kruittorenstraat. From Lichtenvoorde take N313 towards Aalten. Turn left at traffic lights, sp 'N318' and 'Bredevoort'. Turn right, sp 'De Slingeplas'. Follow road to right, then left over bridge, both sp 'De Slingeplas'. At crossroads turn right, sp 'Hamalandroute'. Turn 1st left and Aire on left, signed. Follow directions as GPS may take you to barriered parking with a €4/day charge.

🚐 8; €10/24hrs inc 6amp elec; Pay at Service Point

🚰 Holiday Cleany; Water €1/80L; No drive over drain; Public toilets 200m

ℹ Pleasant Aire in a rural location adj to large recreation area with fishing/leisure lake with swimming beach, no views; no dogs May-Oct. Seasonal toilets and outdoor showers by lake. Very popular on hot days and holidays, isolated rest of year. Village centre with local and tourist commerce 550m. Reinspected 2015.

DE HEURNE　　C5　154　　N51°53.882' E006°30.002'　7095

Caspersstraat. From De Heurne follow main route north for 1.3km. Turn right into farm, sp 'De Haar'. Aire on right.

🚐 10; €10/24hrs inc 6amp elec and WiFi; Reinforced grass parking

🚰 Holiday Cleany; Water €1

ℹ Very pleasant Aire at private farm house on outskirts of village. Don't let the Wolf Project sign put you off, they only have friendly, well trained domestic dogs. A great deal of effort has been made to get this right and it feels like a CL. Restaurant/bar 5 mins. Reinspected 2015.

SILVOLDE · C4 · 155 · N51°54.974' E006°22.317' · 7064

Terborgseveld. From Ulft on N317 turn off at roundabout, sp 'Silvolde'. In town take left fork, not signed. Turn left, sp 'Sportcomplex De Paasberg'. Turn 1st right, then in 450m turn left into car park, sp 'P'. Designated parking on left, signed.

4; Max 72hrs; 10m bays

None; See 156

Designated parking in large car park adj to sports complex. Residential houses and library with free computers/WiFi adj. Numerous sports facilities including open access basketball and skateboard ramps. Walk or cycle 900m through the adj parks to the pleasant centre of Terborg. Inspected 2015.

DINXPERLO · D5 · 156 · N51°51.422' E006°28.583' · 7091

Meniststraat, behind De Rietstap fuel station. Heading towards Germany on N317 turn left on last road before river crossing. Follow road and De Rietstap fuel station is on left.

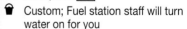

None; See 155

Custom; Fuel station staff will turn water on for you

Service Point only. LPG on site. Reinspected 2015.

ZELHEM — C4 — 157 — N51°59.917' E006°20.703' — 7021

Stikkenweg. Turn off N315 at roundabout, sp 'Halle'. Turn right into car park and designated parking is signed in right-hand corner.

🚐 2; Max 24hrs

🚰 None; See 156

ℹ️ Aire located in car park adj to N315 main route. The designated parking is closest to the road and shaded by deciduous trees. The adj bus stop is no longer used. Small town commerce 1km by foot/cycle path. Simply cross the road and follow Doetinchemseweg to the centre. http://tipzelhem.nl Reinspected 2015.

TOLKAMER — D4 — 158 — N51°51.092' E006°05.918' — 6916

Europakade. Approach from north on N881. Turn right at roundabout, sp 'Europakade' and signed. Follow road, then turn left, sp 'Europakade' and signed. On top of dyke turn right and drive along dyke, signed. At river turn right into Aire, signed.

🚐 15; €7.50/24hrs from noon; Collected; Max 48hrs

🚰 6 16amp Seijsener elec points; At far end; €1

ℹ️ Popular Aire with uninterrupted view across the Rhine river towards Germany. Commercial barges of all shapes and sizes pass by frequently and moor adj. Town adj. Additional commercial Aire at Restaurant de Swaenenbloem 2.6km away: N51°51.749' E006°04.695', €10 without elec, grass parking and adj to Rhine and swimming beaches. Reinspected 2015.

Oosterwijk Leerdam

DOESBURG   ⚓ C4   160   N52°00.658' E006°07.990'   6981

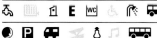

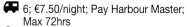

Turfhaven. From Arnhem on A348 turn onto N317, sp 'Doesburg'. Follow N317 for 2km, crossing river, then turn immediately right and right again, both sp 'Doesburg Centrum'. In 750m turn right, sp 'Turfhaven' and signed. Turn 1st right, then left, then right, signed. Designated parking on left along marina edge, signed.

🚰   🏠   E   wc   ♿   🚌   F

⚫   P   🚐   🕯   🎵   🚌   F   ❄

🚐 6; €7.50/night; Pay Harbour Master; Max 72hrs

🔧 Custom; 6 Maryport CEE elec points adj; €0.50/kWh; All other services on pedestrian pontoon; Shower €0.50

ℹ️ Marina Aire with pleasant designated parking in car park on upper quay looking down over pleasure boat moorings. Doesburg city has a pleasant old town with town centre commerce, 600m. www.vvvdoesburg.nl Inspected 2015.

EERBEEK   C4   161   N52°06.196' E006°03.944'   6961

Stationstraat. From Dieren take N786, sp 'Eerbeek'. Stay on N786 by turning left, then 1st right, sp 'Laag Soeren'. Turn right at roundabout, sp 'Eerbeek'. Turn left, sp 'Koenders Bedrijfsauto's'. Service Point on left at motorhome workshop, to right of workshop door, signed: N52°06.133' E006°03.889'. Parking across railway track outside WelKOOP supermarket.

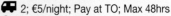

🚐 2; €5/night; Pay at TO; Max 48hrs

🚰 Custom; 150m across railway track on left; Water €2 avail Mon-Fri 8am-5.30pm, Sat 10am-3pm; No drive over drain

i Designated parking adj to small supermarket, garden centre/animal feed shop and railway track. Railway line adj is used, but the rolling stock is stored long term. TO 230m at end of high street. www.vvvbrummen.nl Inspected 2015.

DOORNENBURG   T   D4   162   N51°53.647' E006°00.075'   6686

Kerkstraat. Turn off N838, sp 'Doornenburg'. Turn left, sp 'De Doornenburg', then turn 1st left, sp 'De Doornenburg'. Follow road to right, sp 'Kasteel Doornenburg', then follow road to left and the designated parking is on the right after town boundary, signed.

🚐 3; Max 72hrs; Reinforced grass parking

🚰 None; Toilets at castle when open

i Pleasant parking on the reinforced grass verge of a minor road. Castle Doornenburg opp, but trees obscure views. Restaurant at castle open daily until 6pm. Castle and café open Apr-Sept Tues-Sun 10am-6pm, tours 1-3 times per day, €7.50pp. Small town commerce 500m. www.kasteeldoornenburg.nl Inspected 2015.

ZEVENAAR C4 163 N51°55.879' E006°04.765' 6901

Bommersheufsestraat. At Zevenaar turn off N336 at roundabout, sp 'Centrum'. Follow road to right, sp 'P Route', then to left. Turn left into car park and designated parking to left, signed.

5; €8/night; Pay at machine, by pressing button for motorhome parking, and display ticket; Max 48hrs; Max 8m; Park parallel

None; See 164

Designated parking in town centre car park. Motorhomes are intended to park parallel across the bays; local car drivers may not understand or respect this, but the likelihood is that they will return to their cars within an hour. Town commerce adj inc a Jumbo supermarket opposite. www.zevenaar.nl Inspected 2015.

ARNHEM 1 C4 164 N51°58.237' E005°56.865' 6827

Oude Veerweg. Exit A12, sp 'Arnhem', and follow sp 'Arnhem' onto N325. In 1.8km turn right at traffic lights, sp 'Westervoort' and 'Arnhem-Centrum'. Go straight across next traffic lights, then turn left into central reservation and across road to Shell fuel station. Service Point at end of car wash, signed. Go to shop to get Service Point unlocked before use.

Poss; Roadside

Custom; Get box unlocked by shop attendant; Water €0.50

Service Point only. LPG available at fuel station. Also see 165. Inspected 2015.

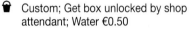

ARNHEM 2   C4   165   N51°58.401' E005°54.948'   6827

Nieuwe Kade. Exit A12, sp 'Arnhem', and follow sp 'Arnhem' onto N325. In 1.8km turn right at traffic lights, sp 'Westervoort' and 'Arnhem-Centrum'. Follow road for 2.3km, passing , then turn left before Aluminium Bennis Arnhem building. Turn 1st left over hump and down to river quay. Aire on right behind Harbour Master's office, signed.

🚐 4; €9/9pm-9am + €1 transaction fee; CC; Pay by phone or online at www.aanuit.net; Max 48hrs; Max 9m, park parallel to wall

🚰 4 16amp CEE Seijsener elec points €0.50/kWh; See 164

ℹ️ Designated quayside parking adj to boat moorings with views along Rhine and the working barges that pass frequently. 300m along river towards centre visit the Airborne memorial and the Battle of Arnhem Information Centre; free entry, open daily Nov-Mar 11am-5pm Apr-Oct 10am-5pm. Inspected 2015.

KEKERDOM (MILLINGEN AAN DE RIJN)   D4   166   N51°51.387' E006°01.862'   6566

Crumpsestraat. From Nijmegen follow sp 'Millingen' onto N840. Turn right off N840 before entering Kerkerdom, signed. Turn 1st left, signed. Aire immediately on left, signed.

🚐 12; €8/night inc WiFi; Max 9m

🚰 Custom; Seijsener WC sink; Water €1/90L; CEE elec €2; Shower €1

ℹ️ Popular rurally located private Aire that feels a bit like a mini campsite. Although the bays are close together, there is some grass to put chairs out. Bike shed with elec. Showers and toilets near house. www.camperplaatshetcrumpsehoekje.nl Inspected 2015.

HUISSEN

D4 | 167 | N51°56.157' E005°56.711' | 6851

Stadsdam. Turn off A325 onto N325 following sp 'Huissen'. Turn off N325, sp 'Huissen', and go right at traffic lights. Go straight on at 1st roundabout, sp 'Huissen'. At 2nd roundabout turn left, sp 'Huissen Centrum'. Follow road for 400m, then after road bends to left turn immediately right into car park, signed. Motorhome parking signed at far end of car park, just before 2hr parking restriction closest to road.

3; Max 72hrs; See info ☗ None; See **164**

ℹ️ Designated parking closest to road, noisy at times and popular with locals, so suggest park elsewhere in car park. Small supermarket adj. Monastery, www.kloosterhuissen.nl, and town centre across road. Huissen was heavily bombed by the allies in 1944; cemetery off Doelenstraat has a mass grave for all civilians who died. Reinspected 2015.

RESSEN

D4 | 168 | N51°53.313' E005°52.343' | 6684

Woerdsestraat. In Ressen turn off main route, sp 'De Woert' and signed. Follow road straight on into 2.3m width restricted road and designated parking is on left and right at farmyard.

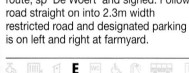

6; €6/night + €1pp tax inc WiFi; Pay at shop
☗ Cont elec €1.50; Pay at shop

ℹ️ Private Aire at fruit farm offering grass and hardstanding parking. Very large, well stocked farm shop open Mon-Sat 8.30am-6pm. Visitors are welcome to wander around the orchards, including the regional speciality cherry trees. The cherries are picked in late Jun-Jul. www.dewoerdt.nl Inspected 2015.

BEMMEL   C4   169   N51°53.384' E005°54.573'   6681

Wardstraat. After A15/A325 junction follow A15 towards Bemmel. Turn right onto N839, sp 'Bemmel'. At traffic lights by BP fuel station turn right, sp 'Bemmel', then 1st left, sp 'de Bongerd' and signed. Follow road and after it bends to right, turn into car park on left.

🚐 3; Max 72hrs

🚻 None; See 164

ℹ️ Designated parking in a residential area, unlikely to ever get busy. High voltage pylon adj and cables pass over the entrance to the Aire. Park with pond and children's play area adj. Town commerce 850m. www.vvvlingewaard.nl Reinspected 2015.

OTTERSUM   D4   170   N51°41.375' E006°00.421'   6595

Siebengewaldseweg. Turn off N291 near Ottersum, sp 'Siebengewald' and signed. Follow road for 2km, then turn left into car park before Old Inn restaurant. Designated parking at far end of car park, signed.

🚐 7; Max 72hrs   🚻 None; See 164

ℹ️ Shaded designated parking to rear of car park adj to walking trails through woods; perfect on a hot day. The adj restaurant was closed due to a vehicle having been parked in the dining room at speed. At the time of publishing a new owner had committed to reopening the restaurant so, the name for example, may change, but the motorhome parking should remain as it appears to be municipal. Inspected 2015.

MILSBEEK　　　D4　171　N51°44.295' E005°57.401'　6596

Zwarteweg. Turn off N271 at roundabout, sp 'Milsbeek' and 'War Cemetery'. Follow road for 2km, then turn right into parking just past restaurant, signed. Designated grass parking to rear.

🚐 5; Max 72hrs; Grass parking

None; See 180

ℹ️ Popular designated parking in large open field, which was oversubscribed at time of inspection but did not feel crowded. Adj restaurant is a pancake house; children's play area and hardstanding parking adj to restaurant. The adj woods are in Germany, and it is possible to cycle along the border. War cemetery, 1.3km in centre, has burials from the push into Germany in 1945: N51°43.529' E005°57.081'. Site 8 on the WWII Liberation Route adj, www.liberationroute.com Inspected 2015.

GENNEP　　　D4　172　N51°41.990' E005°58.459'　6591

Martinushof. Exit A73 at Junction 5, sp 'N264 Haps'. Follow N264, sp 'Oeffelt'. At roundabout turn right, sp 'N264 Gennep'. At roundabout turn left, sp 'Centrum'. At end of road, opp ALDI, turn left, then 1st right into car park. Drive past ALDI and follow road to designated parking at end, signed.

🚐 5; Max 72hrs; Max 9m

None; See 180

ℹ️ Popular, pleasant, partially shaded designated parking at far end of town centre car park overlooking park and defensive dyke along river Niers. Signs obstruct overhang in most bays. Beach volleyball courts opp. ALDI and pedestrian high street 200m. Saturday market. www.gennep.nl Inspected 2015.

WELL 1   D4   173   N51°33.792' E006°03.845'   5855

Recreatie Leukermeer. Turn off N271 north of Knikkerdorp, sp 'Leukermeer'. In 800m turn right. Follow road straight on for 1.2km, then turn left, sp 'Recreatieplaats aan de Maas' and signed. Designated parking in field on right, signed. Service Point and toilets at marina: N51°33.924' E006°03.854'.

🚐 40; €10/night inc 10amp CEE elec and service; Pay at marina/collected; Grass parking; Hardstanding parking Oct-Mar at marina

🛒 Custom; 16amp CEE elec €0.50; Showers €0.50; All at marina; See directions

ℹ Marina Aire with large, pleasant camping field adj to leisure lake with swimming beach, no views. Ideal place to visit in hot weather and enjoy splashing about in the lake. Marina across road has restaurant, closed Tuesdays, and all facilities. www.leukermeer.nl Inspected 2015.

WELL 2 (BERGEN)   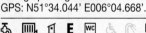 D4   174   N51°33.975' E006°04.770'   5855

Camperplaats Seurenheide. 5km south of Bergen turn off N271 into country lane, sp 'Leukermeer'. Turn 1st right, sp 'Seurenheide'. Turn right at Seurenheide sign, GPS taken here, then follow road through parking field to Aire at end. Actual GPS: N51°34.044' E006°04.668'.

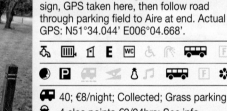

🚐 40; €8/night; Collected; Grass parking

🛒 4 elec points €2/24hrs; See info

ℹ This large, open, municipally owned, grass camping field is popular with motorhomers. Located adj to swimming beach at lake, no views. Suitable for all motorhomes, subject to weather conditions. Very basic facilities at adj campsite/leisure beach, follow sp 'Toiletten'. De Maasduinen National Park with peat bogland and sand dunes on opp side of N271. www.np-demaasduinen.nl Reinspected 2015.

GRAVE 1   D4   175   N51°45.528' E005°44.225'   5360

Trompetterstraat. From east approach Grave on N324. Turn right at 2nd set of traffic lights by Mooiland glass building, sp 'Grave'. At end of car park on left turn right into car park. Designated parking at end of row on left, signed.

🛏 1; Max 8m

⚡ 1 CEE elec point (Not working); See 178

ℹ️ 1 designated parking bay in small car park at foot of fortification mound. Walk to top of the fortification for 5 mins of fun and maybe walk down the other side to have refreshments at the former arsenal, Het Arsenaal. The Graafs Museum is opposite the arsenal, www.graafsmuseum.nl Grave high street commerce 400m. Inspected 2015.

GRAVE 2   D4   176   N51°45.697' E005°44.182'   5361

Pater van de Elsenstraat. Turn off N324 into Grave at traffic lights by Stadhuis Grave. Turn 1st left, then next right, sp 'Camper Parkeerplaats'. Follow road to right and parking in car park on right, signed.

🛏 20; Max 72hrs

⚡ None; See 178

ℹ️ Large gravel car park adj to marina, but partial views only. Easy parking for any sized motorhome and within easy walking distance of the town commerce. The Graafs Museum, 750m, is housed in the old fort, €3pp. www.graafsmuseum.nl Also see Grave 175 and 177. Caravan dealer with accessory shop adj to N324. Reinspected 2015.

p ←
+ camper
parkeerplaats
max 72 uur

2 min lopen
naar centrum

GRAVE 3   D4   177   N51°46.116' E005°43.852'   5361

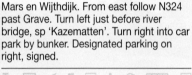

Mars en Wijthdijk. From east follow N324 past Grave. Turn left just before river bridge, sp 'Kazematten'. Turn right into car park by bunker. Designated parking on right, signed.

🏍 ▥ 🏠 E WC ♿ 📶 🚌 F

● P 🚐 ⚓ 🧴 🎵 🚐 F ❋

🚐 2; Reinforced grass parking

🏠 None; See 178

ℹ️ Pleasant designated parking on edge of town adj to pumping station and between two WWII bunkers, now a museum; €1pp, open Apr-Oct weekends 1-5pm. Views across to John S Thompson bridge named after the allied lieutenant who captured it after a fierce gun battle during WWII. Info panels in English at the bridge explain the battle; site 123 on the Liberation Route www.liberationroute.com Bullet impacts are clearly visible on the nearby bunker. Inspected 2015.

VELP   D4   178   N51°44.808' E005°42.715'   5363

Beukenlaan. Turn off N324 at traffic lights, sp 'Velp'. Turn 1st left, sp 'Trefpunt'. Follow road to left past 't Trefpunt building. Aire in far end of car park on left, signed.

🏍 ▥ 🏠 E WC ♿ 📶 🚌 F

● P 🚐 ⚓ 🧴 🎵 🚐 F ❋

🚐 2; 10m bays plus overhang

🏠 Custom; Max 1hr on Service Point

ℹ️ Pleasant, shaded Aire within car park adj to school and park. Because of its wooded setting, it may feel isolated if alone. Velp is a small village with local commerce at N324 crossroads. Once you have exhausted those, catch a bus into Grave. Inspected 2015.

SP 🌳 ⛺ ⛷ 📷 🗑 🚶 🚲 🦆 🦃 🐦

OSS 1   D4   179   N51°46.640' E005°31.381'   5346

Rusheuvelstraat. Turn off N329 at traffic lights, sp 'Oss'. Follow road straight on, sp 'Centrum', then at roundabout with triangular statues turn right, sp 'P Rusheuvel'. Follow road, then turn right into car park, sp 'P Rusheuvel'. The designated parking is on the left in the 2nd row, signed.

 10; Max 72hrs 🔒 None; See **180**

ℹ️ Designated parking in large car park next to sports facilities and bowling alley. The parking is overlooked by residential housing and there is some road noise. Skateboard park adj. This parking can take motorhomes of all sizes and is always likely to have space. The large high street is 1km. Inspected 2015.

OSS 2   D4   180   N51°45.588' E005°33.361'   5349

Van Venrooy Motorhomes. Turn off N329 for 2.4km then turn off, sp 'Berghem-Zuid'. Turn right at traffic lights, sp 'Berghem-Zuid', then turn 1st left into Galliërsweg. Follow road to Van Venrooy Motorhomes on left. Parking by reception, signed. Service Point on corner of building nearest parking.

 2

🔒 Custom; 2 4amp CEE elec points

ℹ️ At Neismann-Bischoff motorhome dealer with service workshop. Service Point and parking available for anyone to use, no need to report to reception. Reception open 9am-5.30pm, English spoken, Tel: 0412 455307, www.vanvenrooymotorhomes.nl www.toerismeoss.nl Reinspected 2015.

HETEREN C4 181 N51°57.274' E005°43.836' 6666

N837. Exit A50 at Junction 18 and follow sp 'Heteren'. At the roundabout by McDonald's turn right, sp 'Heteren'. At next roundabout turn left onto N837, sp 'Zetten'. Follow road to Aire on right in small lay-by car park under trees, signed.

🚐 4; Max 72hrs; Hardstanding; Poss grass parking subject to weather

🚻 None; See 164

ℹ️ Pleasant, rural Aire adj to road. Parking is under deciduous trees. The adj park houses a ruined fortification with a footpath meandering around the moat and defences. Bus stop adj and cycle path to town, 2.5km. Reinspected 2015.

APPELTERN ★ D4 182 N51°50.563' E005°33.781' 6629

Molenstraat. Exit N322 at roundabout onto N329, sp 'Appeltern'. In 2.9km turn right, sp 'Alphen'. Turn left, sp 'Fietstop'. Aire on right, signed.

🚐 30; €5/night inc WiFi; Collected; Grass parking

🚻 Custom; Seijsener WC sink; 4amp CEE elec €2/night

ℹ️ This is a popular, pleasant, commercial Aire that feels like a rally field for motorhomes only. Grass parking suitable for any size motorhome. The charming facilities are located in a rustic cabin. Half of the parking overlooks a large grassy area onto carp and sturgeon fishing lakes. An ideal place for fisherman and their families. Inspected 2015.

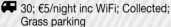

TIEL   C4   183   N51°53.113' E005°26.431'   4001

Waalkade. Exit A15 at Junction 33, sp 'Tiel', and follow sp 'Tiel'. At the roundabout turn right, sp 'P Centrum'. Follow road past Total fuel station, then in 100m turn left, sp 'P Waalkade'. Follow signs in car park to bays.

🚐 4; €1.36/hr or €8.20/day Mon-Wed/Fri-Sat 8am-6pm, Thurs 8am-9pm; Sun noon-5pm; Pay at machine; CC/€; Max 48hrs

⛽ None; See 164

ℹ️ This large car park has wide views over a busy navigation and the 4 motorhome bays are nowhere near enough to meet demand. Café adj; town centre with numerous commerce, 500m. Pedestrian ferry across river. www.uitintiel.nl Appelpop, the biggest free music festival in the Netherlands, held annually in 2nd week of Sept; www.appelpop.nl Reinspected 2015.

SCHIJNDEL   D4   184   N51°36.991' E005°25.818'   5481

Bunderstraat. Enter on N618 from Boxtel. Turn left immediately before large monastery style building, sp 'Past v Erpstraat'. The parking is at sports centre on left in 200m, sp 'De Dioscuren'.

🚐 3; €4/24hrs; Pay in reception; Max 48hrs; Max 7m

⛽ Toilets and pay showers in sports centre

ℹ️ Shaded designated parking adj to sports facility. Overpriced for location and facilities unless you require access to a shower. Town centre, 400m, has a Saturday market in the central square 10am-4pm. www.schijndel.nl Reinspected 2015.

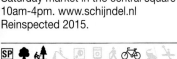

SINT OEDENRODE   D4   185   N51°34.019' E005°27.452'   5492

Dommelpark. From Schijndel follow N637 to St Oedenrode. At St Oedenrode go straight over roundabout, sp 'Centrum', then turn right, sp 'Olland'. At roundabout turn left, then turn right, sp 'P De Neul'. Follow road to designated parking in car park, signed.

3; Max 48hrs   None; See 187

Pleasant open parkland, watercourses and sports facilities surround this designated parking area. Adj trees provide some welcome shade in summer. Swimming pool with waterslide on opp side of stream. The town centre with high street commerce and numerous popular eateries is 500m through park and across bridge. Inspected 2015.

BEST   D3   186   N51°31.276' E005°23.631'   5682

P Carpool de Wilg. Exit A2 at Junction 27, sp 'Best-West', and follow sp 'P Carpool' to the Aire in the carpool parking, signed.

3; Max 24hrs
None; See 187

Motorhomes allowed in carpool car park just off A2. CCTV over parking area. Town centre 1.2km, follow road to left. Pleasant day parking 5km: N51°30.823' E005°27.868'. Follow N620 east from Best to a woodland recreation area on left with lake and sand dune. Reinspected 2015.

EINDHOVEN D4 187 N51°26.134' E005°25.488' 5657

Meerhoven P&R, Sliffertsestraat. Exit A2 at Junction 31 and follow sp 'P&R Meerhoven'. Enter through barrier. Service Point and parking to left of barrier, signed.

🚐 10; 1st 15 mins free; 1st day €4.50, then €5/day; CC; Pay at booth by café

🚽 Custom; Pay toilets in café, open during day

ℹ️ Designated parking at park and ride. 15 mins free access is just enough time to empty toilet and drain waste tanks. No freshwater on site. WiFi in café. There is a constant hum from adj motorway. McDonald's nearby. Bus to Eindhoven centre €0.50pp. www.thisiseindhoven.nl Inspected 2015.

NUENEN D4 188 N51°27.821' E005°33.807' 5673

Pastoorsmast. In Nuenen follow sp 'Nuenen-Zuid', then at roundabout with 6 tall bushes turn onto Maatschappijweg. Follow road to right. After passing Nuenen boundary sign, designated parking in car park on left, signed.

🚐 5; Max 5 days; Reinforced grass parking

🚽 None; See 187

ℹ️ Designated, partially reinforced grass parking on verge adj to sports grounds and scout hut; hardstanding parking also adj. This Aire is in woodland on the edge of town and may feel isolated if alone. Van Gogh lived locally for two years and painted the local rural life. Visit the Vincentre, 2.5km in town: N51°28.609' E005°33.061', the TO and Van Gogh museum or follow a walking trail around the old village. www.vangoghvillagenuenen.nl www.vvvnuenen.nl Inspected 2015.

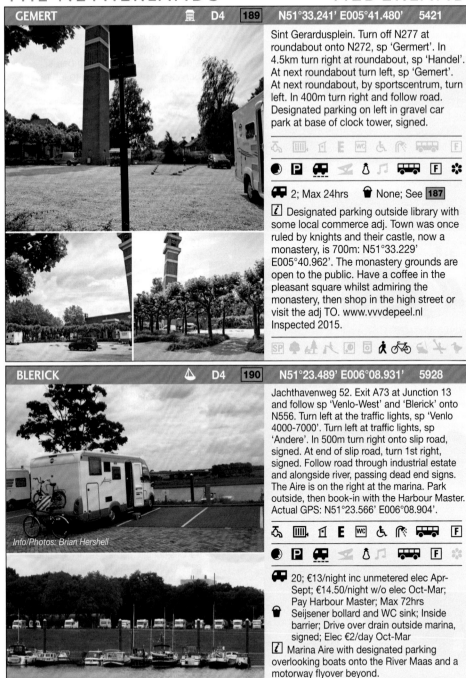

GEMERT 🏛 D4 [189] N51°33.241' E005°41.480' 5421

Sint Gerardusplein. Turn off N277 at roundabout onto N272, sp 'Germert'. In 4.5km turn right at roundabout, sp 'Handel'. At next roundabout turn left, sp 'Gemert'. At next roundabout, by sportscentrum, turn left. In 400m turn right and follow road. Designated parking on left in gravel car park at base of clock tower, signed.

🚐 2; Max 24hrs 🔔 None; See [187]

ℹ Designated parking outside library with some local commerce adj. Town was once ruled by knights and their castle, now a monastery, is 700m: N51°33.229' E005°40.962'. The monastery grounds are open to the public. Have a coffee in the pleasant square whilst admiring the monastery, then shop in the high street or visit the adj TO. www.vvvdepeel.nl Inspected 2015.

BLERICK △ D4 [190] N51°23.489' E006°08.931' 5928

Jachthavenweg 52. Exit A73 at Junction 13 and follow sp 'Venlo-West' and 'Blerick' onto N556. Turn left at the traffic lights, sp 'Venlo 4000-7000'. Turn left at traffic lights, sp 'Andere'. In 500m turn right onto slip road, signed. At end of slip road, turn 1st right, signed. Follow road through industrial estate and alongside river, passing dead end signs. The Aire is on the right at the marina. Park outside, then book-in with the Harbour Master. Actual GPS: N51°23.566' E006°08.904'.

Info/Photos: Brian Hershell

🚐 20; €13/night inc unmetered elec Apr-Sept; €14.50/night w/o elec Oct-Mar; Pay Harbour Master; Max 72hrs
🔔 Seijsener bollard and WC sink; Inside barrier; Drive over drain outside marina, signed; Elec €2/day Oct-Mar

ℹ Marina Aire with designated parking overlooking boats onto the River Maas and a motorway flyover beyond. www.wsvdemaasvenlo.nl Reinspected 2015.

NEER　　　🏭⛵　E4　191　N51°15.461' E006°00.256'　6086

Hanssum. Turn off N273 north of Neer, sp 'Soerendonck'. Follow this road for 1.4km. After passing WC emptying point: N51°15.458' E006°00.169' (sp on WSV Clubhouse), turn right into Jachthaven Hanssum, sp 'WSV Hanssum'. Designated parking adj to river, signed.

🚐 10; €12.50/night inc CEE elec;
　　Collected; Max 48hrs
🛒 Custom; CEE elec and water at
　　parking; Showers €0.50
ℹ️ Designated parking in section of grass reinforced parking area. 8 bays overlook the navigation and the passing barges and pleasure boats. This is the best view of all the marina Aires locally. Pedestrian ferry across adj River Meuse. Cycle routes displayed on information board. Cafés adj to river; local commerce 1.5km. www.wsvhanssum.nl Reinspected 2015.

THORN　　　🏭　E4　192　N51°09.503' E005°50.631'　6017

Waterstraat. Exit A2 at Junction 42, sp 'Wessem'. Follow road for 4km following sp 'Thorn' and 'Waterstraat'. At roundabout turn right. Turn right into car park before no entry signs, sp 'P Waterstraat'. Motorhome parking immediately on left, signed.

🚐 3; €2.50/9am-6pm; Free 6pm-9am; Pay
　　at machine
🛒 None; See 191
ℹ️ Pleasant parking located 300m from the pretty village with local, but mostly tourist, commerce. The village centre was, until 1797, a convent and the smallest independent state in the Holy Roman Empire Swimming beach, 650m, has extensive unrestricted gravel/grass parking: N51°09.232' E005°50.402'. Turn left out of Aire, then right at roundabout and follow road. Reinspected 2015.

BRUNSSUM E4 193 N50°56.755' E005°59.065' 6443

Heidestraat. From Brunssum follow sp 'Landgraaf' and 'Parkstad 1200-2100'. At the roundabout with swords in middle turn off, sp 'Parkstad 1200-2100'. In 50m turn left, sp 'Schutterspark'. Follow road and turn right into 'Schutterspark P1'. Motorhome parking behind coach parking, signed.

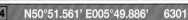

8; Max 72hrs None; See 196

Designated section of car park at leisure park. There is a large children's play area/adventure park adj and a supporting café. The park has walking and mountain biking trails and large lake. www.schutterspark.com. Residential street opp. Town commerce 1.2km. Nato HQ and airbase nearby. Reinspected 2015.

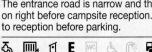

VALKENBURG T E4 194 N50°51.561' E005°49.886' 6301

Camping Den Driesch. Approach Valkenburg from north on N298. After crossing railway line turn right at traffic lights at end of road. Turn left, sp 'Thermae 2000', and follow sp 'Thermae 2000', then 'Den Driesch'. It is necessary to drive past entrance and turn around as the entrance turn is too steep. The entrance road is narrow and the Aire is on right before campsite reception. Report to reception before parking.

30; €15-€22/night; Pay at campsite; Max 5 nights
Marycamp XL; Water €1; Elec €0.60/kW

Popular commercial Aire run by the campsite. The whole site is on a steep hill with extensive terracing. Toboggan slide to one side, castle to the other. Town centre with tourist commerce and many restaurants 800m downhill. Day parking €7: N50°51.790' E005°50.204'. www.valkenburg.nl Reinspected 2015.

MAASTRICHT E4 195 N50°52.505' E005°40.861' 6291

Bosscherweg. North of Maastricht exit A76/A2/E314 at Junction 33 (in Belgium) onto N78 and follow sp 'Lanaken'. Just before Lanaken turn left at roundabout onto N766, sp 'Maastricht'. In 1.6km turn left at traffic lights, sp 'Kayakverhuur'. Aire 1km on left, signed. Enter through barrier.

🚐 100; €15/noon-noon; CC; Pay at machine before barrier

☂ Custom; Water €0.50/50L; 16amp CEE elec €2.50/24hrs; Inside barrier

ℹ Landscaped commercial Aire between river, road and canal. Reinforced grass bays, 67 with elec. Front row has views over the Meuse. Cycle path to Maastricht, 3km. Some local commerce 900m. Motorhome dealer at Gronsveld (south) allows parking outside Mon-Fri 6pm-10am and anytime at weekends: N50°48.337' E005°43.333'. www.vvvmaastricht.nl Inspected 2015.

SITTARD E4 196 N51°00.502' E005°52.891' 6136

Sportcentrumlaan, at swimming pool. Easiest approach on L228 from Germany. Cross border into the Netherlands, then at roundabout turn right into Sportcentrumlaan. In 350m turn right at next roundabout and the Aire is immediately on the left, signed. Well signed in town, follow sp 'De Nieuwe Hateboer'.

🚐 10; Max 48hrs; Text vehicle reg to number on sign

☂ Custom

ℹ Large designated bays on edge of swimming pool car park, backing onto a very large grassy verge. Affordable café at swimming pool. Town centre, 1.5km, has large covered market surrounded by cafés and bars; large market Thurs 8am-1pm, organic food market Sat. www.insittardgeleen.nl Inspected 2015.

ROERMOND E4 197 N51°11.619' E005°58.826' 6041

De Ster. From west approach on N280. Turn 1st right at traffic-lighted junction, sp 'Centrum West'. In 500m turn right at roundabout, sp 'Voorstad'. The Aire is 200m on the left, signed. Park outside gate and book in at Helenawerf chandlers opposite to obtain access code.

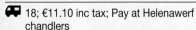

18; €11.10 inc tax; Pay at Helenawerf chandlers

Custom; WC point behind basic portable toilet block; No drive over drain; Unmetered CEE elec €1

i Marina Aire with designated parking inside compound adj to a pleasure boat marina, unfortunately there is no view of water due to high wall which spoils the ambiance. Advise look around before paying. Town centre 550m. www.helenawerf.nl Inspected 2015.

WEERT E4 198 N51°15.272' E005°41.575' 6002

Suffolkweg. Exit A2 at Junction 39 and follow sp 'Weert'. Follow road straight on following sp 'Ring West' and signed. After 4.3km turn left at roundabout, sp 'N564 Budel'. Turn 1st left, signed. Aire at end of road, signed. Enter through gate and speak to guardian.

19; €12/night inc 6amp elec and WiFi; Pay guardian

Custom; No drive over drain

i Popular landscaped commercial Aire opp working canal in industrial area on outskirts of town. Former winner of the NKC camperplaats of the year. Poss to walk to town from Aire: Turn left and follow canal path 800m, then cross over bridge to town centre. www.metonsinweert.nl Inspected 2015.

VESSEM   ☖   D3   199   N51°24.731' E005°16.483'   5512

Zwembadweg 1. From Eindhoven exit A67/E34 at Junction 30 following sp 'Vessem', then sp 'Eurocamping'. The Aire is 7.7km from Junction 30 on the right, opp the Service Point, 130m before the campsite reception.

🛁 35; €7/night Oct-Apr; €10/night May-Sept

💧 Marycamp XL; Water €1/80L; Free water inside Aire; No drive over drain; CEE elec €0.60/kWh

ℹ️ Commercial Aire in large, open grass field adj to and run by Eurocamping campsite. There is some shade at the west end. Limited hardstanding pitches. Use of campsite facilities, including showers, toilets, swimming pool and crazy golf, is included. Mini market and café onsite. WiFi €1/24hrs. Bus stop at entrance. www.eurocampingvessem.nl Visited 2015.

Info/photos: Martin & Joanne Rennie

Tolkamer

Discover the best of Holland!

Camping

Glamping

Caravanning

Chalets

DAY PARKING

The following towns offer designated motorhome day parking. Overnight parking in these locations is prohibited.

BELGIUM

WESTENDE BAD   E1   `121`   **N51°10.050' E002°45.995'**

Koning Ridderdijk. From south on N34 turn off at 1st traffic lights before town. Drive past Hotel St Laureins and parking is on right, hidden behind sand dunes. Must park between motorhome signs on right-hand side of car park.

🚐 8; €15/day 9am-7pm (half day 9am-2pm or 2pm-7pm €8)

OSTEND 1   E1   `122`   **N51°13.421' E002°55.273'**

Zinnialaan. Approach Ostend on A10. At end of A10 go straight over roundabout onto N340, sp 'Centrum'. At next roundabout turn right and follow road to right. Turn left opposite bus parking and follow road. Turn left at 2.5t truck weight restriction. Motorhome parking on right, signed.

🚐 8; Narrow bays

OSTEND 2   E1   `123`   **N51°14.184' E002°56.169'**

Forstraat, near lighthouse at northern side of town in marina/dock/industrial area. As exit Ostend on N34 turn left at science attraction Explorado, sp 'Earth Explorer' and 'Fort Napoleon'. Parking at end of road on right.

🚐 40; 6am-10pm

BREDENE   D1   `124`   **N51°13.798' E002°57.905'**

Spuikomlaan, at sports centre, signed. Follow sp 'Sportcentrum'.

🚐 2; Max 6m

MIDDELKERKE   E1   `125`   **N51°11.004' E002°49.400'**

Klein Kasteelstraat. Turn off N318 at church onto N325, sp 'Diksmuide' and 'Politie'. In 400m turn left into Parking Klein Kasteel, sp 'Brandweer'. Designated parking on left opposite fire station, signed.

🚐 3; 9am-7pm

DAY PARKING/MOTORWAYS

| DAMME | D1 | 126 | N51°14.899' E003°16.597' |

Damse Vaart-Zuid. Aire on right as enter village from Bruges, 200m before windmill. Parking to rear of car park, signed.

 2; See notice at entrance

| BLANKENBERGE | D1 | 127 | N51°19.114' E003°08.899' |

Emiel Moysonpad. Turn off N34 opp aquarium, signed.

 20; €1/hr; Max 10hrs

THE NETHERLANDS

| KATWIJK | C3 | 200 | N52°11.664' E004°23.444' |

Sportlaan. Turn off N206, sp 'Katwijk aan Zee', then turn left, sp 'Katwijk aan Zee'. Follow road for 2km to seafront, then turn left. Follow road along seafront for 1.3km, then follow the road around to the left. Turn right, sp 'P Zuidduinen', then immediately left into car park. Designated parking is on the far side of the car park, signed. Motorhomes over 6m must be parked in designated bays.

Unlimited less than 6m; 3 over 6m; €2/hr or €10/day 10am-10pm; Max 6hrs; 7am-11pm only

MOTORWAY SERVICE STATIONS

The following motorway service areas all have a motorhome Service Point. Vicarious Media recommends that you never park overnight at motorway services and maintain vigilance at all times when using them.

BELGIUM

| A7/E42 ST GHISLAIN | F2 | A | N50°27.092' E003°48.400' (East) |
| | | | N50°27.160' E003°48.192' (West) |

A7/E42 motorway service station. Located between Junctions 25 and 26. Service Points on both sides of motorway, located in parking past fuel station.

LUXEMBOURG

| A6 CAPELLEN (West) | G4 | B | N49°38.262' E005°58.256' |

A6 westbound. 10km west of Luxembourg City travelling towards Belgium. Service Point just behind fuel on left, drive through car pumps. There is no Service Point at service station on opposite side of motorway.

Boom CLOSED 2015.

Zeebrugge CLOSED 2015.

CLOSED AIRES

This list of closed Aires is provided to prevent unnecessary journeys. The Aires have been confirmed closed by inspectors on location. Closed Aires that have no alternative Aire are marked with an **X** on the mapping. The map reference number from the edition in which they were published is also provided. Alternative Aires, when available, are listed in the final column.

TOWN	GPS	ALTERNATIVES
BELGIUM		
ZEEBRUGGE 1, 10, 2nd ed	N51°20.020' E003°11.926'	6
ZEEBRUGGE 2, 11, 2nd ed	N51°19.692' E003°11.084'	6
ROESELARE 1, 22, 2nd ed	N50°56.860' E003°08.075'	17
AALTER, 25, 2nd ed	N51°05.595' E003°28.983'	13, 33, 34
BOOM, 38, 2nd ed	N51°05.305' E004°22.611'	43
LIER 2, 40, 2nd ed	N51°07.819' E004°34.918'	52
TIHANGE, 71, 2nd ed	N50°31.981' E005°15.568'	110, 120, 121
NISRAMONI, 76, 2nd ed	N50°08.466' E005°40.258'	101
THE NETHERLANDS		
HEUSDEN, 19, 2nd ed	N51°44.085' E005°08.025'	26
BORNE, 96, 2nd ed	N52°17.976' E006°45.486'	128,130
ALMELO, 97, 2nd ed	N52°21.595' E006°39.408'	128,130
VALKENBURG 1, 128, 2nd ed	N50°51.791' E005°50.213'	194

Vicarious Shop

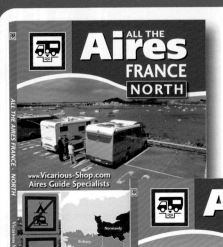

- Inspected and photographed Aires
- Easy directions, on-site GPS co-ordinates
- LPG stations
- Aires for big motorhomes

Motorhomes have the privilege of staying on Motorhome Stopovers, known as Aires.

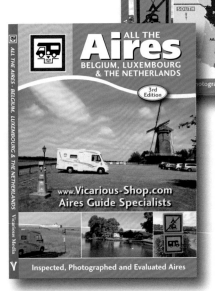

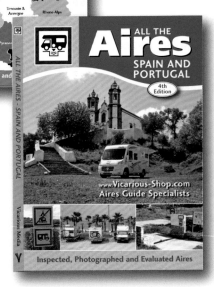

To order, give us a call or visit our website to buy online.

0131 208 3333   www.Vicarious-Shop.com

Sandelingen

LPG

Steenenhoek/de Bout

LPG

428 fuel stations with LPG pumps are listed here, comprising of: 208 in Belgium, 207 in the Netherlands and 13 in Luxembourg. This list was compiled by inspection and from information kindly provided by DKV and ESSO. LPG is widely available in the Netherlands and Flemish Belgium. LPG has limited availability in Luxembourg and in the hilly Ardennes region of Belgium, although stations are never further than 50km apart. The ACME screw connector is used in Belgium and Luxembourg. The Netherlands uses the bayonet connector.

LPG is inexpensive in Belgium and Luxembourg. In March 2016 both countries charged 40 cents per litre, the Netherlands and France charged 72 cents and Germany was 55 cents. Source: mylpg.eu

TOWN	Grid Ref	Map Ref	GPS	DIRECTIONS
LPG BELGIUM				
VEURNE	E1	1	N51°03.693' E002°40.540'	Total. N390/Albert I Laan. 1.4km south of town.
WESTENDE	E1	2	N51°09.106' E002°45.587'	Texaco. N318/Lombardsijdelaan. 1km southwest of town.
OSTEND	E1	3	N51°11.947' E002°54.132'	Total. N33/Torhoutsesteenweg, south of roundabout junction with N341. 2.5km east of Ostend Airport.
A10 JABBEKE (East)	E1	4	N51°11.123' E003°06.376'	Total. A10/E40 eastbound at Junction 6b. 800m northeast of town. Open 24hrs.
A10 JABBEKE (West)	E1	4	N51°11.254' E003°06.396'	Total. A10/E40 westbound at Junction 6. 1km northeast of town. Open 24hrs.
TORHOUT	E1	5	N51°03.981' E003°05.526'	Texaco. R34/Vredelaan, 230m south of roundabout junction with N33. 750m west of town. Open 24hrs.
OOSTKAMP	E1	6	N51°09.606' E003°14.479'	Gulf. N50/Albrecht Rodenbachstraat. 800m northeast of town.
HEIDELBURG	E1	7	N51°08.916' E003°09.900'	Power. N32/Torhoutsesteenweg, adj to roundabout junction with N309. 2km east of town. Open 24hrs.
LISSEWEGE	D1	8	N51°17.210' E003°11.618'	Esso. Zeelaan. 800m south of town. Open 24hrs.
ZEEBRUGGE	D1	9	N51°19.704' E003°11.605'	Octa+. N34/Kustlaan. Open 24hrs.
BEERNEM	E1	10	N51°07.382' E003°19.548'	Power. N370/Wingene Steenweg. 250m north of A10/E40 Junction 10. Open 24hrs.
EEKLO	E2	11	N51°10.645' E003°34.677'	Power. N9/Gentsesteenweg. 1.4km southwest of town. Open 24hrs.
MALDEGEM	E2	12	N51°12.378' E003°25.973'	Total. N9/Koningin Astridlaan, 500m southeast of roundabout junction with N9d and N498. 1km southwest of town.
POPERINGE	E1	13	N50°48.784' E002°38.124'	Q8. D948/Callicanneweg. 7.5km southwest of town. Adj to French border.
YPRES	E1	14	N50°52.305' E002°53.237'	Power. Pilkemseweg, 50m north of junction with N38. 2.5km north of town.
YPRES	E1	15	N50°50.938' E002°54.749'	Lukoil. N8/Meenseweg, 300m west of roundabout junction with N345 and N37. 2.5km east of town.
PLOEGSTEERT	E1	16	N50°43.737' E002°52.725'	Total. N365/Rue de Messines. 250m north of town.
ROESELARE	E1	17	N50°55.701' E003°06.408'	Total. N37/Meiboomlaan, 50m east of junction with R32. 2.9km southwest of town.
A14 KORTRIJK (North)	E1	18	N50°47.949' E003°15.125'	Shell. A14/E17 northbound between Junctions 1 and 2. Open 24hrs.

TOWN	Grid Ref	Map Ref	GPS	DIRECTIONS
A14 KORTRIJK (South)	E1	18	N50°48.050' E003°15.159'	Shell. A14/E17 southbound between Junctions 2 and 1. Open 24hrs.
MOUSCRON	E1	19	N50°44.435' E003°15.302'	Power. Chaussée de Dottignies. 2.5km east of town adj to roundabout junction with N58. Open 24hrs.
EVREGNIES - MOUSCRON	E1	20	N50°42.944' E003°16.389'	Texaco. N511, at roundabout. 1.7km east of A17/E40 Junction 2. Open 24hrs.
A17 ROESELARE (North)	E1	21	N50°53.754' E003°10.598'	Esso. A17/E403 northbound between Junctions 5 and 6. Open 24hrs.
A17 ROESELARE (South)	E1	21	N50°53.795' E003°10.496'	Esso. A17/E403 southbound between Junctions 6 and 5. Open 24hrs.
RUDDERVOORDE	E1	22	N51°05.986' E003°11.674'	Power. N368/Sijslostraat. 1km northwest of town. Open 24hrs.
HARELBEKE	E1	23	N50°51.757' E003°19.411'	Power. N43/Gentsesteenweg, southwest of junction with N36. 1km northeast of town. Open 24hrs.
TIELT	E2	24	N50°57.720' E003°21.784'	Total. N327/Wakkensesteenweg, 500m northwest of junction with N305. 5km southeast of town. Open 24hrs.
WAREGEM	E2	25	N50°52.561' E003°25.854'	Octa+. N382/Expresweg. 1km northwest of A14/E17 Junction 5. 1.3km southwest of town. Open 24hrs.
DEERLIJK	E2	26	N50°50.802' E003°22.718'	Shell. N36. 350m southeast of A14/E17 Junction 4. 2km southeast of town. Open 24hrs.
A8 FROYENNES (East)	E1	27	N50°37.120' E003°20.440'	Q8. A8/E42 eastbound between Junctions 35 and 34. Open 24hrs.
A8 FROYENNES (West)	E1	27	N50°37.197' E003°20.364'	Q8. A8/E42 westbound between Junctions 34 and 35. Open 24hrs.
TOURNAI	E2	28	N50°36.233' E003°25.000'	Lukoil. N7/Chaussée de Bruxelles. 1.25km west of A16/E42 Junction 32. 2km east of town.
OUDENAARDE	E2	29	N50°49.775' E003°36.188'	Esso. N60, south of roundabout junction with N8. Open Mon-Fri 6am-10pm; Sat-Sun 8am-10pm.
GAVERE	E2	30	N50°55.807' E003°37.694'	Q8. N60, adj to junction with N35 and N439. 2.2km west of town. Open 24hrs.
A14 NAZARETH (East)	E2	31	N50°58.245' E003°36.571'	Total. A14/E17 eastbound between Junctions 7 and 8. Open 24hrs.
A14 NAZARETH (West)	E2	31	N50°58.371' E003°36.739'	Total. A14/E17 westbound between Junctions 8 and 7. Open 24hrs.
SINT MARTENS LATEM	E2	32	N51°00.339' E003°37.501'	Desimpel. N43/Kortrijksesteenweg. 500m southwest of town. Open 24hrs.
A10 DRONGEN (North)	E2	33	N51°02.084' E003°38.331'	Texaco. A10/E4 northbound between Junctions 14 and 13. Open 24hrs.
SINT DENIJS - GHENT	E2	34	N51°01.312' E003°41.554'	Lukoil. N43/Kortrijksesteenweg. 450m northeast of A10/E40 Junction 14. 4km south of Ghent.
WOLFPUT - GHENT	E2	35	N51°06.607' E003°45.856'	Texaco. R4/J.F. Kennedylaan. 9km north of town. Open 24hrs.
A14 KALKEN (East)	E2	36	N51°04.198' E003°55.233'	Total. A14/E17 eastbound between Junctions 11 and 12. Open 24hrs.
A14 KALKEN (West)	E2	36	N51°04.308' E003°55.268'	Total. A14/E17 westbound between Junctions 12 and 11. Open 24hrs.

LPG

TOWN	Grid Ref	Map Ref	GPS	DIRECTIONS
A11 ZELZATE (West)	E2	37	N51°11.543' E003°50.077'	Texaco. A11/E34 westbound at Junction 13. 200m east of R4. Open 24hrs.
LOKEREN	E2	38	N51°06.728' E003°59.205'	Lukoil. N70/Bergendriesstraat. 1.25km north of town.
LOKEREN	E2	39	N51°05.443' E004°01.063'	Texaco. N47/Zelebaan. 450m northwest of A14/E17 Junction 12. Open 24hrs.
SINT NIKLAAS	E2	40	N51°10.665' E004°11.505'	Q8. N70/Heidebaan. 3.5km northeast of town.
A14 KRUIBEKE (East)	E2	41	N51°10.994' E004°17.287'	Texaco. A14/E17 eastbound between Junctions 16 and 15a. 2.2km northwest of town. Open 24hrs.
A14 KRUIBEKE (West)	E2	41	N51°11.121' E004°17.398'	Texaco. A14/E17 westbound between Junctions 15a and 16. 2.2km northwest of town. Open 24hrs.
ANTWERP	D2	42	N51°16.200' E004°22.602'	Texaco. N180/Noorderlaan. Exit A12 at Junction 16 onto N180 following sp 'Haven' for 4km. North of Ekeren. Open 24hrs.
EKEREN - ANTWERP	D3	43	N51°16.253' E004°27.516'	Texaco. N11. 300m north of A1/E19 Junction 5. 3km east of town. Open 24hrs.
A13 RANST (East)	E3	44	N51°12.477' E004°32.973'	Q8. A13/E313 eastbound between Junctions 18 and 19. Open 24hrs.
A13 RANST (West)	E3	44	N51°12.603' E004°32.791'	Q8. A13/E313 westbound between Junctions 19 and 18. Open 24hrs.
KONTICH	E3	45	N51°08.330' E004°26.283'	Texaco. N173/Prins Boudewijnlaan, 300m north of junction with N171. Open 24hrs.
A1 WAARLOOS (North)	E3	46	N51°05.895' E004°26.267'	Total. A1/E19 northbound between Junctions 8 and 7. Open 24hrs.
A1 WAARLOOS (South)	E3	46	N51°05.862' E004°26.181'	Total. A1/E19 southbound between Junctions 7 and 8. Open 24hrs.
TEMSE	E2	47	N51°07.739' E004°13.963'	Lukoil. N419/Krijgsbaan. 800m east of junction with N16. 1.4km east of town.
BORNEM	E2	48	N51°05.297' E004°16.536'	Maes. N16/Rijksweg Temse Breendonk, at N16/N159 junction. 2.5km southeast of town. Open 24hrs.
BUGGENHOUT	E2	49	N51°01.881' E004°11.763'	VdB Energie. N17/Provincialebaan. 2km north of town.
MECHELEN	E3	50	N51°00.424' E004°28.425'	Q8. N1/Brusselsesteenweg. 150m north of N1/B101. 2km south of town. Open 24hrs.
LIER	E3	51	N51°07.422' E004°34.605'	Octa+. N10/Hoogveldweg. 100m north of junction with R16. 750m south of town.
NIJLEN	E3	52	N51°09.910' E004°40.982'	Pollet. N13/Bouwelsesteenweg. 1km northeast of town.
HERENTALS	E3	53	N51°09.900' E004°50.753'	Lukoil. N152/Aarschotseweg. 500m south of N152/N13 junction. 1.5km southeast of town.
WECHELDERZANDE	D3	54	N51°15.485' E004°48.037'	Van Raak. N153/Gebroeders de Winterstraat. 300m northwest of A21/E34 Junction 21. 750m south of town. Open 24hrs.
KALMTHOUT	D3	55	N51°23.132' E004°30.188'	Q8. N117/Brasschaatsteenweg. 2km east of town. Open 24hrs.
ESSEN	D3	56	N51°27.716' E004°28.453'	Dekkers. N133/Kapelstraat. 150m north of junction with N117. 750m south of town.

L P G

TOWN	Grid Ref	Map Ref	GPS	DIRECTIONS
A1 MINDERHOUT (North)	D3	57	N51°25.213' E004°42.416'	Texaco. A1/E19 northbound between Junctions 2 and 1. Open 24hrs.
A1 MINDERHOUT (South)	D3	57	N51°25.198' E004°42.226'	Total. A1/E19 southbound between Junctions 1 and 2. Open 24hrs.
BRASSCHAAT	D3	58	N51°19.758' E004°31.405'	Texaco. N1/Bredabaan. 50m north of N1/N117 junction. 4.5km northwest of town.
MINDERHOUT	D3	59	N51°25.626' E004°45.600'	Pollet. N14/Bredaseweg. 100m east of junction with N146. 1km north of town.
BEERSE	D3	60	N51°19.512' E004°49.881'	Kenis. Rijkevorselseweg, north of canal. 1.7km northwest of town. Open 24hrs.
POPPEL	D3	61	N51°28.254' E005°02.872'	Van Raak. N12/Tilburgseweg. 2.7km north of town.
A21 GIERLE (East)	D3	62	N51°17.480' E004°52.288'	Texaco. A21/E34 eastbound between Junctions 22 and 23. Open 24hrs.
A21 GIERLE (West)	D3	62	N51°17.562' E004°52.312'	Texaco. A21/E34 westbound between Junctions 23 and 22. Open 24hrs.
TURNHOUT	D3	63	N51°16.833' E004°57.226'	Total. N19/Steenweg op Diest. 3km south of A21/E34 Junction 24. 4.8km south of town. Open 24hrs.
GEEL	E3	64	N51°08.833' E004°57.660'	Van Raak. N19/Antwerpseweg. 2.6km southwest of town. Open 24hrs.
OLEN	E3	65	N51°08.846' E004°51.484'	Total. N152/Koning Boudewijnlaan. 400m south of A13/E313 Junction 22. 400m north of town.
GEEL OOST	E3	66	N51°06.669' E005°01.300'	Total. N174/Nieuwe Baan at Geel-Oost Industrial Estate. 350m north of A13/E313. Junction 24.
MOL	E3	67	N51°10.836' E005°06.269'	Texaco. N103/Ginderbroek. 1.3km southwest of town. Open 24hrs.
A13 TESSENDERLO (North)	E3	68	N51°04.312' E005°08.819'	Total. A13/E313 northbound at Junction 25a. Open 24hrs.
A13 TESSENDERLO (South)	E3	68	N51°04.215' E005°08.763'	Total. A13/E313 southbound at Junction 25a. Open 24hrs.
HEPPEN - LEOPOLDSBURG	E3	69	N51°06.698' E005°14.181'	Esso. N73. Located 500m from both Heppen and Leopoldsburg. Open 24hrs.
KATTENBOS - LOMMEL	E3	70	N51°12.133' E005°18.373'	Q8. N746/Kattenbos. 3km south of Lommel. Open 24hrs.
LOMMEL	E3	71	N51°14.065' E005°22.482'	Gulf. N715/Luikersteenwag. 140m south of N790. 4.5km east of town.
HAMONT	E4	72	N51°14.830' E005°30.727'	Texaco. N71/Bosstraat. 2.7km west of town. Open 24hrs.
BOCHOLT	E4	73	N51°10.771' E005°32.617'	Esso. Kaulillerweg. 2.5km west of town.
PEER	E4	74	N51°08.136' E005°30.336'	Esso. N73. 3.5km east of town.
GRUITRODE	E4	75	N51°05.741' E005°35.378'	Esso. N730. 600m north of town. Open 7am-8pm.
OPITTER - BREE	E4	76	N51°07.075' E005°38.721'	Q8. N721/Opitterkiezel. In central Opitter.
BREE	E4	77	N51°08.534' E005°39.954'	Q8. N73/'t Hasseltkiezel. 4.5km east of town.
OPHOVEN	E4	78	N51°07.853' E005°48.245'	Esso. N78. 550m north of town.
NEEROETEREN	E4	79	N51°04.111' E005°43.615'	Total. N757. 3km southeast of town.
DILSEN	E4	80	N51°03.371' E005°44.584'	Q8. N78. 2.5km northeast of town. Open 24hrs.
MAASMECHELEN	E4	81	N50°57.327' E005°41.684'	Esso. N78. 300m north of A2/E314 Junction 33. 3km south of town. Open 24hrs.

LPG

TOWN	Grid Ref	Map Ref	GPS	DIRECTIONS
REKEM	E4	82	N50°55.820' E005°41.306'	N78. 3km south of A2/E314 Junction 33. 1km northwest of town.
HOUTHALEN (North)	E3	83	N51°01.165' E005°22.416'	Esso. N715/Grote Baan northbound. 750m north of Junction 29. 1.5km south of town. Open 24hrs.
HOUTHALEN (South)	E3	83	N51°01.248' E005°22.406'	Lukoil. N715/Grote Baan southbound. 900m north of A2/E314 Junction 29. 1km south of town.
GENK	E4	84	N50°57.860' E005°28.503'	Esso. N75. 2km west of town.
DIEPENBEEK	E4	85	N50°54.353' E005°25.784'	Shell. N2/Grendelbaan. 1.2km east of town.
KORTESSEM	E3	86	N50°51.585' E005°23.067'	Esso. N20. 300m northwest of junction with N76. 1.6km southwest of town. Open 24hrs.
HOESELT	E4	87	N50°51.420' E005°29.868'	Q8. N730/Bilzensteenweg. 200m southwest of A13/E313 Junction 31. 800m northeast of town. Open 24hrs.
HASSELT	E3	88	N50°56.640' E005°19.990'	Esso. N794. 1km north of R71 junction. 1.5km north of town. Open 24hrs.
KURINGEN	E3	89	N50°56.324' E005°18.670'	Lukoil. N2/Kuringersteenweg. 1km east of A13/E313 Junction 27. 1km northwest of town.
HEUSDEN ZOLDER	E3	90	N51°00.719' E005°17.853'	Texaco. N72. 550m northwest of A2/E314 Junction 28. 1km southwest of Zolder. Open 24hrs.
DIEST	E3	91	N50°58.130' E005°04.471'	Lukoil. N2/Halensebaan. 750m north of A2/E314 Junction 25. 2km south of town.
RILLAAR	E3	92	N50°58.628' E004°56.109'	Esso. N10/Mannenberg. 3km east of town. Open 24hrs.
A2 ROTSELAAR (East)	E3	93	N50°57.018' E004°47.518'	Esso. A2/E314 eastbound between Junctions 21 and 22. Open 24hrs.
A2 ROTSELAAR (West)	E3	93	N50°57.103' E004°47.561'	Esso. A2/E314 westbound between Junctions 22 and 21. Open 24hrs.
WEZEMAAL	E3	94	N50°57.491' E004°46.284'	Avia. N19/Aarschotsesteenweg. 1.6km northeast of town. Open 24hrs.
BOORTMEERBEEK	E3	95	N50°58.466' E004°33.797'	Texaco. N26/Leuvensesteenweg. 1km southwest of town. Open 24hrs.
A3 HEVERLEE (East)	E3	96	N50°51.125' E004°39.508'	Texaco. A3/E40 eastbound between Junctions 22 and 23. Open 24hrs.
A3 HEVERLEE (West)	E3	96	N50°51.254' E004°39.490'	Texaco. A3/E40 westbound between Junctions 23 and 22. Open 24hrs.
ZAVENTEM	E3	97	N50°52.554' E004°29.724'	Q8. N2/Leuvensesteenweg. 2km southeast of town and Brussels airport. Open 24hrs.
VILVOORDE	E3	98	N50°56.532' E004°26.285'	Lukoil. N1/Mechelsesteenweg. 550m south of R22. 1.9km northeast of town.
BRUSSELS	E2	99	N50°52.296' E004°21.318'	Total. N260a/Avenue du Port. 350m southwest of junction with N277 and N260. In town centre.
A10 GROOT BIJGAARDEN (East)	E2	100	N50°52.820' E004°15.134'	Texaco. A10/E40 eastbound between Junctions 20 and 21. Open 24hrs.
A10 GROOT BIJGAARDEN (West)	E2	100	N50°52.858' E004°15.333'	Texaco. A10/E40 westbound between Junctions 21 and 20. Open 24hrs.
AALST	E2	101	N50°55.798' E004°03.817'	Total. N9/Brusselsesteenweg. 700m east of R41 junction. 2km southeast of town.
A10 WETTEREN (East)	E2	102	N50°58.201' E003°50.432'	Shell. A10/E40 eastbound between Junctions 17 and 18. Open 24hrs.

TOWN	Grid Ref	Map Ref	GPS	DIRECTIONS
A10 WETTEREN (West)	E2	102	N50°58.228' E003°50.716'	Shell. A10/E40 westbound between Junctions 18 and 17. Open 24hrs.
ERPE MERE	E2	103	N50°55.451' E003°57.100'	Lukoil. N46. 550m south of A10/E40 Junction 18. 1.1km north of town.
LESSINES	E2	104	N50°42.710' E003°49.503'	Total. N57/Boulevard Emile Schevenels, adj to roundabout junction with N42, N57 and N529. On west edge of town.
A8 SILLY (East)	E2	105	N50°40.993' E003°53.855'	Total. A8/E429 eastbound between Junctions 29 and 28. Open 24hrs.
A8 SILLY (West)	E2	105	N50°41.058' E003°53.860'	Total. A8/E429 westbound between Junctions 28 and 29. Open 24hrs.
SOIGNIES	F2	106	N50°34.419' E004°03.981'	Q8. N6/Boulevard Roosevelt. 400m southwest of town. Open 24hrs.
HALLE	E2	107	N50°44.626' E004°16.227'	Texaco. Alsembergsesteenweg. 350m north of R0/E19 Junction 20. 2.75km northeast of town. Open 24hrs.
R0 RUISBROEK (North)	E2	108	N50°46.667' E004°18.081'	Total. R0/E19 northbound between Junctions 19 and 18. Open 24hrs.
R0 RUISBROEK (South)	E2	108	N50°46.756' E004°18.014'	Total. R0/E19 southbound between Junctions 18 and 19. Open 24hrs.
A7 NIVELLES (North)	E2	109	N50°36.908' E004°18.049'	Total. A7/E19 northbound between Junctions 19 and 18. Open 24hrs.
A7 NIVELLES (South)	E2	109	N50°36.934' E004°17.960'	Total. A7/E19 southbound between Junctions 18 and 19. Open 24hrs.
WATERLOO	E3	110	N50°42.551' E004°24.094'	Q8. N5/Chaussée de Bruxelles. 500m south of town. Open 24hrs.
BRUSSELS	E3	111	N50°49.019' E004°23.840'	Texaco. N206/Boulevard du Triomphe. 4.5km southeast of town. Open 24hrs.
A4 BIERGES (North)	E3	112	N50°43.161' E004°35.031'	Esso. A4/E411 northbound at Junction 5. Open 24hrs.
A4 BIERGES (South)	E3	112	N50°43.040' E004°35.023'	Esso. A4/E411 southbound at Junction 5. Open 24hrs.
OTTIGNIES	E3	113	N50°39.398' E004°33.768'	Lukoil. N237/Avenue Provinciale. 2km southwest of town.
A4 AISCHE-EN-REFAIL (North)	F3	114	N50°35.978' E004°47.569'	Shell. A4/E411 northbound between Junctions 12 and 11. Open 24hrs.
A4 AISCHE-EN-REFAIL (South)	F3	114	N50°35.986' E004°47.396'	Q8. A4/E411 southbound between Junctions 11 and 12. Open 24hrs.
RAMILLIES	E3	115	N50°38.078' E004°51.892'	Avia. N91/Chaussée de Namur. 3.6km west of town. Open 24hrs.
GLIMES	E3	116	N50°40.403' E004°49.594'	Esso. N29. 200m northeast of roundabout junction with N91. 1km southwest of town.
JODOIGNE	E3	117	N50°43.950' E004°49.728'	Esso. N240. 3km west of town. Open 24hrs.
A3 TIENEN (West)	E3	118	N50°45.202' E004°57.076'	Total. A3/E40 westbound between Junctions 25 and 26. Open 24hrs.
ST TRUIDEN	E3	119	N50°48.147' E005°10.785'	Esso. N80. 400m south of N3 junction. Open 24hrs.
ST TRUIDEN	E3	120	N50°49.088' E005°12.413'	Q8. Rellestraat, off N80. 1.5km west of town.
A3 BETTINCOURT (East)	E3	121	N50°42.349' E005°14.999'	Total. A3/E40 eastbound between Junctions 28a and 29. Open 24hrs.

LPG

TOWN	Grid Ref	Map Ref	GPS	DIRECTIONS
A3 BETTINCOURT (West)	E3	121	N50°42.488' E005°15.157'	Total. A3/E40 westbound between Junctions 29 and 28a. Open 24hrs.
TONGEREN	E4	122	N50°45.892' E005°28.305'	Esso. N20. 2km south of town. Open 7am-10pm.
TONGEREN	E4	123	N50°47.046' E005°28.950'	Texaco. N79/Maastrichtersteenweg. 500m east of town. Open 24hrs.
RIEMST	E4	124	N50°48.590' E005°35.370'	Total. N79/Tongersesteenweg. 450m west of N745/N79 junction. 870m northwest of town.
VISE	E4	125	N50°43.868' E005°41.769'	Lukoil. N653/Rue de Jupille. 200m east of A25/E25 Junction 2. 150m west of A25.
HERSTAL	E4	126	N50°41.616' E005°37.677'	Q8. Rue de Hermée. 500m north of A3/E25 Junction 34. 3km north of town. Open 24hrs.
A3 TIGNEY (East)	E4	127	N50°39.274' E005°42.535'	Shell. A3/E42 eastbound between Junctions 36 and 37. Open 24hrs.
A3 TIGNEY (West)	E4	127	N50°39.282' E005°42.658'	Shell. A3/E42 westbound between Junctions 37 and 36. Open 24hrs.
A3 LICHTENBUSCH (East)	E4	128	N50°43.076' E006°07.285'	Total. A3/E40 eastbound at the German border. 4.5km north of town. Open 24hrs.
A3 LICHTENBUSCH (West)	E4	128	N50°43.117' E006°07.176'	Total. A3/E40 westbound at the German border. 4.5km north of town. Open 24hrs.
EUPEN	E4	129	N50°38.812' E006°00.303'	Lukoil. N67/Herbesthaler Strasse. 350m south of A3/E40 Junction 38. 3km north of town.
SOUMAGNE	E4	130	N50°37.983' E005°44.583'	Texaco. N3/Avenue de la Résistance. 550m southwest of A3/E40 Junction 37. 500m east of town. Open 24hrs.
LIEGE	E4	131	N50°37.262' E005°35.700'	Texaco. N30. 700m north of junction with N633.
SERAING	F4	132	N50°36.165' E005°29.563'	Lukoil. N90/Rue de Many, south of river. 2.2km north of town.
LIEGE	E4	133	N50°38.996' E005°30.612'	Texaco. Rue de Laguesse, off N367. 600m southwest of A602/E25 Junction 31a. Open 24hrs.
AWANS	E4	134	N50°40.488' E005°28.970'	Q8. N3/Rue de Bruxelles. 1.7km northeast of town.
A15 VERLAINE (East)	F3	135	N50°35.522' E005°18.238'	Q8. A15/E42 eastbound between Junctions 6 and 5. Open 24hrs.
A15 VERLAINE (West)	F3	135	N50°35.598' E005°18.166'	Q8. A15/E42 westbound between Junctions 5 and 6. Open 24hrs.
NEUPRE	F4	136	N50°32.549' E005°28.632'	Total. N63/Route du Condroz. 200m west of town.
HUY	F3	137	N50°30.494' E005°15.910'	Cado. N66/Route de Hamoir. 2km southeast of town.
NANINNE	F3	138	N50°25.213' E004°56.301'	Lukoil. N4/Chaussée de Marche, adj to roundabout junction with N941. 1km east of town.
BELGRADE - NAMUR	F3	139	N50°28.349' E004°49.268'	Texaco. N4/Avenue Joseph Abras. 3.6km west of Namur.
A15 SPY (East)	F3	140	N50°29.658' E004°42.131'	Total. A15/E42 eastbound between Junctions 14 and 13. Open 24hrs.
A15 SPY (West)	F3	140	N50°29.727' E004°42.068'	Total. A15/E42 westbound between Junctions 13 and 14. Open 24hrs.
FLEURUS	F3	141	N50°27.799' E004°32.033'	Esso. N29. 950m south of A15/E42 Junction 15. 2.5km south of town. Open 24hrs.
GOSSELIES - CHARLEROI	F2	142	N50°27.767' E004°24.731'	Lukoil. N582. 350m west of A54/E420 Junction 22. 1.5km west of Gosselies.

TOWN	Grid Ref	Map Ref	GPS	DIRECTIONS
CHARLEROI	F3	143	N50°25.755' E004°27.509'	Texaco. N569/Chaussée de Chatelet. 350m east of A54/E420 Junction 26. 2.25km north of town. Open 24hrs.
COUILLET - CHARLEROI	F3	144	N50°23.086' E004°27.839'	Esso. N5/Route de Philippeville. 120m north of R3 Junction 8. 3km south of Charleroi. Open 24hrs.
BINCHE	F2	145	N50°24.564' E004°12.237'	Scipioni. N90/Route de Charleroi. 2.7km east of town.
LA LOUVIERE	F2	146	N50°27.846' E004°11.981'	Lukoil. N27/Chaussée de Mons. 1.8km southeast of town.
A7 HAUTS BOIS (East)	F2	147	N50°29.277' E004°05.747'	Q8. A7/E42 eastbound between Junctions 22 and 21. Open 24hrs.
A7 HAUTS BOIS (West)	F2	147	N50°29.415' E004°05.754'	Q8. A7/E42 westbound at Junction 21a. Open 24hrs.
MONS	F2	148	N50°27.198' E003°55.679'	Total. N51/Rue Grand Route, between junctions with R5 and R50. 2km west of town. Open 24hrs.
A7 ST GHISLAIN (East)	F2	149	N50°27.102' E003°48.288'	Texaco. A7/E19 eastbound between Junctions 26 and 25. Open 24hrs.
A7 ST GHISLAIN (West)	F2	149	N50°27.155' E003°48.343'	Texaco. A7/E19 westbound between Junctions 25 and 26. Open 24hrs.
QUIEVRAIN	F2	150	N50°24.286' E003°40.782'	Texaco. N51/Route de Valenciennes. 400m east of French border.
FRAMERIES	F2	151	N50°24.277' E003°55.153'	Texaco. N543. 200m north of junction with N546. 1.8km east of town. Open 24hrs.
HAVAY	F2	152	N50°21.923' E003°58.025'	Esso. N6. 1km west of town. Open 24hrs.
ERQUELINNES	F2	153	N50°18.744' E004°08.129'	Texaco. N40, adj to roundabout junction with N561. 2km east of town. Open 24hrs.
BEAUMONT	F2	154	N50°13.838' E004°14.109'	Esso. N53. 700m south of town. Open 24hrs.
BEAUMONT	F2	155	N50°14.241' E004°14.648'	Texaco. N40/Chaussée Fernand Deliège. 300m east of junction with N53. Open 24hrs.
SOMZÉE	F3	156	N50°19.829' E004°28.565'	Texaco. N5. 4km north of town. Open 24hrs.
METTET	F3	157	N50°18.734' E004°39.744'	Esso. N98. 1km south of town. Open 24hrs.
CELLES	F3	158	N50°13.937' E005°00.218'	Texaco. At N910/N94 crossroads on northeast edge of town.
GRANDHAN	F4	159	N50°19.607' E005°25.540'	Octa+. N833/Rue de Givet. 1km east of town.
BARVAUX SUR OURTHE	F4	160	N50°20.664' E005°29.220'	Lukoil. N86/Route de Marche. 800m south of town Open 24hrs.
A26 SPRIMONT (North)	F4	161	N50°31.418' E005°40.024'	Q8. A26/E25 northbound between Junctions 45 and 44. Open 24hrs.
A26 SPRIMONT (South)	F4	161	N50°31.408' E005°39.873'	Q8. A26/E25 southbound between Junctions 44 and 45. Open 24hrs.
ENSIVAL - VERVIERS	F4	162	N50°34.682' E005°50.237'	Lukoil. N61. 850m from Junctions 5 and 6 of A27/E42. 2.4km southwest of Verviers.
BALMORAL - SPA	F4	163	N50°30.917' E005°54.520'	Texaco. N629/Balmoral. 2.3km northeast of town.
SPA	F4	164	N50°29.438' E005°50.908'	Shell. N62/Avenue Reine Astrid. 1.1km west of town. Open 24hrs.
MALMEDY	F4	165	N50°25.381' E006°01.000'	Shell. N62/Avenue des Alliés. 750m southwest of town. Lukoil station 90m east on N62 also has LPG: N50°25.412' E006°01.068'.

LPG

TOWN	Grid Ref	Map Ref	GPS	DIRECTIONS
AYWAILLE	F4	166	N50°28.698' E005°41.742'	Lukoil. N633/Avenue de la Porallée. 2km northeast of town.
ROCHEFORT	F3	167	N50°09.925' E005°12.740'	Esso. N949, adj to junction with N911. 650m northeast of town. Open 6am-11pm.
A4 WANLIN (North)	F3	168	N50°08.584' E005°04.818'	Total. A4/E411 northbound between Junctions 23 and 22. Open 24hrs.
A4 WANLIN (South)	F3	168	N50°08.586' E005°04.674'	Total. A4/E411 southbound between Junctions 22 and 23. Open 24hrs.
PHILIPPEVILLE	F3	169	N50°11.968' E004°33.012'	Octa+. Rue de Namur. 450m west of junction with N40 and N97. 500m northeast of town. Open 24hrs.
PHILIPPEVILLE	F3	170	N50°09.330' E004°30.458'	OPEN. N5/Rue de Maiembourg. 5km south of town.
MOMIGNIES	F2	171	N50°01.748' E004°08.721'	Esso. Rue Mandenne, on the French border. 1.5km west of town. Open 24hrs.
COUVIN	F3	172	N50°04.029' E004°29.993'	Total. N5/Route Charlemagne. 1.7km north of town.
BASTOGNE	F4	173	N50°00.135' E005°41.710'	Total. N84/Route de Marche. 550m east of A26/E25 Junction 54. 1.3km west of town.
NOIREFONTAINE	G3	174	N49°48.875' E005°05.173'	Total. N89/Rue du Croise. 800m southwest of town.
LIBRAMONT - CHEVIGNY	G3	175	N49°54.962' E005°21.852'	Total. N826. 800m east of N40/N826 roundabout. 1km west of town.
LA ROCHE EN ARDENNE	F4	176	N50°11.397' E005°32.384'	Q8. Adj to N888/N833 junction. 3.5km west of town.
BIEVRE	G3	177	N49°56.636' E005°01.131'	Shell. N95/Rue de Dinant. 350m north of N95/N913 roundabout. 350m north of town.
LPG LUXEMBOURG				
ALLERBORN	F4	1	N50°02.184' E005°53.210'	Esso. 12. Adj to 12 and 20 road junction. 1.2km east of town.
HOSINGEN	F4	2	N50°00.358' E006°05.031'	Gulf. 7/E421. 1.5km south of town.
DIEKIRCH	G4	3	N49°53.093' E006°08.223'	Aral. 7/E421. Adj to the B7/7 roundabout. 3km north of town.
ECHTERNACH	G5	4	N49°48.596' E006°26.124'	Esso. 10/E29, near German border. Accessible from both sides.
A4 WASSERBILLIG	G5	5	N49°43.615' E006°29.537'	Esso. A1/E44 northbound at Junction 15, near German border. 1.5km north of town.
GREVENMACHER	G4	6	N49°40.773' E006°23.679'	Esso. 1. 280m from A1/E44 Junction 13. 3km west of town. Open 24hrs.
LUXEMBOURG	G4	7	N49°35.264' E006°08.292'	Shell. Rangwee, 450m northeast of roundabout junction with A3 and B3. 2.8km south of town.
A6 CAPELLEN (East)	G4	8	N49°38.123' E005°58.208'	Q8. A6/E25 eastbound between Junctions 1 and 2.
A6 CAPELLEN (West)	G4	8	N49°38.232' E005°58.324'	Q8. A6/E25 westbound between Junctions 2 and 1.
A3 BERCHEM (North)	G4	9	N49°32.554' E006°07.068'	Aral. A3/E25 northbound between Junction 2 and 1.
RUMELANGE	G4	10	N49°27.131' E006°01.564'	Esso. D59/Rue de Rumelange. 1km south of town, adj to French border.
SCHENGEN	G4	11	N49°28.813' E006°21.859'	Q8. 10/Schengerwiss 3. 400m north of A13 Junction 13. 1.1km north of town.

TOWN	Grid Ref	Map Ref	GPS	DIRECTIONS
LPG THE NETHERLANDS				
SLUIS	D2	1	N51°18.874' E003°21.636'	Tamoil. N253/Rondweg. On Belgian border 2km west of town. Open 24hrs.
MIDDELBURG	D2	2	N51°28.946' E003°37.570'	Total. Schroeweg. 900m north of A58/E312 Junction 39. 2km south of town.
A58 ARNEMUIDEN	D2	3	N51°29.797' E003°40.669'	Shell. A58/E312 northbound at Junction 37. Accessible from both sides. Open 24hrs.
TERNEUZEN	D2	4	N51°18.375' E003°51.273'	Picobello. Guido Gezellestraat. 300m north of junction with N290 and N61. 3.25km southeast of town.
AXEL	D2	5	N51°16.028' E003°53.612'	Total. N686/Buthdijk. 1.1km west of town.
KLOOSTERZANDE	D2	6	N51°21.502' E004°01.499'	Aers. N689. 1.4km south of town. Open 24hrs.
A58 VOELPOMP (East)	D2	7	N51°25.533' E004°05.257'	BP. A58/E312 eastbound between Junctions 32 and 31. Open 24hrs.
A58 VLIETE (West)	D2	7	N51°25.366' E004°05.795'	BP. A58/E312 westbound between Junctions 31 and 32. Open 24hrs.
PUTTE	D3	8	N51°21.838' E004°23.453'	Texaco. N289/Antwerpsestraat. 600m north of town.
A58 WOUWSE TOL - ZUID (East)	D2	9	N51°30.266' E004°20.919'	Esso. A58/E312 eastbound between Junctions 27 and 26. Open 24hrs.
A58 WOUWSE TOL - NOORD (West)	D2	9	N51°30.321' E004°20.998'	Total. A58/E312 westbound between Junctions 26 and 27. Open 24hrs.
A58 MASTPOLDER (East)	D3	10	N51°32.858' E004°31.697'	BP. A58/E312 eastbound between Junctions 22 and 21. Open 24hrs.
A58 HOEZAAR (West)	D3	10	N51°32.930' E004°31.876'	Shell. A58/E312 westbound between Junctions 21 and 22.
WERNHOUT	D3	11	N51°27.372' E004°38.741'	Total. N263/Wernhoutseweg. On northeast edge of town.
A58 ETTEN LEUR - BREDA (East)	D3	12	N51°34.408' E004°41.067'	Shell. A58/E312 eastbound between Junctions 18 and 16.
A58 ETTEN LEUR - BREDA (West)	D3	12	N51°34.454' E004°41.225'	Esso. A58/E312 westbound between Junctions 16 and 18. Open 24hrs.
A17 KELZERSHOF (North)	D3	13	N51°38.513' E004°33.341'	BP. A17 northbound between Junctions 24 and 25. Open 24hrs.
A59 DE FENDERT (West)	D3	14	N51°38.473' E004°28.883'	Total. A59 westbound between Noordhoek Junction and Junction 24. Open 24hrs..
ZIERIKZEE	D2	15	N51°39.246' E003°55.024'	Texaco. N59/Nieuwe Koolweg. 300m west of roundabout junction with N654. 850m northwest of town.
DIRKSLAND	D2	16	N51°44.975' E004°07.261'	BP. Korteweegje, adj to roundabout junction with N215. 2km east of town.
A29 BUTTERVLIET (South)	D3	17	N51°44.185' E004°24.618'	Shell. A29 southbound between Junctions 22 and 23.
A16 ZUIDPUNT (South)	D3	18	N51°44.105' E004°37.962'	Shell. A16/E19 southbound between Junctions 20 and 18.
A15 PORTLAND (East)	D3	19	N51°51.734' E004°27.782'	Shell. A15 eastbound between Junctions 18 and 19a. Open 24hrs.
A16 SANDELINGEN - OOST (North)	D3	20	N51°50.021' E004°37.259'	Shell. A16/E19 northbound at Junction 23. Open 24hrs.

L P G

TOWN	Grid Ref	Map Ref	GPS	DIRECTIONS
A16 SANDELINGEN - WEST (South)	D3	20	N51°50.222' E004°36.952'	BP. A16/E19 southbound at Junction 23. Open 24hrs.
A20 DE VINK (East)	C3	21	N51°57.977' E004°35.303'	BP. A20/E25 eastbound between Junctions 16 and 17. Open 24hrs.
A20 MAATVELD (West)	C3	21	N51°58.057' E004°35.366'	Shell. A20/E25 westbound between Junctions 17 and 16. Open 24hrs.
SPIJKENISSE	D2	22	N51°51.462' E004°18.272'	Texaco. N218/Hartelweg eastbound. 210m east of N493. 2km north of town. Open 24hrs.
SPIJKENISSE	D2	22	N51°51.482' E004°18.258'	Texaco. N218/Hartelweg westbound. 210m east of N493. 2km north of town. Open 24hrs.
OOSTVOORNE	C2	23	N51°54.847' E004°06.910'	Shell. Brielseweg, adj to roundabout junction with N218. 1.5km east of town. Open 24hrs.
MAASDIJK	C2	24	N51°57.014' E004°13.834'	Shell. Coldenhovelaan. 400m southeast of A20 Junction 6. 1.5km southeast of town.
A20 AALKEET (East)	C2	25	N51°55.151' E004°18.499'	Total. A20/E25 eastbound between Junctions 7 and 8. Open 24hrs.
A20 RIJSKADE (West)	C2	25	N51°55.134' E004°18.947'	BP. A20/E25 westbound between Junctions 8 and 7. Open 24hrs.
A12 KNORRESTEIN (West)	C3	26	N52°03.088' E004°26.276'	Texaco. A12/E30 westbound between Junctions 6 and 5. Open 24hrs.
A12 DE ANDEL (East)	C3	27	N52°02.370' E004°42.318'	Shell. A12/E30 eastbound between Junctions 11 and 12. Open 24hrs.
A12 BODEGRAVEN (West)	C3	27	N52°03.974' E004°44.518'	Total. A12/E30 westbound at Junction 12a. Open 24hrs.
ALPHEN AAN DEN RIJN	C3	28	N52°07.499' E004°37.613'	BP. Leidse Schouw. 150m east of N11 Junction 4. 3km west of town.
A4 AURORA (North)	C3	29	N52°09.594' E004°33.266'	Total. A4/E19 northbound at Junction 6. Open 24hrs.
A4 BOSPOORT (South)	C3	29	N52°09.765' E004°33.308'	Shell. A4/E19 southbound at Junction 6. Open 24hrs.
A44 ELSGEEST (North)	C3	30	N52°11.865' E004°28.191'	BP. A44 northbound between Junctions 7 and 6. Open 24hrs.
A4 DEN RUYGEN HOEK (North)	C3	31	N52°15.513' E004°41.130'	Shell. A4/E19 northbound between Junctions 4 and 3. Open 24hrs.
A4 DEN RUYGEN HOEK (South)	C3	31	N52°15.681' E004°41.227'	BP. A4/E19 southbound between Junctions 3 and 4. Open 24hrs.
VOGELENZANG	C3	32	N52°18.854' E004°34.130'	Texaco. N206/Bartenweg. 750m south of town.
A9 AMSTELVEEN (North)	C3	33	N52°18.353' E004°50.187'	Shell. A9 northbound between Junctions 5 and 6. Open 24hrs.
A9 AMSTELVEEN (South)	C3	33	N52°18.311' E004°50.220'	Tango. A9 southbound between Junctions 6 and 5. Open 24hrs.
A2 RUWIEL (North)	C3	34	N52°11.008' E004°59.277'	Shell. A2/E35 northbound between Junctions 5 and 4. Open 24hrs.
A1 HONSWIJCK (East)	C3	35	N52°19.309' E005°04.796'	Shell. A1/E231 eastbound between Junctions 4 and 5. Open 24hrs.
A1 HACKELAAR (West)	C3	35	N52°19.302' E005°05.024'	BP. A1/E231 westbound between Junctions 5 and 4. Open 24hrs.
LANDSMEER	C3	36	N52°24.999' E004°54.752'	BP. S117/IJdoornlaan. 130m south of A10 Junction 17. 1.4km south of town. Open 24hrs.

TOWN	Grid Ref	Map Ref	GPS	DIRECTIONS
LANDSMEER	C3	36	N52°25.176' E004°54.737'	BP. S117/IJdoornlaan. 130m north of A10 Junction 17. 1.4km south of town
BEVERWIJK	C3	37	N52°28.545' E004°39.435'	BP. N197/Parallelweg. 400m east of A22/N197 junction. 1.2km south of town. Open 24hrs.
ALKMAAR	B3	38	N52°36.875' E004°44.363'	Shell. N9/Heilooër Tolweg, adj to AFAS Stadium. 200m from N242 junction. 2.1km south of town. Open 24hrs.
A7 KRUISCOORD (South)	B3	39	N52°34.843' E004°58.665'	BP. A7/E22 southbound between Junctions 7 and 6. Open 24hrs.
HEERHUGOWAARD	B3	40	N52°38.670' E004°47.578'	BP. N242/Westerweg northbound. 500m north of N508 junction. Open 24hrs.
ENKHUIZEN	B3	41	N52°42.461' E005°16.509'	BP. Lindenlaan. 50m east of N302 junction. 1km west of town.
SCHAGEN	B3	42	N52°47.453' E004°47.000'	Supertank. De Fok. 300m east of 56 in industrial estate. 1.5km west of town. Open 24hrs.
DEN HELDER	B3	43	N52°54.748' E004°47.594'	Total. N9 southbound. 150m south of N99/N250 junction. 4.5km southeast of town.
A7 HOGEKWEL (North)	B3	44	N52°51.392' E005°01.265'	Shell. A7/E22 northbound between Junctions 13 and 14. Open 24hrs.
A7 ROBBENOORDBOS (South)	B3	44	N52°54.439' E005°01.834'	Texaco. A7/E22 southbound between Junctions 14 and 13. Open 24hrs.
A7 BREEZANDDIJK	B3	45	N53°01.315' E005°12.640'	Texaco. A7/E22 northbound between Junctions 14 and 15. Accessible from both sides.
A7 LAERD (East)	B4	46	N53°03.117' E005°33.136'	Shell. A7/E22 eastbound between Junctions 18 and 19. Open 24hrs.
HARLINGEN	A4	47	N53°10.431' E005°26.352'	Texaco. Almenumerweg. Adj to but not accessible from, N31. 1km east of town. Open 24hrs.
FRANEKER	A4	48	N53°11.157' E005°31.774'	Texaco. N384/Burgemeester J Dijkstraweg. 1.8km west of town.
A32 SMARPOT (South)	B4	49	N53°02.300' E005°50.926'	Tamoil. A32 southbound between Junctions 13 and 12. 1.5km south of town. Open 24hrs.
N31 STIENKAMP (East)	B4	50	N53°08.599' E006°02.715'	OK. N31/Waldwei eastbound. Open 24hrs.
N31 DE KRELLEN (West)	B4	50	N53°08.610' E006°02.903'	Q8. N31/Waldwei westbound. Open 24hrs.
LEEUWARDEN	A4	51	N53°10.259' E005°49.616'	Q8. Drachtsterweg southbound. 450m north of N31 Junction 26. 3.8km south of town.
DOKKUM	A4	52	N53°19.069' E005°59.455'	Texaco. N356/Rondweg West. 1km southwest of town.
A7 OUDE RIET (West)	B4	53	N53°10.030' E006°18.789'	Shell. A7/E22 westbound between Junctions 33 and 32. Open 24hrs.
A32 MANDALAN (North)	B4	54	N53°07.707' E005°48.272'	Shell. A32 northbound between Junctions 15 and 16. Open 24hrs.
A7 DIKKE LINDE (East)	A5	55	N53°11.672' E006°42.029'	Texaco. A7/E22 eastbound between Junctions 40 and 39.
A7 VEENBORG (West)	A5	55	N53°11.220' E006°42.999'	Total. A7/E22 westbound between Junctions 40 and 39. Open 24hrs.

LPG

TOWN	Grid Ref	Map Ref	GPS	DIRECTIONS
A7 MEEDENERTOL (East)	A5	56	N53°10.854' E006°55.921'	Shell. A7/E22 eastbound between Junctions 44 and 45.
NIEUWE PEKELA	B5	57	N53°05.323' E006°57.304'	Total. N366/Provincialeweg eastbound. 2.75km northwest of town. Open 24hrs.
STADSKANAAL	B5	58	N52°58.873' E006°58.207'	BP. Steenhouwer. 100m south of roundabout junction with N374. 1.9km southeast of town. Open 24hrs.
N33 NIJLANDERVELD (West)	B5	59	N52°58.248' E006°36.892'	Texaco. N33/Rijksweg westbound. 2.75km southwest of Rolde. Open 24hrs.
A28 PEELERVELD (North)	B5	60	N53°01.323' E006°33.254'	A28/E232 northbound between Junctions 33 and 34. Open 24hrs.
A28 ZEYERVEEN (South)	B5	60	N53°01.016' E006°32.735'	Tamoil. A28/E232 southbound between Junctions 34 and 33. Open 24hrs.
TYNAARLO	B5	61	N53°04.809' E006°36.396'	Total. N386/Dorpsstraat. 200m east of A28/E232 Junction 35. 560m west of town.
A7 DE WALDEN (North)	B4	62	N53°01.756' E006°01.174'	Texaco. A7/E22 northbound between Junctions 27 and 28. Open 24hrs.
A7 DE VONKEN (South)	B4	62	N53°01.913' E006°01.263'	Shell. A7/E22 southbound between Junctions 28 and 27. Open 24hrs.
A28 SMALHORST (North)	B5	63	N52°50.700' E006°29.263'	Shell. A28/E23 northbound between Junctions 29 and 30.
A28 DE MUSSELS (South)	B5	63	N52°50.766' E006°29.247'	Q8. A28/E232 southbound between Junctions 30 and 29.
A7 DE HORNE (East)	B4	64	N52°57.509' E005°50.773'	BP. A7/E22 eastbound between Junctions 24 and 25. Open 24hrs.
DONKERBROEK	B4	65	N53°00.891' E006°13.973'	Q8. N381. 400m south of junction with N380. 300m southwest of town.
A32 DORPSHELLEN (South)	B4	66	N52°55.172' E005°58.185'	Gulf. A32 southbound between Junctions 10 and 9.
A32 PAARDEWEIDE (North)	B4	67	N52°45.074' E006°11.368'	Texaco. A32 northbound between Junctions 4 and 5.
A32 BOVENBOER (South)	B4	67	N52°45.211' E006°11.207'	BP. A32 southbound between Junctions 5 and 4. Open Mon-Fri 6am-9pm; Sat 7am-9pm; Sun 8am-9pm.
MEPPEL	B4	68	N52°40.756' E006°11.526'	Total. Werkhorst. 300m north of A32 Junction 1. 1.4km south of town.
A28 DEKKERSLAND (North)	B4	69	N52°37.436' E006°12.460'	Shell. A28/E232 northbound between Junctions 22 and 23. Open 24hrs.
A28 LAGEVEEN (East)	B4	70	N52°40.771' E006°21.508'	Texaco. A28/E232 eastbound between Junctions 24 and 25. Open 24hrs.
A28 PANJERD (West)	B4	70	N52°40.968' E006°22.220'	BP. A28/E232 westbound between Junctions 25 and 24. Open 24hrs.
A37 GROOTE VELDBLOKKEN (East)	B5	71	N52°42.914' E006°38.673'	Total. A37/E233 eastbound between Junctions 2 and 3. Open 24hrs.
A37 ZWINDERSCHEVELD (West)	B5	71	N52°42.971' E006°38.619'	Total. A37/E233 westbound between Junctions 3 and 2. Open 24hrs.
ZWOLLE	C4	72	N52°29.960' E006°06.295'	BP. N337/IJsselallee. 2.4km southeast of town. Open 24hrs.

TOWN	Grid Ref	Map Ref	GPS	DIRECTIONS
KLAZIENAVEEN	B5	73	N52°43.974' E006°58.828'	Shell. N862/Pollux. 400m south of A37/E233 Junction 6. 1km southeast of town. Open 24hrs.
ERM	B5	74	N52°45.341' E006°49.157'	Firezone. N376/Oosterlangen. 850m north of N34 junction. 850m north of town.
KAMPEN	B4	75	N52°33.393' E005°54.183'	BP. Flevoweg. 1km north of **113**. 850m west of town. Open 24hrs.
A6 DE ABT (North)	B4	76	N52°37.538' E005°39.949'	Texaco. A6 northbound between Junctions 11 and 13. Open 24hrs.
A6 HAN STIJKEL (South)	B4	76	N52°39.683' E005°41.446'	Texaco. A6 southbound between Junctions 14 and 13.
A6 LEPELAAR (North)	C4	77	N52°25.977' E005°25.345'	Total. A6 northbound between Junctions 8 and 10.
A6 AALSCHOLVER (South)	C4	77	N52°26.141' E005°25.502'	Total. A6 southbound between Junctions 10 and 8.
A28 DRIELANDER (South)	C4	78	N52°19.882' E005°35.459'	Texaco. A28/E232 southbound between Junctions 12 and 11. Open 24hrs.
't HARDE	C4	79	N52°24.558' E005°53.474'	BP. N309/Eperweg. 100m south of A28/E232 Junction 16. 800m southwest of town.
A50 KOLTHOORN (North)	C4	80	N52°23.392' E006°00.944'	Total. A50 northbound between Junctions 28 and 29.
RAALTE	C4	81	N52°22.283' E006°15.809'	Texaco. N348/Nieuwe Deventerweg. 1.75km southwest of town.
N36 HAZEPAD (North)	C5	82	N52°25.991' E006°37.793'	Gulf. N36 northbound. Open 24hrs.
N36 SMOKKELPAD (South)	C5	82	N52°26.078' E006°37.746'	Gulf. N36 southbound. Open 24hrs.
DENEKAMP	C5	83	N52°22.237' E006°59.992'	BP. Oldenzaalsestraat, adj to roundabout junction of N349/N342. 600m southwest of town. Open 24hrs.
A1 HET LONNEKERMEER (North)	C5	84	N52°16.859' E006°51.064'	Avia. A1 northbound between Junctions 31 and 32. Open 24hrs.
A1 HET VEELSVELD (South)	C5	84	N52°17.191' E006°51.685'	Texaco. A1 southbound between Junctions 32 and 31. Open 24hrs.
HENGELO	C5	85	N52°14.586' E006°45.898'	Texaco. Platinastraat. 600m north of A35 Junction 27. 2.5km southwest of town. Open 24hrs.
HAAKSBERGEN	C5	86	N52°09.206' E006°42.857'	Texaco. N347/Westsingel. 2.3km west of town. Open 24hrs.
A1 BOLDER (East)	C4	87	N52°15.161' E006°25.825'	BP. A1/E30 eastbound between Junctions 26 and 27. Open 24hrs.
DEVENTER	C4	88	N52°14.303' E006°12.660'	Texaco. N348/Siemelinksweg. 300m north of A1/E30 Junction 24. 4.9km southeast of town. Open 24hrs.
ZUTPHEN	C4	89	N52°09.545' E006°12.167'	Brand Oil. N348/Oostzeestraat. 1.8km north of town.
A50 DE BRINK (South)	C4	90	N52°10.277' E006°01.598'	Texaco. A50 southbound between Junctions 24 and 23, south of A1 junction. Open 24hrs.
A1 LUCASGAT (East)	C4	91	N52°11.742' E005°50.082'	Shell. A1/E30 eastbound between Junctions 18 and 19.
A1 DE HUCHT (West)	C4	91	N52°11.120' E005°53.487'	BP. A1/E30 westbound between Junctions 19 and 18. Open 24hrs.

LPG

TOWN	Grid Ref	Map Ref	GPS	DIRECTIONS
A1 PALMPOL (East)	C4	92	N52°09.789' E005°32.031'	Total. A1/E30 eastbound between Junctions 14 and 15. Open 24hrs.
A1 DE MIDDELAAR (West)	C4	92	N52°09.942' E005°28.631'	Total. A1/E30 westbound between Junctions 15 and 14. Open 24hrs.
A1 DE SLAAG (East)	C3	93	N52°12.727' E005°20.432'	Shell. A1/E231 eastbound between Junctions 11 and 12. Open 24hrs.
A1 NEERDUIST (West)	C3	93	N52°12.328' E005°23.078'	Shell. A1/E231 westbound between Junctions 13 and 12. Open 24hrs.
A27 't VEENTJE (South)	C3	94	N52°15.933' E005°15.267'	Tango. A27 southbound between Junctions 35 and 34.
A27 VOORDAAN (North)	C3	95	N52°07.737' E005°09.036'	BP. A27 northbound between Junctions 31 and 32. Open 24hrs.
A12 BIJLEVELD (East)	C3	96	N52°04.799' E004°58.801'	BP. A12/E25 eastbound at Junction 14a. Open 24hrs.
A12 HELLEVLIET (West)	C3	96	N52°04.873' E004°59.056'	Shell. A12/E25 westbound at Junction 14a. Open 24hrs.
A2 JUTPHAAS (South)	C3	97	N52°00.986' E005°04.116'	Total. A2/E25 northbound between Junctions 10 and 9. Open 24hrs.
A2 DE IJSSEL	C3	97	N52°01.728' E005°03.782'	BP. A2/E25 southbound at Junction 9. Open 24hrs.
A27 DE KNOEEST (North)	C3	98	N52°00.823' E005°07.268'	OK. A27/E311 northbound at Junction 28. Open 24hrs.
A27 DE KROON (South)	C3	98	N52°00.941' E005°07.278'	BP. A27/E311 southbound at Junction 28. Open 24hrs.
A12 DE FORTEN (East)	C3	99	N52°03.701' E005°10.736'	Texaco. A12/E35 eastbound between Junctions 18 and 19. Open 24hrs.
AMERSFOORT	C4	100	N52°07.598' E005°21.892'	Texaco. N227/Doornseweg southbound. 300m south of A28 Junction 5. 4.5km southwest of town.
A12 BLOEMHEUVEL (East)	C4	101	N52°03.020' E005°27.699'	Shell. A12/E35 eastbound between Junctions 22 and 23. Open 24hrs.
A12 OUDENHORST (West)	C4	101	N52°03.057' E005°27.939'	Total. A12/E35 westbound between Junctions 23 and 22. Open 24hrs.
A30 DE POEL (North)	C4	102	N52°03.822' E005°36.680'	BP. A30 northbound between Junctions 2 and 3. Open 24hrs.
A30 DE VEENEN (South)	C4	102	N52°03.840' E005°36.573'	BP. A30 southbound between Junctions 3 and 2. Open 24hrs.
HENGELO	C4	103	N52°02.435' E006°18.330'	BP. Molenenk, off N316. 1.3km south of town. Open 24hrs.
RUURLO	C5	104	N52°04.834' E006°27.496'	Tamoil. De Venterkamp. 400m west of N315/N319 roundabout. On southern edge of town. Open 24hrs.
WINTERSWIJK	C5	105	N51°56.324' E006°47.451'	Texaco. N319/Kottenseweg. 6.2km southeast of town. Open 24hrs.
LICHTENVOORDE	C5	106	N51°59.237' E006°33.008'	Texaco. N18/Europaweg. 1.25km west of town. Open 24hrs.
DOETINCHEM	C4	107	N51°56.902' E006°18.442'	BP. Terborgseweg. 350m north of A18 Junction 4. 2km south of town.
A18 STILLE WALD (East)	C4	108	N51°56.341' E006°11.030'	Texaco. A18 eastbound between Junctions 1 and 2.

TOWN	Grid Ref	Map Ref	GPS	DIRECTIONS
A18 GEULENKAMP (West)	C4	108	N51°56.383' E006°11.027'	Shell. A18 westbound between Junctions 2 and 1.
A12 OUDBROEKEN (East)	C4	109	N51°57.137' E006°03.091'	BP. A12/E25 eastbound between Junctions 28 and 29. Open 24hrs.
A12 DE SCHAARS (North)	C4	110	N52°01.464' E005°52.806'	Shell. A12/E35 northbound between Junctions 26 and 25. Open 24hrs.
A325 HOGEWEI (North)	C4	111	N51°55.985' E005°52.673'	Shell. A325 northbound between Elst Junction and Elden Junction.
A325 KEMPKE (South)	C4	111	N51°55.918' E005°52.603'	Shell. A325 southbound between Elden Junction and Elst Junction.
A50 WEERBROEK (South)	C4	112	N51°56.038' E005°46.046'	Texaco. A50 southbound between Junction 18 and Valburg Junction. Open 24hrs.
A15 VARAKKER (West)	C4	113	N51°55.417' E005°36.431'	Shell. A15/E31 westbound between Junctions 36 and 35. Open 24hrs.
A2 LINGEHORST (North)	C3	114	N51°54.720' E005°10.834'	BP. A2/E25 northbound between Junctions 14 and 13. Open 24hrs.
A2 BISDE (South)	C3	114	N51°54.756' E005°10.708'	Texaco. A2/E25 southbound between Junctions 13 and 14. Open 24hrs.
A27 BLOMMENDAAL (North)	C3	115	N51°54.645' E004°59.058'	Shell. A27/E311 northbound between Junctions 25 and 26. Open 24hrs.
GORINCHEM	D3	116	N51°50.538' E004°57.190'	Texaco. Banneweg. 1.6km west of town. Approach town from west on N216.
A15 EIGENBLOK (West)	D3	117	N51°50.929' E005°11.517'	Tango. A15/E31 westbound between Junctions 30 and 29. Open 24hrs.
A27 DE KEIZER (North)	D3	118	N51°44.785' E004°55.260'	BP. A27/E311 northbound between Junctions 21 and 22. Open 24hrs.
A59 DE HESPELAAR (East)	D3	119	N51°40.413' E004°49.159'	Texaco. A59 eastbound between Junctions 32 and 33. Open 24hrs.
A59 STEELHOVEN (West)	D3	119	N51°40.575' E004°49.637'	Texaco. A59 westbound between Junctions 33 and 32. Open 24hrs.
A27 GALGEVELD (South)	D3	120	N51°36.191' E004°50.514'	Texaco. A27/E311 southbound between Junctions 17 and 16. Open 24hrs.
A59 LABBEGAT (East)	D3	121	N51°41.664' E005°00.505'	Shell. A59 eastbound between Junctions 36 and 37. Open 24hrs.
A59 DE SPRANG (West)	D3	121	N51°41.650' E005°01.121'	Shell. A59 westbound between Junctions 37 and 36. Open 24hrs.
KAATSHEUVEL	D3	122	N51°38.532' E005°03.533'	Gulf. N261/Midden-Brabantweg southbound. 2.8km southeast of town. Open 24hrs.
's HERTOGENBOSCH	D3	123	N51°42.594' E005°18.008'	Total. Hambakenweg. 950m south of A59 Junction 47. 1.3km north of town. Open 24hrs.
A2 DE LUCHT - OOST (North)	D3	124	N51°46.492' E005°15.628'	Shell. A2/E25 northbound between Junctions 19 and 17.
A2 DE LUCHT - WEST (South)	D3	124	N51°46.610' E005°15.452'	Shell. A2/E25 southbound between Junctions 17 and 19. Open 24hrs.
A59 DE LUCHT (East)	D4	125	N51°43.712' E005°28.515'	Shell. A59 eastbound between Junctions 51 and 52.
A59 DE GEFFENSE BARRIERE (West)	D4	125	N51°44.080' E005°29.638'	BP. A59 westbound between Junctions 52 and 51. Open 24hrs.

LPG

TOWN	Grid Ref	Map Ref	GPS	DIRECTIONS
REEK	D4	126	N51°44.218' E005°40.432'	Texaco. N324. 500m east of N277/N324 roundabout. 1km southwest of town. Open 24hrs.
AFFERDEN	D4	127	N51°52.430' E005°38.343'	Texaco. N322/Maas en Waalweg. 700m southeast of town. Open 24hrs.
A73 HONDSIEP (North)	D4	128	N51°40.997' E005°53.590'	Shell. A73/E31 northbound between Junctions 6 and 5. Open 24hrs.
A73 LOKKANT (South)	D4	128	N51°41.077' E005°53.478'	Total. A73/E31 southbound between Junctions 5 and 6. Open 24hrs.
WELL	D4	129	N51°33.339' E006°05.901'	BP. N271/Moleneind. 100m west of N270/N271 roundabout. 1km northeast of town.
A73 ROM-EINSE PUT (North)	D4	130	N51°30.341' E006°01.337'	Texaco. A73 northbound between Junctions 10 and 9. Open 24hrs.
A73 DE WUUST (South)	D4	130	N51°30.278' E006°01.314'	Texaco. A73 southbound between Junctions 9 and 10. Open 24hrs.
VREDEPEEL	D4	131	N51°32.404' E005°52.080'	Tamoil. N277/Ripseweg. On south edge of town. Open 24hrs.
N50 SONSE HEIDE	D4	132	N51°32.155' E005°28.771'	BP. A50 southbound between Junctions 9 and 8. Open 24hrs.
A2 OOIENDONK (North)	D3	133	N51°33.313' E005°21.712'	Texaco. A2 northbound between Junctions 27 and 26. Open 24hrs.
A2 VELDER (South)	D3	133	N51°33.656' E005°21.387'	Texaco. A2 southbound between Junctions 26 and 27. Open 24hrs.
TILBURG	D3	134	N51°35.083' E005°06.597'	BP. N261/Burgemeester Bechtweg. 3km northeast of town. Open 24hrs.
A58 MOLENHEIDE (West)	D3	135	N51°33.282' E004°54.780'	Shell. A58/E312 westbound between Junctions 12 and 13. Open 24hrs.
BAARLE NASSAU	D3	136	N51°25.863' E004°55.926'	Texaco. N119/Turnhoutseweg. South of town adj to Belgian border.
A58 KLOOSTERS (East)	D3	137	N51°29.525' E005°20.965'	Shell. A58/E312 eastbound between Junctions 8 and 7.
EINDHOVEN	D4	138	N51°26.061' E005°27.157'	Texaco. Limburglaan, on west side of ring road. 1.5km southwest of town.
EINDHOVEN	D4	139	N51°27.275' E005°31.330'	BP. N270/Eisenhowerlaan westbound. 3.7km east of town.
A67 OELJENBRAAK (West)	D4	140	N51°25.435' E005°40.060'	Shell. A67/E34 westbound between Junctions 35 and 34. Open 24hrs.
A67 DEERSELS (East)	D4	141	N51°22.687' E006°00.037'	Shell. A67/E34 eastbound between Junctions 38 and 39. Open 24hrs.
A67 REIJNEN (West)	D4	142	N51°23.771' E006°09.694'	BP. A67/E34 westbound between Junctions 40 and 39. Open 24hrs.
TEGELEN	D4	143	N51°21.117' E006°09.011'	Total. N271/Venloseweg. 100m southwest of A73 Junction 16. 1.3km northeast of town.
KESSEL	D4	144	N51°18.197' E006°03.680'	BP. Baarloseweg, adj to traffic-lighted crossroads with N273 and N277. 1.3km northeast of town.
A2 DE GROOTE BLEEK (South)	D4	145	N51°19.350' E005°35.619'	Total. A2/E25 southbound between Junctions 35 and 36. Open 24hrs.
BERGEIJK	D3	146	N51°16.227' E005°23.887'	Tamoil. N69. 400m from the Belgian border. 6.4km southeast of town. Open 24hrs.

TOWN	Grid Ref	Map Ref	GPS	DIRECTIONS
WEERT	E4	147	N51°13.042' E005°35.061'	Total. N564/Kempenweg. 10.3km southwest of town.
A67 HETGOOR (North)	D3	148	N51°19.276' E005°13.058'	Gulf. A67/E34 northbound. 1.2km east of the Belgian border. Open 24hrs.
A67 DE BEERZE (South)	D3	148	N51°19.468' E005°13.470'	Gulf. A67/E34 southbound. 600m east of the Belgian border. Open 24hrs.
A73 HOOGVONDEREN (South)	E4	149	N51°11.510' E006°01.760'	Total. A73 southbound between Junctions 19 and 20. Open 24hrs.
ITTERVOORT	E4	150	N51°10.568' E005°50.241'	Avia. Torenweg. 50m from roundabout junction with N273. 1.5km northeast of town. Open 24hrs.
ECHT	E4	151	N51°05.566' E005°54.072'	Tamoil. N572/Brugweg. 2km southeast of town.
A2 SWENTIBOLD (North)	E4	152	N51°00.639' E005°47.974'	Shell. A2/E25 northbound between Junctions 48 and 47. Open 24hrs.
SITTARD	E4	153	N50°59.116' E005°50.644'	BP. N276/Middenweg. 3.5km southwest of town.
LANDGRAAF	E4	154	N50°54.990' E006°01.409'	Texaco. Brunssummerweg, off N299. 2.5km north of town. Open 24hrs.
HEERLEN	E4	155	N50°53.830' E005°56.739'	Shell. N281/Antwerpseweg northbound. 2.5km northwest of town. Open 24hrs.
A2 DE KRUIGSBERG	E4	156	N50°53.185' E005°44.372'	Total. A2/E25 northbound. 1.8km north of junction with A79. 1km west of town. Open 24hrs.
HOUTHEM	E4	157	N50°52.484' E005°47.105'	Avia. Vroenhof. 600m southeast of A79 Junction 2. 760m west of town.
HEERLEN	E4	158	N50°52.502' E005°58.546'	Texaco. N281/Keulseweg Oost northbound. 1.5km southwest of town.
VAALS	E4	159	N50°46.447' E006°00.925'	Tamoil. N278/Maastrichterlaan. 300m northwest of town.
A2 PATIEL (North)	E4	160	N50°46.624' E005°43.753'	Gulf. A2/E25 northbound between Junctions 58 and 57. Open 24hrs.
A2 VOSSEDAL (South)	E4	161	N50°56.206' E005°47.061'	BP. A2/E25 southbound between Junctions 49 and 51. Open 24hrs.

USER UPDATES

The Aires situation is constantly changing and customer feedback has proven vital in keeping the guide up to date. Photographs are essential because they provide the supporting evidence we need to confirm that your submissions are accurate. The truth is that submissions without photos are like reading a book in the dark. Filling in a submission form on site is best practice because you are unlikely to remember everything, however it is essential that you record GPS coordinates on site. The best way to keep an accurate record is with your digital camera by following this photographic checklist.

Take photos of the:

- Parking area from several angles
- Surrounding area from several angles
- Service Point showing all working parts/sides
- Close-up of the payment slot to identify token or payment type
- Close-up of the electricity points and trip-switches to identify plug type and amperage
- Designation signs and information boards, including close-ups of text
- Also take GPS coordinates on site

Please name photos by the town name, region, and the person's name to be credited if they are published.

You can submit your text and digital photos online at www.all-the-aires.co.uk/submissions.shtml We cannot process printed photos, but they are still useful as record shots.
If you have lots of submissions and photos, burn them to disk and post them to:
Vicarious Media,
Unit 1, North Close Business Centre,
Shorncliffe Industrial Estate,
Folkestone,
CT20 3UH

Considerable thanks goes to the Aire Heads who have provided photographs and information about the Aires they have visited. Some of them are listed below:

John & Janet Watts, Jean Dew, Donna Garner, Joanne Holmes, Linda Leiper, Peter Cooke, David Tiplady, Alan Stead, Sue Moore, Paul Verniquet, Jeroen Huyen, Martin & Joanne Rennie, Alistair MacFadyen, Andy Barthorpe

INDEX

LUXEMBOURG

THE NETHERLANDS

INDEX

INDEX

AIRE/LPG SUBMISSION FORM

Please use this form to update Aires information in this guide. If the Aire is already listed, complete only the sections where changes apply. Please write in capital letters and circle appropriate symbols.

Town/Village:

Region:

Road name/number:

Date Visited:

Surroundings:

Coastal	Village	Campsite	R Recommended
Residential	Riverside or lakeside	Day parking	! Warning
Urban	Farm	Marina	
Rural	Park/Sports facilities	T Tourism	

Please circle 1 or more symbols as appropriate

Page Number: Postcode – if known:

Number of Spaces:

Time limit: Cost:

Parking symbols:

Overnight parking possible	Sloping	Large motorhomes
P Designated motorhome parking	Illuminated	F Free of charge
Hard surface	Noisy	Open all year

Please circle 1 or more symbols as appropriate

Service Point type: Cost:

Payment/Token type:

Sanitation symbols:

Water	E Electric hook-up	Showers
Waste water disposal	WC Toilets	F Free of charge
Toilet disposal	Disabled toilet	

Please circle 1 or more symbols as appropriate

Leisure Information Symbols:

SP Shaded parking	Children's play area	Marked cycle route
Green space suitable for dogs/children	Washing machine	Fishing
	Boules	Boating (unmotorised)
Picnic tables/benches	Walking - path or trail	Bird watching

Please circle 1 or more symbols as appropriate

Please turn over

AIRE/LPG SUBMISSION FORM

Directions - Brief, specific directions to Aire/LPG:

GPS Coordinates:

Information - Brief description of location and amenities:

Name and email or address - so information can be credited:

Your feedback is vital to keep this guide up to date. Fill in this form whilst you are at the Aire. Please name photos with the town name, region, and the name you want credited if they are published. Please submit your text and digital photos online at **www.all-the-aires.co.uk/submissions.shtml** or post your completed forms and CDs of photos to **Vicarious Media, Unit 1, North Close Business Centre, Shorncliffe Industrial Estate, Folkestone, CT20 3UH.** You can print off more forms at **www.All-the-Aires.co.uk**

Please include at least five photos showing the parking area in different directions and close-ups of any signs. Photograph the Service Point showing working parts, and the token slot, so that we may identify the token type, don't forget the waste drain. Submissions without photos are like reading a book in the dark. We cannot process printed photos, but they are still useful as record shots.

Thank you very much for your time.

By supplying details and photographs you are giving unrestricted publication and reproduction rights to Vicarious Media Ltd.

AIRE/LPG SUBMISSION FORM

Please use this form to update Aires information in this guide. If the Aire is already listed, complete only the sections where changes apply. Please write in capital letters and circle appropriate symbols.

Town/Village:

Region:

Road name/number:

Date Visited:

Surroundings:

Coastal	Village	Campsite	R Recommended
Residential	Riverside or lakeside	Day parking	! Warning
Urban	Farm	Marina	
Rural	Park/Sports facilities	T Tourism	

Please circle 1 or more symbols as appropriate

Page Number: Postcode – if known:

Number of Spaces:

Time limit: Cost:

Parking symbols:

Overnight parking possible	Sloping	Large motorhomes
P Designated motorhome parking	Illuminated	F Free of charge
Hard surface	Noisy	Open all year

Please circle 1 or more symbols as appropriate

Service Point type: Cost:

Payment/Token type:

Sanitation symbols:

Water	E Electric hook-up	Showers
Waste water disposal	WC Toilets	F Free of charge
Toilet disposal	Disabled toilet	

Please circle 1 or more symbols as appropriate

Leisure Information Symbols:

SP Shaded parking	Children's play area	Marked cycle route
Green space suitable	Washing machine	Fishing
for dogs/children	Boules	Boating (unmotorised)
Picnic tables/benches	Walking - path or trail	Bird watching

Please circle 1 or more symbols as appropriate

Please turn over

AIRE/LPG SUBMISSION FORM

Directions - Brief, specific directions to Aire/LPG:

GPS Coordinates:

Information - Brief description of location and amenities:

Name and email or address - so information can be credited:

Your feedback is vital to keep this guide up to date. Fill in this form whilst you are at the Aire. Please name photos with the town name, region, and the name you want credited if they are published. Please submit your text and digital photos online at **www.all-the-aires.co.uk/submissions.shtml** or post your completed forms and CDs of photos to **Vicarious Media, Unit 1, North Close Business Centre, Shorncliffe Industrial Estate, Folkestone, CT20 3UH.** You can print off more forms at **www.All-the-Aires.co.uk**

Please include at least five photos showing the parking area in different directions and close-ups of any signs. Photograph the Service Point showing working parts, and the token slot, so that we may identify the token type, don't forget the waste drain. Submissions without photos are like reading a book in the dark. We cannot process printed photos, but they are still useful as record shots.

Thank you very much for your time.

By supplying details and photographs you are giving unrestricted publication and reproduction rights to Vicarious Media Ltd.